THE
BRONC

CHARLES J. BRUCATO, JR.
WITH JOHN M. BRUCATO

First Stillwater River Publications Edition.

ISBN: 978-1-963296-31-0

Library of Congress Control Number: 2024905562

1 2 3 4 5 6 7 8 9 10
Written by Charles J. Brucato, Jr. and John M. Brucato.
Cover and interior book design by Matthew St. Jean.
Map of Sicily by Cattette, CC BY-SA 4.0, via Wikimedia Commons.
Published by Stillwater River Publications, West Warwick, RI, USA.

Names: Brucato, Charles J., Jr., author. | Brucato, John M., 1955- author.
Title: The Bronc / Charles J. Brucato, Jr., with John M. Brucato.
Description: First Stillwater River Publications edition. | West Warwick, RI, USA : Stillwater River Publications, [2024] | Includes bibliographical references.
Identifiers: ISBN: 978-1-963296-31-0 (paperback) | LCCN: 2024905562
Subjects: LCSH: Brucato, Charles, Sr. | Italian Americans—Massachusetts—Milford—Biography. | Baseball players—Massachusetts—Milford—Biography. | World War, 1939-1945—Veterans—Massachusetts—Milford—Biography. | Post-traumatic stress disorder. | Milford (Mass.)—Biography. | LCGFT: Biographies.
Classification: LCC: F74.M64 B78 2024 | DDC: 974.43092—dc23

This book is dedicated to the memory of the Bronc's wife Concetta,
his brother John, and his sisters Molly and Ninfa,
who were the wind beneath his wings....

And to the memory of the courageous marines
who he battled beside in the Marshall Islands, Saipan,
Tinian, and Iwo Jima during World War II.

Cchi fa 'n liuni p'essiri 'u liuni?
Nenti. Ma 'n omu ha risicari a morti ppi sèntisi poi diri:
Chi liuni! Chiddu daveru, sì, ca è 'n omu forti!

TRANSLATION
What does a lion do to be a lion?
Nothing. But a man must risk death to hear it said of him: "What a lion!
Yes, here we have a strong man!"

Luigi Pirandello

BRUCATO FAMILY TREE

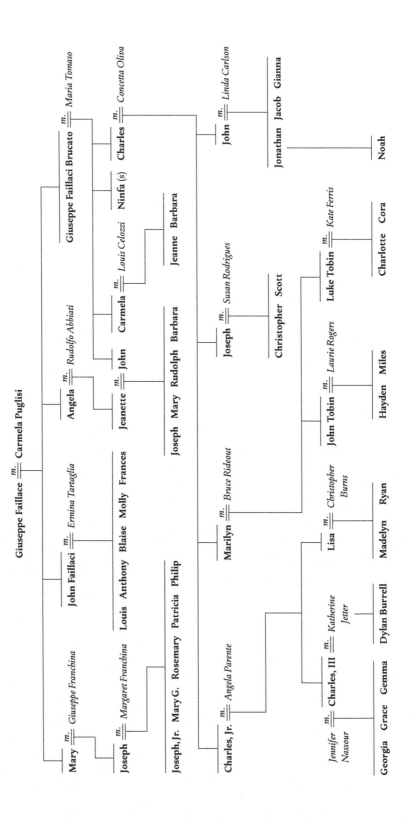

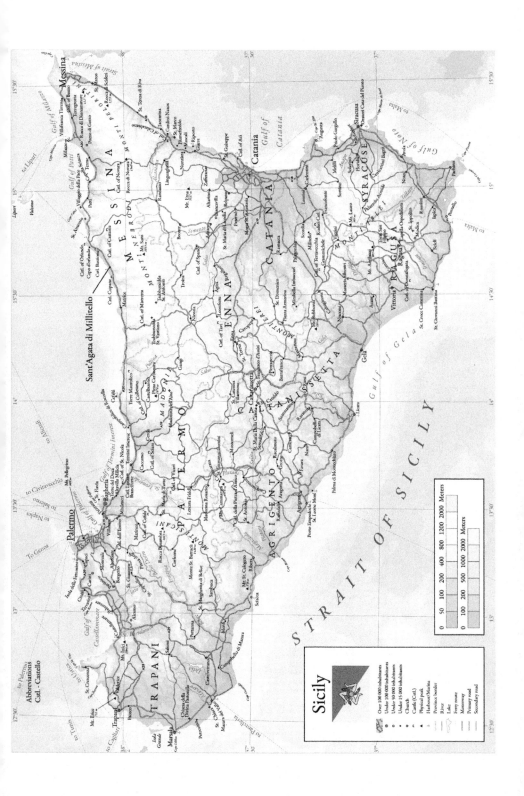

FOREWORD

CHARLES J. "THE BRONC" BRUCATO WAS A COMPLEX MAN who experienced the highest of highs and the lowest of lows in his eighty-three years on earth. In this poignant and captivating biography of their father, the authors take the reader on a journey through the major events of the twentieth century and chronicle his many successes as an athlete and coach. His accomplishments are proof that incredible achievements sometimes occur where least expected.

This book, however, is not just about achievement. Rather, it is a story about Sicilian culture and creed, ethnic prejudice, family, loss, and service to town, country, and the marine corps. Most of all, it is a story about quiet anguish.

The book contains numerous anecdotes not only about the Bronc but also about the many and varied individuals who touched his life. The reader will be both entertained and enlightened by these. The book also contains numerous old photographs which hearken to a time long since passed.

I thoroughly enjoyed the book. It is a great read for anyone seeking to understand the plight of Sicilian immigrants in the early twentieth century and how they persevered to become part of the fabric of America.

Ken Hamwey
Sportswriter
Bellingham, Massachusetts
November 1, 2023

CHAPTER ONE

SICILIAN ROOTS

C HARLES J. BRUCATO WAS BORN ON MARCH 2, 1916, IN Milford, Massachusetts, but his life journey has its genesis with the birth of his father on the island of Sicily in February of 1879. At that time, the Kingdom of Italy was in its nascent years, having only been created in 1861 with the unification of the country.

Prior to unification, though the mainland and the island of Sicily were referred to as Italy, what composed these areas was an expanse of separate territories, regions, empires, and kingdoms, most of which were under the control of other countries. The Austrians ruled Venice and Lombardy; Florence, Modena, and Parma were under Austrian protection; the French ruled Rome; the Bourbons of Spain ruled Naples and Sicily. Only the Piedmont region was independent.

There was no universal Italian language. The people in each of the disparate territories spoke their own language or dialect, and the dialects were so different that people residing in one region had a difficult time understanding those living in the other regions. The attitudes, customs, and even the food differed from territory to territory. Sicily was the most unique and different of all.

The Sicilians were darker skinned than the people on the mainland. They did not speak a dialect; they spoke a language of their own. Their morals and customs were also dramatically different from the other regions. "Nepotism, for example, was not considered remotely wrong; on the contrary, it was the duty of any respectable man to do as much as he possibly could for his family and friends. Patronage, too, was right and natural; it affected all transactions, all agreements, and it extended in a vast network from one end of the island to the other."[1] Most importantly, the attitude and psyche of the Sicilians were unique. Sicily's geography and its history are the main reasons for this.

> "Sicily," says Goethe, "is the key to everything." It is, first of all, the largest island in the Mediterranean. It has also proved, over the years, to be the most unhappy. The stepping-stone between Europe and Africa, the gateway between the East and the West, the link between the Latin world and the Greek, at once a stronghold, clearinghouse, and observation point, it has been fought over and occupied in turn by all the great powers that have striven over the centuries to extend their dominion across the Middle Sea....Even today, despite the beauty of its landscape, the fertility of its fields, and the perpetual benediction of its climate, there lingers everywhere some dark, brooding quality—some underling sorrow of which poverty, the Church, the Mafia, and all the other popular scapegoats may be manifestations but are certainly not the cause. It is the sorrow of long, unhappy experience, of opportunity lost and promise unfulfilled—the sorrow, perhaps, of a beautiful woman who has been betrayed too often and is no longer fit for love or marriage.[2]

The movement toward the unification of Italy, known as the *Risorgimento*, began in 1860. For Sicilians, it brought chaos to an island already

---

1   John Julius Norwich, *Sicily: An Island at the Crossroads of History* (New York: Random House, 2015), 300

2   Norwich, *Sicily*, xxiii

in turmoil. The entire nineteenth century on the island was turbulent. There were four separate rebellions (1820, 1837, 1848 and 1860) by the Sicilians against the hated Bourbons of Spain, who were the last of many to occupy the island and rule its people.

The battle for Risorgimento began in Sicily and later moved to Naples and the mainland of Italy. In the spring and summer of 1860, Giuseppe Garibaldi and his volunteers—dubbed "the Thousand Red Shirts"—began a successful military campaign to wrest control of the island. Most Sicilians were elated. They believed that they would be independent at long last. They were wrong. What followed the freeing of Sicily from the hated Bourbons was the freeing of the Italian main-land from foreign control and ultimately the unification of all regions into the Kingdom of Italy. On March 17, 1861, Victor Emanuel II of Piedmont was proclaimed king. Sicily was not independent much to the dismay of its natives. It was now under the rule of another monarch.

Unification did little to change the mindsets of the Sicilians or the people of the Italian mainland. "The political unification of Italy could neither wipe out centuries of separation nor could it instantly supply a common identity for those who believed themselves to be dif-ferent depending on the region in which they lived."[3] This was espe-cially true in Sicily where the residents were particularly provincial and entrenched in their beliefs and customs. What they yearned for was independence. What they got was more domination.

"In Sicilian eyes, the unification of Italy...got off to a deplorable start. The new Italian government was hated, perhaps even more than that of the Bourbons before it. The people of Sicily deeply resented not only the refusal of their promised autonomy but the summary dis-missal of Garibaldi, with barely a word of thanks or congratulations on his stunning achievement....The officials sent from Turin to set Sic-ily to rights were equally disillusioned by what they found. They had expected a sadder, poorer version of Piedmont; here instead was another

---

3   Stephen Puelo, *The Boston Italians* (Boston: Beacon Press, 2007), 68

world, speaking another language, operating on a completely different system."[4]

The Kingdom of Italy brought with it two major reasons for the Sicilians to hate it—taxation and conscription into military service. Most of the people who lived in Sicily were peasants with little or no ability to pay taxes, and being drafted into the army of a country they felt no loyalty to was repugnant to them. By the 1870s, poverty, high taxes, violence, and suppression of peasant movements by the government plagued the island. Corruption became widespread and brigands terrorized the island. This spawned organized crime, which eventually came to be known as the Mafia or Cosa Nostra.

The Mafia "emerged in the Palermo hinterland when the toughest and smartest bandits, members of the parties' *gabelotti,* smugglers, livestock rustlers, estate wardens, farmers, and lawyers came together to specialize in the violence industry and to share a method for building power and wealth that was perfected in the lemon business. These men extended their method to family members and business contacts....The Mafia had the protection rackets and the powerful political friends, and it also had its cellular structure, its name, its rituals, and an untrustworthy state as a competitor."[5]

In his book, *Cosa Nostra: A History of the Sicilian Mafia,* John Dickie describes its methods. "The Mafia of Sicily pursues power and money by cultivating the art of killing people and getting away with it, and by organizing itself in a unique way that combines the attributes of a shadow state, an illegal business, and a sworn secret society like the Freemasons."[6]

Not trusting the new government, "rural Sicilians...came to rely on the Mafia, rather than the police, 'to ferret out and punish the criminals.' If they needed someone to settle a dispute with a neighbor or to find out who may have rustled their cattle or sheep, they went to the

---

4   Norwich, *Sicily,* 299

5   John Dickie, *Cosa Nostra: A History of the Sicilian Mafia* (n.p.: Holder & Stoughton, 2015), 65, eBook.

6   Dickie, *Cosa Nostra,* 21.

head of their local family, not the authorities, and the capo decided what to do. The winning party then owed the boss a favor, to be collected at some unknown time in the future. The loser accepted the decision and kept quiet. To protest meant problems, perhaps even death, for him and his family."[7] To complicate matters, the Mafia often worked for the government and, after a time, controlled the local officials.

On February 27, 1879, amid this strife, a son was born to Giuseppe Faillace[8] and his wife Carmela (born Puglisi), in Sant'Agata di Millitello, a small village situated on the northeast coast of the Tyrrhenian Sea, ninety kilometers from Messina and 120 kilometers from Palermo. They named him Giuseppe after his father. He was the third of four children in the family. The other children were Angela and Maria Grazia, who were older than Giuseppe, and John, who was born nine years later.

Like most Sicilians, the Faillaces were peasants. They did not own land and had few possessions. There is virtually no information about Giuseppe's parents or how his father supported the family. The only work in the area was farming in the olive groves and lemon orchards or fishing. What is known is that Carmela took care of the household and children as all married women did in Sicily.

In 1887, when Giuseppe was eight years old, Francesco Crispi, a Sicilian, began his rule of Italy. Rather than improving the situation in his native region, he made matters worse. He was particularly cruel to the peasants. From 1893 to 1896, Crispi "ruthlessly suppressed peasant movements in his native Sicily and inaugurated savage laws against the growing movements of socialism and anarchism."[9] In addition to the burdens placed on the Sicilians by the government, there was also the brutality doled out by the Mafia.

7   John Keahey, *Seeking Sicily* (n.p.: Thomas Dunne Press, 2011), loc. 2529 of 4492, Kindle.

8   *Fallacce* was the spelling of the name in the archives in Sant'Agata, but over the years, it changed to *Failacci, Faillaci,* and *Faillacci* in many records. These spellings will appear in later parts of the book.

9   Harry Hearder, *Italy: A Short History* (1990; repr., Cambridge: Cambridge University Press, 2014), 207

Small in stature and very thin, Giuseppe schooled up to the fifth grade and was one of few in his village able to read and write. He aspired to be a teacher, but that would prove to be impossible. When he was nineteen, Giuseppe met Maria (Mary) Tomaso who lived nearby in the village of Tusa. There is no record that the two married while living in Sicily, but on August 25, 1899, Maria gave birth to their first child, Giovanni (John). Giuseppe was twenty and, astonishingly, Maria was just thirteen years old. In the archives (*archiva*) at Sant'Agata, the record of John's birth lists Giuseppe Faillace as father, but there is no mention of his mother. According to one of the clerks there, the mother's name is not listed when she is not married. Whether Maria, Giuseppe, and baby John lived together in Sicily cannot be confirmed. There is also scant information about what Giuseppe did to support them.

At the time of John's birth, corruption was rampant, and there was violence everywhere. Work was scarce, and in addition to the oppressive taxes, the new Italian government was conscripting young men for the army. Many oppressed Sicilians, seeing no other way, had begun a movement toward socialism. Others became anarchists. "As for the 'honored society'—as the Mafia liked to call itself—it filled the gap where government should have been. Crime was the means by which it achieved its ends; those ends were respect, power, and money."[10]

Giuseppe was ill-equipped to weather the storm around him and his family. In addition to being small in stature, he was quiet, sensitive, and introverted. Living in these chaotic times had had a profound effect on him. He had become disillusioned, distrustful, and sad. Fearful of the insensitive new government, the Mafia, and the various ideologues, he became withdrawn and distant. These attitudes would stay with him for the rest of his life, and he would pass them down to his children—his youngest child, Charles, most of all.

Luigi Pirandello, one of the most famous Sicilian writers, who received the Nobel Prize for Literature in 1934 and lived during the same time as Giuseppe, said: "All Sicilians are sad after all, because of

10 Norwich, *Sicily,* 305.

their tragic sense of life.... They perceive with mistrust the contrast between their closed disposition and the open nature around them."

Another contemporary, Giuseppe Tomasi di Lampedusa, said,

> For over twenty-five centuries, we've been bearing the weight of superb and heterogeneous civilizations, all from outside, none made by ourselves, none that we could call our own.
>
> This violence of landscape, this cruelty of climate, this continual tension in everything, and even these monuments of the past, magnificent yet incomprehensible because not built by us and yet standing round us like lovely mute ghosts; all those rulers who landed by main force from every direction who were at once obeyed, soon detested, and always misunderstood, their only expressions works of art we couldn't understand and taxes which we understood only too well and which they spent elsewhere: all these things have formed our character, which is thus conditioned by events outside our control as well as by a terrifying insularity of mind.
>
> —Giuseppe Tomasi di Lampedusa, *The Leopard*

As the nineteenth century ended and the twentieth began, Giuseppe decided that he could no longer live with the lawlessness and uncertainties in his native land. Like thousands of other weary and wary Sicilians, he decided to seek a better life in America. "More than 4 million Italians left Italy to come to the United States between 1880 and 1920, and 80 per cent of those came from southern Italy and Sicily."[11]

According to his naturalization petition filed on November 30, 1938, Giuseppe states, "I immigrated to the United States from Naples, Italy. My lawful entry for permanent residence in the United States was at New York, New York under the name of Joseph Faillaci on May 12, 1903, on the *Duca Di Galliera*." The immigration records show the arrival of Giuseppe Faillaci in New York in two separate registers. The official "List or Manifest of Alien Passengers" at Ellis Island reveals the

---

11 Puleo, *Boston*, 47.

arrival of twenty-three-year-old Giuseppe Faillaci on May 13, 1903, on a ship known as *Citta Di Torino*. That record reveals that he was married, a shoemaker, could read and write, was meeting Giuseppe Franchina, and his destination was Stamford, Connecticut.

The second record is an unofficial abstract of the list of "New York Castle Garden Immigrants," and it shows the arrival of Giuseppe Faillaci on May 18, 1903, on the *Duca Di Galliera* ship. That record contains less information but lists the same age, occupation, and relative joined in the United States as the Ellis Island record. Notwithstanding the different records, it is clear that Giuseppe arrived in New York in mid-May of 1903.

In his naturalization petition, Giuseppe also stated that he had lived in Massachusetts since June 9, 1905. Where he lived and worked for the two years after he arrived in America is unclear. There is no evidence that he was a shoemaker. His first stop was Stamford, Connecticut, but whether he remained cannot be confirmed. He did have family there, so it is reasonable to conclude that he stayed. One unconfirmed story was that he landed in Milwaukee, Wisconsin, for a period but left because he was being pressured to join the Mafia.

After entering the United States, Giuseppe began using the Americanized first name "Joseph." Remarkably, he also started to use "Brucato" as his last name. Why he did this remains a mystery. Many immigrants had their names changed inadvertently. Since most were illiterate, their names would be recorded by clerks at Ellis Island. This led to misspellings and the Americanization of the names. Sometimes the clerks mistakenly recorded the city or town from which the immigrant came as his/her last name. Sometimes the names were changed to their English counterparts (i.e. Bianchi to White) or occupation (Calzolaio to Shoemaker).

None of these reasons apply to the change from Faillaci to Brucato. There are, however, some *sotto voce* theories for the change in family lore. Some family members speculate that Giuseppe's father was involved with the various uprisings in Sicily or some other wrongdoing tarnishing the family name. Others speculate that he was a member of the Mafia or some other illicit group. It is also possible that he was a fugitive. If any of these theories were true, it is possible that Giuseppe was afraid to use his real last name in his new country. There had to be a reason why he adopted the Brucato name. Unfortunately, it will remain a mystery. The people who would know have long since died.

Maria and John did not come to the United States with Giuseppe. This was not uncommon. Many men left their families in Italy to find work in the new world. Once they got jobs, some had no intention of staying and would return to Italy once they had saved some money. Others would remain and bring their other family members over when the time was right. It is likely that this is what Giuseppe did.

In his naturalization petition, he stated that Maria arrived in the United States in 1905. The name "Brocato" appears in the immigration records at Ellis Island, which reveal that a twenty-one-year-old Maria Brocato arrived at Ellis Island with a four-year-old son, Giovanni Brocato on May 11, 1904. They came over on a ship known as *Roma* which sailed from Naples. While their last name is misspelled, and Maria's age is incorrect (she was seventeen and not twenty-one), these errors can be explained. The clerks could have mistakenly placed an *o* where the *u* was, and Maria probably told the authorities she was twenty-one because one would likely have to be of legal age to enter the country when bringing a child.

There are other discrepancies which cannot be explained, so it is impossible to confirm that they were Giuseppe's "wife" and son. Another record shows Maria Braucato born circa 1885 arriving at Ellis Island on March 15, 1905, further complicating matters. (Immigration records are filled with the Brucato name or variations of it, making confirmation impossible. There are far less Faillaci name entries.)

What is reasonably certain is that Giuseppe, Maria, and John ultimately landed in Milford, Massachusetts, where Maria's family from Sicily had settled. Giuseppe's naturalization petition reveals that he began residing in Massachusetts on June 9, 1905, and according to the town's wedding records, Maria Tomasi and Giuseppe Faillaci were married in Milford on October 15, 1905. Where the family lived in Milford after the wedding is unknown. The Milford residence books do not show the Brucato or Faillaci name until 1929. Perhaps they were living with members of Maria's family and did not want their presence in town known because they were not United States citizens, and they could have feared deportation. This makes sense. After all, Giuseppe was a private and distrustful young man.

IN 1905, THEODORE ROOSEVELT WAS IN HIS SECOND TERM as the president of the United States, and the Wright Brothers were trying to prove that man was capable of flying. Milford was a small town near the Rhode Island border, situated about thirty miles west of Boston and eighteen miles south of Worcester. Transportation was either by rail or horse and buggy. Originally inhabited by the English, Milford had become a melting pot in the nineteenth century when Irish immigrants settled there. The town grew even more with the arrival of the Italians in the twentieth century.

When the Brucatos got there, Milford was a thriving industrial and mining community due in large part to its unique geography. The Charles River, Mill River, and Blackstone River watershed ran through the town, making it ideal for manufacturing. There were also large deposits of rare pink granite in Milford which attracted companies to mine it. Additionally, there was easy access to Milford with a railway and roadways running through town from every direction. The presence of the mills and granite companies created a great demand for unskilled labor, and the immigrants from Italy were happy to supply that demand. Giuseppe and the other Italian immigrants had little trouble finding work. Though the work involved hard manual labor, especially in the granite quarries, they were happy to get it—but there was a price they would have to pay. In their later years, countless quarry workers would develop what they called "stone cutter's disease" (medically known as silicosis), a respiratory ailment caused by inhaling dust particles. Those who contracted it suffered from coughing, sputum, and shortness of breath. It often led to premature death. The foundries in the manufacturing companies were equally toxic.

Though getting gainful work was not problematic for the Italian immigrants, assimilating into the community was another story. By the time the Italians arrived, the Irish had already entrenched themselves in the community both socially and politically. It was easy for the Irish to assimilate. Unlike the southern Italians and Sicilians, they were fair skinned and spoke English. The Irish and the "Mericanos" did not like the newly arriving Italians, especially the darker skinned immigrants from southern Italy and Sicily, whom they considered to be inferior.

As a result, hostility between the established Milfordians and the new immigrants from Italy immediately ensued, and the town was split into two separate and distinct communities. The dividing line was a set of railroad tracks, which ran through Milford. The Irish and "Yankees" lived on the uptown side of the tracks, where the retail district, town hall, high school, and "Irish church" (St. Mary's) were located. The Italians resided in a well-defined area on the other side of the tracks called "the Plains," where the granite quarries and manufacturing companies were located. There, they had their own grocery stores, businesses, farms, and church (Sacred Heart). Interestingly, both Roman Catholic churches were located less than a stone throw from each other albeit on opposite sides of the tracks. The Irish would never attend mass at Sacred Heart and vice-versa.

Though the "Mericanos" and Irish would cross the tracks with impunity, this was not the case for the Italians. They did not dare cross the tracks lest they be subjected to stinging insults and taunts. They were called *WOPs, dagos, guineas, spaghetti benders,* and other more vulgar names. They were not welcome at the stores, eateries, bars, and even the banks uptown. This was especially true for the Sicilians. "Southern Italians were viewed as a different race entirely, likely for many reasons: their darker complexions, their inability to speak English, their general illiteracy, and their unusual Catholic religious customs.... Discrimination against Southern Italians was as much racism as xenophobia."[12]

Within the Plains, there was also separation among the Italian immigrants based on the area in Italy from which they came. The Sicilians settled in a one or two block area on either Hayward Street or Mount Pleasant Street, creating their own separate enclave. There were other enclaves in the Plains. The immigrants from Calabria, Foggia, Abruzzo, Bari, Marche, and other regions lived in their own separate areas of the Plains. In each of these enclaves, the people shared the same backgrounds, spoke the same dialects, and had the same customs. The Sicilians on Hayward Street spoke a language so vastly different from the dialects spoken by the immigrants from the other regions in Italy that they could not communicate with them.

As Stephen Puleo says in his book *The Boston Italians*, "The Italian immigration process in Boston and other American cities was characterized most dramatically by the development of these tightly knit enclaves. Italians from the same region or village relocated to America through a process called 'chain migration' and settled on the same block or even the same street."[13] "They belonged not to Italy first, but to their families and then to their villages."[14]

Unfortunately, ". . . the enclaves overall insularity prevented Italians from learning rapidly; to read and speak English; about Americans and their customs; or additional skills to improve their job prospects and their economic plight.... Maybe more important, the fact that Italians so often cloistered in enclaves prevented Americans from learning from *them*."[15]

At some point, Giuseppe, Maria, and their son John took up residence in an apartment on Mount Pleasant Street at the intersection of Hayward Street. Giuseppe got a job in nearby Hopedale at Draper Corporation, which manufactured looms for the textile industry. Draper

---

12 Puleo, *Boston*, 81.
13 Puleo, *Boston*, 67.
14 Puleo, *Boston*, 68.
15 Puleo, *Boston*, 73.

BRUCATO FAMILY CIRCA 1917

Front row, left to right: Charles, Carmela (Molly), Ninfa.
Second row: Maria and Giuseppe. Standing in rear: John.

Corporation was the largest employer in the area. On March 2, 1912, Maria gave birth to a daughter, Carmela (Molly) followed two years later by the birth of another daughter, Ninfa. In the year Ninfa was born, World War I had broken out in Europe, but the United States was not yet involved. Charlie was born two years after Ninfa. All three children were born in Milford, and their last name was Brucato.

A professional photograph of the family taken in late 1916 or early 1917 shows Maria and Giuseppe seated. He has a bushy dark mustache and thick dark hair. Maria has a round face and a much bigger frame than her husband. Baby Charlie is on her lap and Giuseppe has Ninfa on his

Maria Brucato circa 1917

lap. Molly is standing between them. John is behind them, towering over everyone. He was seventeen or eighteen years old at the time. No one in the photo is smiling. Their expressions are somber, almost foreboding.

On April 6, 1917, the United States entered World War I, and not long thereafter, tragedy struck the Brucato family. In the summer of 1917, Maria developed an infection (thought to be caused by breast feeding). Medicine was not what it is now, and the infection could not be controlled. She died on July 19, 1917. Charlie was only sixteen months old. The fact that he had to grow up without the love and nurturing of a mother would prove to be the first of many traumatic episodes for him. When he grew older, Charlie insisted that he had vivid memories of his mother even though he was a baby when she died. He always carried a photograph of her in his wallet. The facial resemblance between the two is striking.

Maria's death was a shock to the entire family, but more importantly, it was a severe blow to the already emotionally fragile Giuseppe. He was left to raise a baby and two little girls. His oldest son, John, departed to join the United States Army and get into World War I. In order to do so, he had to become a citizen. On his naturalization papers, he listed his name as John Brucato. Giuseppe kept the rest of the family in Milford where Maria's sisters (who had also settled on Hayward Street) could help with the children while he worked. One of Maria's sisters, Rosalina (Tomaso) Longo ("Zia Roe"), even wet nursed baby Charlie.

The period between 1903 and 1917 brought with it a multitude of changes in the United States. In 1908, Henry Ford had launched the production and sale of the Model T and William Howard Taft defeated William Jennings Bryan to become the twenty-seventh president of the United States. The year 1910 saw the first public radio broadcast. In 1912, Woodrow Wilson won the presidential election, and in 1913, the sixteenth Amendment, creating an income tax for all Americans, was enacted. The year 1914 marked the beginning of World War I, and the next year, Ford produced one million cars.

America was growing and prospering. Then, in 1918, an influenza pandemic ravaged the world, infecting 500 million people and killing 50 million. First discovered in the United States in military personnel in the spring of 1918, it spread quickly and was particularly deadly to children under five, people in the twenty to forty age range, and those over sixty-five. The Brucatos were spared, but many in the Italian community in Milford were not so lucky.

———

WORLD WAR I ENDED ON NOVEMBER 11, 1918. SHORTLY thereafter, in 1919, when Charlie was three, Giuseppe moved the family to Stamford, Connecticut, where his brother John (who kept the name Faillaci) and his two sisters lived. Stamford was not the bustling modern metropolis it has become in recent years. It was a working-class city where Italian immigrant families had settled. Like Milford, Stamford had its own separate Italian enclaves, and Giuseppe's relatives lived in the Sicilian section of the city. Few, if any of these families, owned their own homes. They lived in rented apartments in wood framed clapboard multifamily structures known as three-deckers.

BRUCATO FAMILY CIRCA 1919

Left to right: Ninfa, Charles, Giuseppe, and Molly.
(Missing: John, who was in the military.)

The Brucatos moved into an apartment on one floor of a three-decker at 45 Beckley Avenue. John, who was now twenty or twenty-one, had been discharged from the army and rejoined his father and siblings in the apartment. The Brucato children were delighted to be reunited with their older brother. Giuseppe's sister, Angela, had married Rodolfo Abbiati, and they lived in the same building in an apartment either above or below them. The Abbiatis had a daughter, Jeannette, who was fourteen or fifteen.

Giuseppe's sister, Mary, had married Giuseppe Franchina, and they also lived in the building at one point or another. In a similar structure, only a few doors away, his brother John Faillaci was living with his family.

Giuseppe immediately sought employment in Stamford. On one employment application, he used the name Joseph Faillaci. He got a job at Yale and Towne Manufacturing Co., but this time he was Joseph Brucato. He also registered for the World War I draft as Joseph Faillaci Brucato.

The Volstead Act took effect in January of 1920, launching Prohibition and ushering in the Roaring Twenties. The Mafia, now in the United States, was among the first to profit from the bootlegging business. They brought with them the lawlessness and violence that Giuseppe knew was their calling card. The Mafia's emergence in America further tarnished the image of the Sicilians.

Soon after he arrived in Stamford, Giuseppe began a relationship with Mary Franchina, a widow, who was also his first cousin. She became his second wife and moved in with the family. (The Franchinas and the Brucato-Faillacis all came from the same area of Sicily, and all were related.) It was not uncommon for Sicilian cousins to marry, which probably speaks to their inherent distrust of people from other regions.

Life in the apartment with their stepmother was not easy for the younger Brucato children. When Giuseppe was away at work or somewhere else, Mary did not treat them well. Ninfa often said of her stepmother, "She was mean to us. Aunt Angela told us to bang on the water pipes if she did anything to us and she would come in and straighten her out." During an interview, one of Mary Franchina's granddaughters denied that this was the case. She claimed that Giuseppe was not a loving husband and he and the children were miserable to Mary.

Molly and Ninfa began their education in the Stamford public schools. Charlie was not yet old enough and remained home with his stepmother. Though the girls learned English in school, they spoke Sicilian at home. Molly and Ninfa doted on their little brother, and John would become his surrogate father and best friend. John was different from the distant and brooding Giuseppe. He was warm and outgoing. Charlie idolized his older brother, who lavished him with toys, sports equipment, and anything else he wanted.

Charlie entered public school in Stamford in 1921. He was small, painfully shy, quiet, and serious. Later in life, in his inimitable way of speaking, he described himself as reticent. Though his sisters and brother tried their best, without the love and nurturing of a mother and with a stoical, pessimistic, cynical, and withdrawn father, Charlie was most likely insecure. This notwithstanding, he soon adjusted to school and life in Stamford with relatives and family friends.

One of his favorite stories about Stamford, which Charlie often recounted, involved an incident at school when he was eight or nine years old. He would chuckle and say, "I was playing at recess one day when a big 'colored boy' named Asa came over to me. He was one of the school bullies, and he began to pick a fight. I was scared, but I knew I couldn't back down from him in front of the other kids, so I agreed to meet him after school to settle things.

"I worried all day and tried to think of ways to avoid fighting him. I was sure that Asa was going to beat me to a pulp. After school, I trudged back to the schoolyard where the fight was to take place. A crowd of kids gathered to watch. Asa seemed surprised I had shown up. Apparently, no one had ever dared to stand up to him. He sauntered toward me with his chest pumped up and glared at me. Somehow, I gathered the courage to look him in the eye, but inside I was terrified. I put up my fists and threw a punch at him as hard as I could. It landed squarely on his chin. He was stunned. He rubbed his chin and looked at me with surprise but did not punch me back. I guess he decided he really didn't want to fight. From that day forward, I had his respect and was a kind of hero to the other kids at school."

There was another story Charlie told about life in Stamford. His brother John had taken a job driving delivery vans and often took Charlie with him. Sometimes, he would even let little Charlie drive. These were times he cherished.

Charlie often recounted what happened on a delivery. "One day, Brother John (as he always referred to him) took me with him on a milk delivery at a house in Stamford. He parked the truck in the driveway and told me to stay there while he made his delivery. A few minutes later, he returned and got back in the truck. He began to back out, but a big 'colored boy' stood in the way. (Charlie was not a racist. This is merely the way people of his generation referred to black people.) Brother John yelled at him to move so he could back out, but the boy just stood there, folded his arms, and scowled. I got really scared. Suddenly, Brother John jumped out of the van and ran back toward the boy. He grabbed the boy by his shirt and flung him about ten feet to the side of the driveway. He returned to the van and backed out onto the street. He never said a word. That was Brother John—one tough son of a bitch."

As time went on, John developed a close relationship with Jeannette Abbiati (his first cousin). She was nearly six years younger than him and was a beautiful girl with a wonderful personality. Since they lived in the same building, they had spent a lot of time together and fell in love. In November of 1924, they were married. Charlie was eight years old at that time.

The best part of living in Stamford for Charlie and his sisters is that they developed close relationships with relatives on the Brucato side of the family. Before they had only known their Tomaso relatives. They would remain close to Uncle John Faillaci, Aunt Angelina Abbiati, and Aunt Maria Franchina and their families for their entire lives.

Charlie also became very close with cousin Joe Franchina. Following the Sicilian tradition, Joe had married his first cousin, Margaret Franchina, who didn't even have to change her name. With his big nose, dark hair, and imposing presence, Joe could have passed as Charlie's brother. Interestingly, they both became career educators. In later years, each summer, Charlie would return to Stamford for a couple of weeks to reconnect with his relatives and Brother John.

On August 29, 1925, Brother John and Jeanette had their first child, a boy named Joseph. At nine years old, Charlie had become an uncle. Now that Brother John had his own family, the apartment was getting too small for Giuseppe and his three other children, so he decided to move back to Milford.

CHAPTER TWO

GROWING UP IN MILFORD

I N 1926, CHARLIE, HIS FATHER, AND TWO SISTERS RETURNED to Milford where they would live for the remainder of their lives. Giuseppe's new wife did not accompany them. Sadly, for Charlie and his sisters, Brother John remained in Stamford with his wife and baby son. When they arrived back in Milford, the Brucatos took up residence in a small apartment at 29 Mount Pleasant Street at the intersection of Hayward Street in the Sicilian neighborhood in the Plains. Like the other residences in the area, the apartment was in a two-floor, wood framed, shingled structure with little land around it. Few Italian immigrants owned the homes they lived in and virtually none owned a car. In fact, during his lifetime, Giuseppe never owned a house or a car.

Molly was now fourteen, Ninfa twelve, and Charlie ten. The two girls shared the household chores and took care of their brother while Giuseppe worked at Draper Corporation in Hopedale. Charlie entered the Milford public school system but neither Molly nor Ninfa resumed their educations. Ninfa said, "Charlie was so shy that he would not go to school until he had looked out the window and was sure nobody was watching."

Ninfa also said that Molly was very smart but was ashamed to go to school because she had a "deformed" arm. (Her arm had been broken at childbirth and was never set correctly) Ninfa said she didn't go to school because she had to do the cooking.

In the traditional Sicilian family, women were relegated to the household while the men would go to school and then off to work when old enough. Molly would, however, enter the work force to help with the family's finances when she was eighteen. She got a job at one of the mills located on Central Street, a stone's throw from the apartment. At that point, Ninfa did the cooking and all the household chores.

The prejudices against Italians in Milford remained. Among other things, the impression which pervaded the Italian community in Milford, was that Italians were lawless, especially those from Sicily where the Mafia and Cosa Nostra had their roots. ". . . The gangsters helped stall and stunt the full acceptance of Italians into American society, even as the 1930s approached"[16] It did not help that Nicola Sacco, one of two immigrants executed in 1927 after the historic Sacco and Vanzetti trial, was from Milford.

Since the Italians were unwelcome on the other side of the tracks, they had to find places where they could socialize. This led to one of the unique features of life in the Italian enclaves in Milford, which exists to the present day— the creation of social clubs. In the Plains, each area had its own club. There was the Marchegiano Club on Meade Street, the Foggiano Club on Granite Street, the Sons of Italy, the Italian American Veterans Club, and the Hoboken Citizens Club on Bear Hill. The Sicilians had their own small club off Hayward Street, but in later years became members of the Hoboken Citizen's Club which was created by the Arbëreshë (Albanians from Italy euphemistically called *gagadas*.). There were strict rules for membership in these clubs. To be a member of the Marchegiano Club, for example, your father had to be a *marche* (a descendant of that province).

16   Puleo, *Boston*, 159.

Some of the club buildings were modest, but others were quite elaborate. All were situated on lots within the various enclaves and were purchased with the money of the members. Construction of the club buildings was done with the labor of the artisans from the respective neighborhoods. Weddings, baptisms, holidays, and other social events were held at the clubs.

The Italian men would also gather at the clubs after work or on weekends to meet, eat, drink, shoot pool, play cards, bocce, or *morra*. The bookies were always at the clubs to accept bets from the club members. Morra (pronounced *mor-ta* in Italian) games fit the Italian personality best. Invented over three thousand years ago, it is a game played by two individuals and involves the prediction of numbers. The two players reveal their hand simultaneously (like rock, scissors, paper), presenting a number of fingers between *uno* (one) and *cinque* (five) while shouting out a number between *due* (two) and *dieci* (ten). The player who successfully guesses the summation of fingers revealed by both players scores a point. The game is played to eleven, and the winner generally gets a beer from the loser. Anyone who has seen a morra game will never forget it. The yelling and screaming of numbers are deafening, and the contestants get so angry that they often come to blows.

DISCRIMINATION AGAINST ITALIANS WAS NOT RESTRICTED to adults. Even though they were born in the United States, ten-year-old Charlie and his *paisanos* felt the sting of prejudice early and often when they left their enclaves to attend school. "Public school officials engaged in a startling level of anti-Italian bigotry when it came to their students. Teachers ridiculed Italian schoolchildren for their broken English, the clothing they wore, or their parents' inability to speak English or read at all."[17] This was a fact of life in Milford in the 1920s and '30s, and it was another damaging and disturbing experience that would impact Charlie's emotional development.

---

17 Puleo, *Boston*, 86.

Sensitive to how Americans perceived Sicilians, Giuseppe instilled in his young boy the cynicism that he had developed in the old country.

"Be careful who you trust. Keep your feelings to yourself," Giuseppe would tell him in dialect. "Don't let anyone know what you are thinking."

Giuseppe ingrained in him another set of values from the old country. Charlie learned the Sicilian code of silence, or *omerta*, which had been adopted and propagated by the Mafia.

Literally, omerta means "manliness." In practice, it means that "whoever appeals to the law against his fellow man is either a fool or a coward. Whoever cannot take care of himself without police protection is both. It is as cowardly to betray an offender to justice, even though his offenses be against yourself, as it is not to avenge an injury by violence. It is dastardly and contemptible in a wounded man to betray the name of his assailant, because if he recovers, he must naturally expect to take vengeance himself."[18] These attitudes were imbedded in Charlie, and he lived by them his entire life.

Playing baseball became the way young Charlie was able to distinguish himself. Even as a ten-year-old, he possessed incredible agility and athleticism. Though he was small, he was an exceptionally fast runner. In later years he attributed this to the fact that "[he] ran everywhere. [He] just loved running." He also possessed extraordinary eye-hand coordination, a trait that made him an outstanding hitter. He said this was because he "spent hours throwing rocks in the air and hitting them with a makeshift bat." The truth was that he was simply a natural athlete with God-given ability.

Soon after he arrived in Milford, Charlie gravitated to his cousin, Sammy Tomaso, who was about the same age. The two developed a friendship which lasted a lifetime. They spent all their free time on the town's playgrounds. Both loved baseball, and both excelled in the sport. At the playgrounds, Charlie met two more lifetime friends, albeit from other enclaves in the Plains—Henry "Tate" Bodio and Frank "Sooey"

---

18 "Omerta," *The Godfather* Wiki, Fandom Wikipedia, https://godfather.fandom.com/wiki/Omert%C3%A0.

DeGaetano. (Everyone in the Milford Italian communities had a nickname.) The four kids were inseparable. Sports drew them together, to kids from other enclaves in the Plains, and even to kids on the uptown side of the tracks. They did not share their parents' desire to stay "with their own." The Plains became a breeding ground for athletes, especially talented baseball players. There was no little league then and no school teams until high school. The boys learned the game from older kids.

There were four parks in Milford where kids played baseball. The Irish and Yankee kids played at Town Park on Spruce Street on the uptown side of the tracks. Oliver Park on Oliver Street featured a mix of ethnicities. Tomaso Field on Hayward Street hosted mainly Sicilian kids and Plains Playground on East Main Street hosted Italian kids. Charlie spent most of his time honing his skills with the Sicilian kids at Tomaso Field and the Italian kids at the Plains Playground. The kids in all four parks welcomed kids from the other parks to play ball with them. Shortly before he died, Charlie gave an interview where he said, "The playgrounds became a mix, and besides, when all your friends were ballplayers, you got along and didn't care about anyone's origin."[19]

One of Charlie's high school and college teammates, Arthur Kenny, put it best, "'It didn't matter who was on the playground,' Kenny, said. 'What we as kids were looking for was ability. ...As kids, we never thought about one's ethnic origin.'"[20] This was the dawning of Milford's dominance in baseball which would continue into the twenty-first century. "(Henry) Bodio, Kenny, (Bernie) Marcus, Charlie Brucato, Hank Comolli, and Sam Tomaso, just to name a few, were the young aspiring athletic kids in the 1920s who soon became the varsity stars of the early 1930s."[21] Charlie developed into one of the best, if not the best baseball player in town. He was fast on the basepaths and nimble in the field, but what set him apart was his ability to hit for average and hit with power.

As in other areas of the country, athletes from immigrant families

---

19   Ken Hamwey, "Milford's League of Nations," *Milford Daily News,* October 16, 1999.
20   Hamwey, "League of Nations."
21   Hamwey, "League of Nations."

gained elevated status in Milford when they had success. Joe DiMaggio, a fellow Sicilian who would become an American icon, is just one example. Lawrence "Yogi" Berra is another. While the Milford Italian kids could not cross the railroad tracks for most activities, the athletic fields were an exception. In an era when there were no televisions, Milfordians from all ethnicities loved to spend their leisure time watching and cheering for the local baseball teams.

In 1929, when he was thirteen years old, Charlie tried out for the newly formed Milford Junior Legion team but was cut. The boy who made the team at his position (second base) was Fred Tredeau, who played at St. Mary's, Milford's Catholic high school. This was a shock to many baseball observers in Milford. Ken Hamwey, a Milford sportswriter, wrote about it on July 29, 1988, in the "Sports Extra" section of the *Milford Daily News*. In the article, which carried the headline "Tredeau Beats Out Brucato in 1929," Hamwey says, "His (Tredeau's) selection to the Legion Team by Frank Berry probably raised a few eyebrows fifty-nine years ago." Tredeau says, "I beat out one of the greatest players Milford High ever had.... I kept Charlie Brucato off the first Legion team. And I'll tell you without hesitation that he was a truly great athlete and player." [22]

The 1929 Legion team ultimately made it to the state finals at Fenway Park where they lost to New Bedford. According to longtime *Milford Daily News* sportswriter Stanley Jones, "The success of the 1929 team was no fluke. It signaled the beginning of Milford's first golden baseball era."[23]

Baseball was not the only entertainment for the Italian kids in the Plains. One of the favorite summer activities for the boys was swimming at the "ledge holes." There were several granite quarries within the Plains where the famous Milford pink granite was mined. In order

22 Ken Hamwey, "Tredeau Beats Out Brucato in 1929," Sports Extra Section, *Milford Daily News*, June 29, 1988.

23 Staley Jones, "Greater Milford Area Sports," *Milford Daily News*, Souvenir Edition, June 7, 1980.

Jumping at ledge hole.

to mine the granite, it was necessary to cut into the rock and remove it in large blocks. The removal of these blocks created large craters, and since the best granite was deep below the surface, the craters were sometimes over one hundred feet deep and hundreds of feet wide. Water from springs in the ground filled the craters creating natural swimming holes.

The swimming holes in the quarries were called ledge holes by the townspeople. It was a rite of passage for the boys to gather at the nonworking quarries, which were in wooded areas, strip their clothes off, and jump into the cold water bare ass. Many boys learned to swim there. It was literally sink or swim, as the ledge holes were often over fifty feet deep. After playing ball in the hot summer sun, swimming at the ledge holes was as good as it gets. Needless to say, it was also very dangerous.

In some areas, the walls of granite extended high above the water. The "daredevils" would climb to the top and then leap from these granite cliffs into the water, holding on to their testicles to protect them from impact. There were even contests to see whose jump was riskier.

In addition to the obvious inherent dangers at the quarries, there was no adult supervision. There were no lifeguards and no safety equipment. In some places, the granite walls were jagged, and slabs of stone protruded out, both above and below the water. The granite surfaces in the ledge holes created the potential for slipping causing scrapes, broken bones, and concussions. The most significant danger was drowning. Charlie and his buddies didn't worry about these things until tragedy struck.

Tate Bodio's brother was swimming at one of the ledge holes with some friends. It was a warm day, and they were having a good time. He jumped in and began swimming underwater. He never came up. He was found wedged under a ledge which protruded into the water. He must have become disoriented or ran out of breath. He was dead when he was pulled out of the water. This very traumatic event also shaped Charlie's adult life. He forbid my brothers and me from going to the ledge holes. We did, however, sneak there on occasion.

In the winter, there was sledding and snowball fights. There were other fun things the Italian boys picked up from the older kids. They learned how to play cards, shoot craps, and gamble on the horses. There was always a poker or gin rummy game in a basement or abandoned building in the area. These were "skills" that Charlie carried with him for his entire life. Growing up in the Plains bestowed on him not only a strong sense of family and community but also street smarts.

This was extremely important to him later in life as he ventured out of his enclave and on to college, played on teams, joined the marines, and became a teacher and coach. It enabled him to make friends easily, hold his own in difficult situations, and gain the respect of those he encountered. Playing cards and handicapping horses would also become essential diversions from the pressures of his career.

CHAPTER THREE

THE HIGH SCHOOL YEARS —
A STAR IS BORN

I N THE FALL OF 1929, CHARLIE ENTERED MILFORD HIGH School as a thirteen-year-old freshman. Many of his Italian friends had quit school after eighth grade to enter the work force and help their families survive. Charlie, Tate Bodio, Sooey DeGaetano, and Sammy Tomaso were four lucky enough to start high school. They did not have much interest in education, but going to school enabled them to play on the sports teams. Bodio said, "No one had cars at school, and there was no television. Having a radio was a big deal. Growing up and going to school meant books and baseball."[24]

Unfortunately, many of the Italian kids who started high school dropped out after a year or two. A college education was not even a possibility. There was little guidance from the teachers and school administrators for these kids. The high school was on the uptown side of the tracks and most of the teachers and administrators were Irish or Yankees. The prejudices held by them against Italians was obvious. Charlie received virtually no counseling and, as a result, chose the easiest classes

24 Hamwey, "League of Nations."

and not the college preparatory courses. This would cause him problems when he graduated.

In October, shortly after Charlie started school and ten months into the presidency of Herbert Hoover, Milford along with the entire country was thrust into years of suffering when the Stock Market crashed and set off the Great Depression. Charlie often talked about this time.

"We had nothing," he reflected. "There were lines of people at places where food was distributed. I pulled a little cart, in the cold, to stand in a long line so I could pick up coal for the stove which heated our apartment. It was tough. A lot of people started doing some very bad things to get by." According to one of his cousins, Charlie once pilfered a bottle of milk from a delivery truck, but Charlie never admitted to doing that.

At the time, men could buy business suits for just over $20, and ladies' dresses were not much more. A pair of shoes cost between $1 and $3. Beef, pork, and chicken sold for less than thirty cents per pound, and cars were selling for under $1,000. In these trying economic times, few people in the Plains could afford any of these things. Oddly, however, people did find enough money to buy cigarettes. The major advertisers in the *Milford Daily News* were cigarette companies. Not a day went by without quarter page ads extolling the virtues of Lucky Strikes or Chesterfields.

The Italian immigrants had experienced poverty in the old country, and one lesson they had learned was how to keep their families well-nourished without having to spend much money. Everyone had a vegetable garden even in very small backyards. They harvested tomatoes, onions, garlic, and parsley, which formed the basis for what they called gravy (pasta sauce). Almost anything was palatable when smothered in gravy.

They had learned to make foods that were cheap but filling. The women made bread, macaroni, pizza fritta (fried dough), and polenta, which were hardy starches. They would get protein from beans, fish they could catch, and animals they could kill. Squirrels, blackbirds, and rabbits with gravy over polenta were favorites. *Pasta fagioli* (pasta and beans) was another, as was tripe (made from the innards of animals) smothered with gravy. They may have been poor, but they were rarely hungry.

At Milford High, freshmen generally did not participate in varsity sports, so Charlie and his friends did not play on the 1929 football or the 1930 baseball teams. They were, however, able to play organized baseball in the summer. When the school year ended, Charlie and Sammy tried out for the Junior Legion team which had been formed in 1929 by Frank Berry, then the Milford High assistant principal and former baseball coach. The team was sponsored by Milford's Legion Sgt. John W. Powers, Post 59.

AS THE SUMMER OF 1930 BEGAN, ECONOMIC CONDITIONS IN Milford were dire. Just eight months into the Depression, there was widespread unemployment, and the legal notice sections of the daily newspapers were filled with foreclosure notices and tax takings. Paying a quarter to see a movie was out of the question, and there were not a lot of other entertainment options available. For Milfordians, the Junior Legion games provided both enjoyment and a welcome respite from their real world problems.

Baseball was the most popular sport in the United States in the 1930s, and Milford loved its baseball teams. Other than the fact that the mitts were smaller, there was no designated hitter, no batting helmets, and no metal bats, the game was no different than the one played now. A great player in the 1920s and '30s would be likely be a great player in 2023.

The Powers Post 59 baseball team brought the Italian boys from the playgrounds in the Plains together with the boys from the playgrounds on the uptown side of the tracks. The team was made up of boys from St. Mary's High School and Milford High. The starting lineup was as ethnically diverse as it was talented on the field. There were Italians, Yankees, Irish, Polish, and Jewish kids on the roster—and one, Hite

Lutfy, was Lebanese. Sammy Tomaso was at third base, Charlie at short-stop, Lutfy at second base, Duke Higgiston at first, Tommy Trautwein caught, Maurice Fitzgerald was in right, Bernie Marcus in center, and Danny Consoletti in left field. The pitching staff consisted of Arthur Kenny, Rube Kurlansky, and Joe Curley.

The team played its home games at venerable Town Park, which was located uptown on Spruce Street, next to Milford High School and a stone's throw from the retail district. The park was used for both football and baseball. Milford High and St. Mary's used it during the school year for both games and practices.

It was unique. There was a large bleacher which extended from behind home plate and along the first base line. There were no fences in the outfield. Right field to center field was bounded by Spruce Street. The right field foul pole was about 350 feet from home plate while dead centerfield was well over four hundred feet from home. The left field foul pole was about three hundred feet from the plate and the boundary from there to center was wide open. If a ball were hit through that area, it would roll down a steep embankment. Due to the amount of play it got, growing good grass on the field was nearly impossible. During games, spectators who couldn't find seats in the bleacher would stand along each foul line and along the outfield boundaries. Though Milford was a small town, the games played at Town Park would often have over five thousand spectators.

The 1929 Legion state championship team had been great, but this 1930 edition of the Powers Post team would prove to be even better. It possessed all the ingredients for winning—excellent coaching, pitching, defense, speed, and hitting. More importantly, the players were disciplined and loved to play baseball. "'We had plenty of discipline at home,' Bodio said. 'We knew all about it, before we got to high school. And since our parents had come from foreign lands, we were kids of blue-collar people. We were basically poor and that was a bond that made us close in everyday life and sports.'"[25]

---

25 Hamwey, "League of Nations."

The Legion season became a coming out party for Charlie. In an account of an early season game against Whitinsville, it was reported in the *Milford Daily News*,

> The little fellows of the Milford Junior Legion Baseball team showed real diamond talent as they energetically punched out an 8-1 victory over Whitinsville on Town Park Saturday afternoon before a fair sized and appreciative assemblage of spectators.
>
> This game, aside from bringing the Milford Legionnaires a victory, threw into the limelight young Brucato, who was just about the big bang of the contest in every department of the game. This little shortstop became a batting *Bambinette* as he took his vicious swipes at Minkema's delivery. In four trips to the platter, Brucato slammed out one single that rolled through Sauve's legs for a home run, another timely single in the fourth, a rousing triple in the sixth, and a peerless home run in the eighth.
>
> In the field, he handled twelve chances, varying from teasing rollers to hard smashes, with only one misplay.[26]

The success of the entire team was remarkable. The Milford nine started the season fast and then went on a roll. After beating Whitinsville, Kurlansky shut out Worcester 9-0 with "splendid support from Brucato."[27] Rube pitched another shutout as Milford beat Millbury 3-0. After eight games, they qualified for the Massachusetts Legion Championship. Higgiston was leading the team in hitting with a .419 average, Charlie was third on the team with a .357 average, and though not hitting for a high average, Sammy was playing good defense and delivering clutch hits.

Milford had to win three best of three series to secure the state championship. In the first game of the first series, the Powers Post 59

---

26 "Brucatto [sic] Stars As Junior Legion Team Beats Whitins 8-1," *Milford Daily News,* July 7, 1930.

27 "Local Jr. Leaguers Plaster Worcester," *Milford Daily News,* July 10, 1930.

team beat Chicopee Falls 6-1 at Town Park. Kurlansky pitched, and Charlie executed a perfect double squeeze in that game. They then traveled seventy miles and beat Chicopee Falls 8-2 the next day in a game in which "Milford came back vigorously in the second (inning) as Brucato drove the ball almost out of the park for a triple."[28] Young Arthur Kenney pitched an outstanding game in the win. The boys weren't the biggest news however. The front-page headline in the *Milford Daily News* a day later read, "Two Federal Men and Milford Police Get 60-Gallon Haul." The byline read "Moonshine in Garage of Joseph Iannitelli."[29] It was a sign of the times.

Milford next faced Malden in the semifinal round. In the first game at Town Park, the newspaper reported "a record crowd of baseball enthusiasts filling the stands to capacity and crowding both foul lines saw the Milford Legion team snatch a victory from Malden..."[30] Kurlansky pitched, and Sammy got two hits in the 3-2 win. They beat Malden the next day in Malden to sweep the series and qualify for the state championship.

The team had to wait for the other semifinal series to end, and when it did, Milford learned that Brockton would be their opponent in the finals. In the first game of the state championship series, Milford edged Brockton 9-8. It was an error filled contest. Milford committed ten of them, and only Charlie and Sammy escaped without one. The second game was much cleaner. With Arthur Kenney pitching, Milford hammered Brockton 11-4 to capture the state championship.

Winning the state championship qualified the team for the Regional Legion Tournament in New Hampshire. The entire town was abuzz. A tag sale was held for the benefit of the players, and despite the woeful economic conditions in town, enough money was raised to purchase a new outfit of civilian clothes for each player to travel in. When the team

---

28 "Milford Junior Leaguers Down Chicopee Falls Team 6-1, 8-2," *Milford Daily News*, July 28, 1930.

29 "Two Federal Men and Milford Police Get 60-Gallon Haul," *Milford Daily News*, July 29, 1930.

30 "Local Juniors Squeeze Out Victory 3-2," *Milford Daily News*, July 31, 1930.

left by train for their trip to New Hampshire, the Milford fandom gave them a rousing send off. The lead story on the front page of the *Milford Daily News*, "Hundreds Journey to Manchester to See Regional Game," chronicled the hysteria and pride the local fans had for their team.[31]

The team routed Bangor, Maine, 20-2 in the regional semifinal only to lose to Manchester, New Hampshire, in the finals. The headline of the story of the Manchester game said it all: "2 Disastrous Innings Bring Defeat to Milford Legion Team 9-6."[32] Fourteen-year-old Charlie was the third hitter and got three hits in five at bat in the semifinal. When the team returned home, their success was celebrated at a fete at Town Hall where four hundred were in attendance, and the players received medals. It was a heady time for the young men.

Brother John and Jeanette, who were still living in Stamford, now had another child, Rudolph, born on May 9, 1930. John was now a police officer in the Stamford Police Department. He wanted to come to Milford to see his little brother play, but work and family obligations did not permit it. Though he knew nothing about baseball, Giuseppe would go to the games when he was able. Nobody was prouder of Charlie's accomplishments than those two men. Brother John began to receive and collect newspaper articles about Charlie and his games. He put together a scrapbook. Over the years, he assembled multiple scrapbooks detailing Charlie's feats in athletics. Regrettably, with the passage of time, they have either been lost, destroyed, or too damaged to be readable. What remains are several yellowed and tattered pictures and newsclips.

IN SEPTEMBER, CHARLIE, NOW A SOPHOMORE, TRIED OUT for the Milford High School varsity football team, which was coached by Albert "Hop" Riopel, a tough, no-nonsense taskmaster. Football was

---

31 "Hundreds Journey to Manchester To See Regional Game," *Milford Daily News*, August 16.
32 "2 Disastrous Innings Bring Defeat to Milford Legion Team 9-6," *Milford Daily News*, August 18, 1930.

a vastly different game than it is now. The players wore high top black cleats and leather headgear with no face masks. The shoulder pads provided little protection and the pants were baggy and had little padding. There was no free substitution, which meant that all eleven men had to play offense, defense, and special teams. They never came off the field.

Charlie's high school sports career started with a bang on the football field. He was a small fourteen-year-old kid, but in his first inter-squad scrimmage, he "showed himself as the liveliest ball carrier on either squad...." [33] He and his friend Sooey also pulled off several nice passes in the scrimmage. Charlie became a starter at halfback on both offense and defense. His speed and elusiveness made him an excellent ball carrier and his toughness and instincts made him an outstanding defender.

Charlie raced for Milford's only two touchdowns in a game played against Maynard in the mud. Both came within the first five minutes of a game Milford won 13-9. This was a theme which continued throughout the year as in game after game, Charlie used his exceptional speed and shiftiness to evade would be tacklers. He also excelled as a defensive back.

The team finished the season with four wins, four losses, and a tie but won the Midland League Championship with a 3-0 record. The tie came against Walpole on Thanksgiving Day before a crowd of two thousand. Neither team managed to score, and the contest ended 0-0. The headline of the *Milford Daily News* report of the game read, "M.H.S. Squad Ends Its Season By Holding Big Walpole Eleven To Tie—Balzarini, Brucato And Murray Star For Milford Team In Scoreless Game." The article recounted several good runs by Charlie and reported, "Little Brucato, with three fingers burned through some misfortune several days ago, sifted through the bulky Walpole line like snow sifted down in intervals into the collars of the cold-storaged onlookers." [34]

---

33 "H.S. Grid Squad Has Taste of Scrimmage; Brucato Shows Well," *Milford Daily News*, September 1930.

34 "M.H.S. Squad Ends Its Season by Holding Big Walpole Eleven to Tie," *Milford Daily News*, November 28, 1930.

Even though Charlie was beginning to gain notice in town for his athletic prowess, he remained a quiet and humble young man. His father kept him not only grounded but also circumspect. There is a Sicilian proverb which Giuseppe uttered more than once: "*La troppa confidenze termina in mala creaza.*" The English translation is, "Too much confidence results in disaster."

AS THE WINTER OF 1930-1931 GAVE WAY TO SPRING, THE leading sports story in the country was the death of beloved Notre Dame football coach Knute Rockne in an airplane crash on March 31, 1931. The *Milford Daily News* ran a series in the sports section celebrating his life and highlighting his incredible career. In local news of the day, the owner of Haskel's Quarry in Milford and the Quarryman's Union had come to an agreement raising wages to seventy-five cents per hour. It seems almost unimaginable today that men received such little pay for work that was not only arduous but dangerous as well. The country's big sports story in April was that Yankee slugger Babe Ruth would miss a month of the season after suffering torn ligaments in his left leg.

On April 8, both the Milford High and St. Mary's baseball teams began preseason practices. The Milford High team was coached by Riopel. Though he was an exceptional football player, Charlie's true love was baseball, and he was excited to start his varsity baseball career. Several upperclassmen returned from the 1930 team, but the opening day lineup had four sophomores starting. The Plains was well represented with Sammy as the leadoff hitter, playing third, Charlie playing shortstop and batting second and Sooey starting at first, batting cleanup. Bernie Marcus, the fourth starting sophomore, was the centerfielder.

The season opened with a loss to Dedham 3-2 on April 21 in a game where veteran Robert "Rube" Kurlansky allowed only six hits, but Milford made four costly errors. They then eked out an 11-10 win against Attleboro when Sooey stroked a line drive single scoring Sammy with two outs in the bottom of the ninth inning. Sooey, Charlie, and Sammy each had two hits in the game. The next two games were wins against Norwood (7-6) and Natick (15-4). Marcus homered in the game against Natick.

After the Natick game, an impatient Coach Riopel moved Charlie to second base and dropped him to seventh in the batting order. He brought up freshman Henry "Camel" Comolli, another son of the Plains, to catch, and Tate began getting time in the outfield. On May 10, Milford suffered a 13-0 humiliating loss to Walpole. The headline to the story of the game said it all: "Milford Blows Up as Walpole Parades 13-0."[35] In the next two games, Charlie had three hits and Sooey pitched well in an 8-2 win against Attleboro, and Sammy had three hits in a 5-2 loss to Marlboro.

"Sooey Twirls Great Game as H.S. Wins 5-4"[36] was the headline in a win against Walpole. Milford then lost to Franklin 5-3 and defeated Clinton 4-3. "Charlie Brucato became a hero in the hour of need yesterday as he sliced a dancing triple to chase Consoletti over the plate with the run that ended a ten-inning battle and gave Milford a narrow 4-3 victory over Clinton...."[37]

After eleven games, Sammy was hitting .325, and Charlie and Bernie Marcus were batting .313. Sooey was not hitting for a high average, but he had pitched well and displayed power and clutch hitting. The Town Series against crosstown rival St. Mary's on Memorial Day was next. The newspaper devoted a full-page advertisement to the series, which listed the starting lineups of both teams. Anticipation in town intensified. "Given the proper conditions, Town Park should see one of the biggest sport crowds in its history Saturday. There is no other event around these parts to rival it for the holiday afternoon. Both high schools are banking on this day to help fill coffers that have little but air in them."[38]

---

35 "Milford Blows Up as Walpole Parades 13-0," *Milford Daily News*, May 11, 1931.
36 "Sooey Twirls Great Game as H.S. Wins 5-4," *Milford Daily News*, May 19, 1931.
37 "Milford High Beats Clinton High in 10th 4 to 3," *Milford Daily News*, May 28, 1931.
38 "Saints' Stock Rises for Big Saturday Game," *Milford Daily News*, May 26, 1931.

Before crowds of over three thousand, Milford was swept by an outstanding St. Mary's team 9-5 and 8-1. In the first game, St. Mary's got fifteen hits and Milford High committed six errors. Sooey was hit hard, but it did not affect his hitting as he blasted a triple and got two other hits. In the second game, St. Mary's collected nine hits off Kurlansky and Milford committed five more errors. Charlie provided the only highlight in the bitter defeat. "A rousing triple into centerfield just barely escaped being a home run for Brucato as Nolan knocked the ball down on its way in the sixth to Spruce Street."[39]

The sports page of the *Milford Daily News* on Monday after game one had a detailed report of the game, but the headline on the front page read, "Fire Uncovers Still in Milford Barn."[40] According to the paper, ninety gallons of alcohol were found at Louise Sessa's property on 6 North Terrace. It was another sign of the times.

While baseball was capturing the hearts of Milfordians and Charlie was making a name for himself, there was other big news in town. On June 11, 1931, the lead story on the first page of the newspaper was a report that Hopedale resident George Draper, who died on February 7, left an estate valued at $11,703, 907.39. As one of the owners of Draper Corporation, the Depression obviously had little impact on him. Following this news was the killing of Thomas Holland, who, along with two others, had broken into a grocery store in the Prospect Heights section of Milford where the Portuguese immigrants had settled. The break-in occurred in the wee hours of the morning. Jose Pereira, who was later exonerated on charges of manslaughter, told police, "I shot because I was hearing footsteps."

Milford finished the season by beating Framingham 22-5 and Clinton 15-2. Sammy had two hits, Sooey three, and Bernie three, including a home run in the Framingham win. Charlie and Sooey each had three hits and a home run against Clinton. Their record was 12-5. Throughout

---

39 "St. Mary's Team Downs Milford High 8-1, to Capture Daily News Cup," *Milford Daily News*, June 8, 1931.

40 "Fire Uncovers Still in Milford Barn," *Milford Daily News*, June 1, 1931.

the year, Charlie showed power at the plate, speed on the basepaths, and agility in the field. The play of all the young sophomores was a preview of what was to become the "golden era of Milford baseball."

THAT SUMMER THE THIRD EDITION OF THE POWERS POST Junior Legion team began its season almost immediately after the high school games ended. The starting nine had Sammy leading off and playing third base, Charlie batting third and playing shortstop, and Camel catching and hitting eighth. Tate would pitch and play some outfield and Arthur Kenny, Rube Kurlansky, and Bill Belluntonio were the pitchers. Neither Sooey nor slugger Bernie Marcus played on the team. Either they were not eligible or had to work during the summer.

The Powers Post team began the season by pounding Fisherville 11-2 in a game where Sammy, Camel, and Charlie each had two hits. "Cheered by one of its largest crowds of the season and serenaded by two bands the...Junior baseball team scored its second consecutive victory in the district eliminations by pinning a 6-5 defeat on the Dudley post club of Webster on Town Park yesterday."[41] Charlie collected two more hits in that game. Arthur Kenney shut out Millbury 9-0, allowing only two hits as Sammy had a double and single and Charlie had a double in the win.

The Legion team celebrated Independence Day by again crushing Fisherville 11-2 with Charlie collecting two more hits. Bill Bellantuonio shut out Millbury in a 3-0 win before the team finally lost to Webster in a wild game 10-8. The newspaper report of the game began "The bad taste that seems destined to fill the mouth at least once during the Junior Legion baseball season is today afflicting the large number of Milford fans who saw wretched umpiring help defeat its team in Webster Saturday afternoon...."[42] "Sammy Tomaso and Charlie Brucato were threatened with expulsion by the pompous ump, and the game

---

41 "Junior Legion Squeezes Out Victory, 6-5," *Milford Daily News*, June 30, 1931.
42 "Local Juniors Lose Wild Game to Websterites," *Milford Daily News*, July 13, 1931.

was delayed several times while coaches and umpires mixed it up—verbally."[43] Sammy and Camel had three hits in the loss. Finishing at 5-1, Milford qualified for the State Championship Series yet again. Charlie was eleven for twenty-three in the six games for a .479 average.

On July 1, the census revealed that the population of Milford was 14,711. The Milford Resident Lists that year contained a listing of Joseph "Brucata," employed by Draper Corporation, and daughter Molly, employed as a shoe worker, residing at 29 Mount Pleasant Street. Minors were not listed in the report, so Charlie and Ninfa's names were not recorded.

The postseason started with a bang. In a game at Town Park before two thousand spectators, Powers Post pounded Lowell. The headline of the story of the game on the front page of the paper read, "Junior Legion Puts Calcimine on Lowell 14-0, Arthur Kenney Hurls No-Run, No Hit Game On Town Park, Teammates Clout Like Battering Rams."[44] The hitting stars were Charlie and Sammy once again. "Charlie Brucato and Sammy Tomaso will be remembered by Lowell. Sammy poked out four singles in five times at bat while Charlie Brucato dispatched two home runs in his first two trips to the plate. The first was a howling line drive between left and center that fled from the left fielder's pursuit and slithered down the left field embankment to let Charlie romp in at his leisure."[45]

They lost the next game at Lowell 2-1, setting up an all or nothing rubber game to be played at Lynn Stadium. Bill Bellantuonio pitched well in the game, and Charlie had two of the team's six hits. With Kenney allowing only two hits, Milford defeated Lowell 6-0 to advance to the next round. Camel was the hitting leader with two hits, and Charlie had a hit and knocked in a run. In the three games, Lowell managed to get only four hits. The win sent Milford to the semifinal round and was headlined on the first page of the newspaper.

---

43 "Diamond Notes," *Milford Daily News*, July 13, 1931.

44 "Junior Legion Puts Calcimine on Lowell, 14-0," *Milford Daily News*, July 25, 1931.

45 "Junior Legion...Lowell," *Milford Daily News*.

In the next series, Milford swept Springfield 7-6 and 3-2. The first game was a nailbiter in which Sammy hit a three run homer in the fifth and then Charlie knocked in two in the last inning with Milford trailing 6-5. "A record crowd that jammed every bit of standing and sitting space on spacious Town Park rooted itself hoarse as the fortunes vacillated from inning to inning." [46] In the second game, Kenney pitched masterfully, Sammy hit another home run, and Charlie got two more hits. The team had once again made it to the finals and would be playing Brockton for the second year in a row.

On July 31, the *Milford Daily News* reported that "Scarface" Al Capone, the notorious gangster in Chicago, had changed his plea from guilty to not guilty in his income tax evasion case. Another Sicilian gangster who had cast a dark shadow on the immigrants from his region, Capone would subsequently be convicted and spend the rest of his life in federal prison. Perhaps this is overreaching, but it appears that the local newspaper was taking a shot at the community on Hayward Street.

Locally, all eyes were focused on the Junior Legion baseball team. The first game against Brockton was at Town Park, and the store owners uptown voted to close early so that everyone could get to the game without missing an inning. A few merchants who had to remain open agreed to work their businesses alone and allow their clerks to leave early so that they could get to the game on time. A crowd of over three thousand watched as Milford was shut out by Brockton 4-0. Charlie got two of the only six hits allowed by the Brockton hurler. Milford won the second game 7-6, knotting the series at one game apiece and setting up a final game where the loser's season would end. Sammy had three hits, and Bellantuonio pitched with relief from Kenney.

In the finale, Milford overcame Brockton's four run early lead and beat their opponent 10-6 for their second consecutive state title. The win was headlined on the first page of the *Milford Daily News* with a picture of the team. Kenney allowed seven hits and struck out seven. Every Milford player except Kenney got a hit, and five of them had two.

46 "Milford Wins in Last Inning Rally, 7-6," *Milford Daily News*, August 1, 1931.

"Despite the fireworks the game itself afforded, the most spectacular aspect of the battle was the crowd which attended it. It was perhaps the biggest crowd ever to witness a ball game in Milford; it certainly was the most frenzied. Estimated at five thousand, it spilled over the bleachers and ringed the playing enclosure five deep."[47]

After the game, the celebration poured onto Main Street and continued into the night. Both teams were guests of Quality Cafeteria for a "feed." "During the course of the meal, the street outside the restaurant was filled with a crowd big enough to elect a president. So great was the crush that the door leading to the restaurant was literally torn from its hinges and the glass paneling smashed."[48]

Before going on to play in the regionals, the boys on the team were again given new civilian clothes and were hosted by the Boston Braves at a game in that city. "The chamber of commerce distributed cards for its member stores bearing the legend 'Boost the Boys to Houston (where the national championship was to be held). Tag Day Today.'" Stickers identifying Milford on cars going to the regionals were also distributed. The newspaper published a list of donors to the Junior Legion Baseball Fund. There were four donations of $15.00, nine of $10.00, several of $5.00, but the vast majority were $1.00. The drive raised $583.00. Tag sales raised another $140.00, and two exhibition games added $71.70 to the cause.

The regionals were held in the Eastern League ballpark in Springfield, and it was anticipated that three thousand fans from Milford would be in attendance. The State Theater planned to announce the score by innings both in the theater and at Draper Park in the retail district. Milford beat Rumford, Maine, 6-0 in a game pitched by Bellantuonio, but the next day they lost to Manchester 4-3, and the season came to a crushing end.

Charlie had an excellent season, playing good defense, batting over .400 with three home runs, several extra-base hits, and a number of

---

47 "5000 See Local Legion Team Win State Title," *Milford Daily News*, August 11, 1931.
48 "5000 See Local," *Milford Daily News*.

stolen bases. Sammy captained the team and was one of the best hitters and defenders. Camel was a reliable catcher who had a good season offensively as well. Arthur Kenny emerged as a dominant starting
pitcher to complement Bill Bellantuonio. The success of the team made
the boys local heroes, but more importantly, it drew the people of Milford, long divided along ethnic lines, closer together.

"Milford sports stars of the early 1930s were youths with true grit.
They came from a variety of backgrounds but always considered themselves as one. They promoted harmony, expanded the melting pot, and
helped Milford to be a town rich in blue-collar spirit. Success came quickly
and easily for them. And as a result, Milford grew and prospered."[49]

IN THE FALL OF 1931, COACH RIOPEL GREETED FIFTY-FIVE
candidates trying out for the Milford High School football team. It
would prove to be one of the best seasons in the school's history. Unfortunately, Sammy, who was hoping to make the team, was unable to play
because he broke his leg in a scrub game in mid-September. Charlie
was now a junior and returned to the starting eleven at left halfback.
At the end of tryouts, Bill Bellantuonio, Camel, who was a sophomore,
and Domenic "Doc" Lombardi earned positions in the backfield with
him. Bernie Marcus was a starter at end. In a *Milford Daily News* cartoon
titled "Milford's 1931 Aggregation Which Finds The Bigger They Are
The Harder They Fall," Charlie is portrayed, in uniform, inside the
image of a star. The caption reads, "Charley Brucato 15-Year-Old Triple
Threat of The Team."

On September 26, Milford opened the season by beating Attleboro
12-6 with Camel doing most of the ball carrying and scoring one of the
touchdowns. Doc Lombardi scored the other. The Milford Eleven next
beat Clinton 18-0 at Town Park. Bellantuonio scored two touchdowns
and Charlie got the third. They then defeated Marlboro 14-0 in a hard
fought game. The newspaper reported, "Leaving a trail of would-be

49 Hamwey, "League of Nations."

1931 MILFORD FOOTBALL STARTERS

Second row: Bill Bellantuonio, third from left; Charlie, fourth from left.

tacklers sprawling over the greenswood, Charlie Brucato streaked fifty-five yards for a touchdown to climax Milford High's stiffly earned
victory over Marlboro in that high and windy city...."[50]

The front page headline on October 19 was, "World Mourns the
Passing Of Thomas Alva Edison,"[51] and that same week, ticket prices
for Milford High football games were raised from twenty-five cents to
fifty cents. Milford beat Franklin 33-7 and Groton (Connecticut) 28-0
in the next two games. In the Groton game, "Charlie Brucato, as in
previous games, was the big ground gainer of the day with 140 yards to
his credit."[52] Milford beat Natick 19-0 for its sixth straight win before
losing to Framingham 6-0 before 7,500 spectators in that town. After
the Natick game, a sportswriter commented, "If Brucato had Lombardi's momentum and Comolli's weight, he'd be one of the best college
prospects in the country."[53]

Against Wellesley, Charlie scored both touchdowns and had several
good runs in a 13-0 win. In the final game on Thanksgiving morning,
Milford took Walpole's measure. "Volatile Charlie Brucato and crack-
ling interference ran wild to give Milford a genuine reason for Thanksgiving as they conspired in the business of piling up a 38-0 victory over
Walpole on Town Park...before a crowd of 2,500 very much interested
men, women, and children....Milford's regulars scored almost at will,
and Charlie Brucato, by virtue of his brilliant open field work, scored
four of Milford's touchdowns himself."[54]

The team finished the regular season with eight wins (six shutouts)
and one loss. Charlie was the leading scorer with sixty-four points followed by Camel with forty-four. Milford then won the "mythical" state
championship by defeating Norwood 20-12 in a December 5 postseason game, which was arranged to benefit the unemployed of both towns.

---

50 "Milford Stops Stubborn Marlboro Defence [sic] 14-0," *Milford Daily News*, October
    13, 1931.
51 "World Mourns the Passing of Thomas Alva Edison," *Milford Daily News*, October 19, 1931.
52 "Milford Gridders Top Groton by 28-0 Score," *Milford Daily News*, October 26, 1931.
53 "Gridiron Gossip," *Milford Daily News*, November 2, 1931.
54 "Milford High Squad Tramples Walpole, 38-0," *Milford Daily News*, November 27, 1931.

(At that time, there was no official state champion, but the locals in both communities and surrounding towns believed that the teams were the best in the state and the winner of the game would be the *de facto* state champ.) Two-thousand hearty fans withstood freezing temperatures in Norwood to watch Milford beat a much heavier and more powerful team. The highlight of the game came in the first few seconds when Charlie returned the opening kickoff eighty-five yards for a touchdown. He also punted the team out of danger and intercepted two passes in the game. At the end of the season, Charlie was selected as the left halfback on the All-Central Massachusetts Scholastic Team.

————————

IN THE WINTER, CHARLIE TRIED HIS HAND AT BASKETBALL, and the results were predictable. He was one of, if not the best, hoopster on the team. He was elected captain and earned his sixth varsity letter. But basketball was just a sport he played to stay in shape.

On March 1, 1932, the twenty-month-old son of famous aviator, Charles Lindbergh, was kidnapped, and stories of the heinous crime and subsequent investigation dominated the newspapers for the next several weeks. The Depression had not abated, and there were no signs that it would ever end. Every day, the newspaper reported the failure of another bank. Milford, along with the rest of the nation, was feeling the brutal effects of the economic disaster.

Early in April, thirty-eight candidates tried out for the Milford High baseball team. A *Milford Daily News* preseason article declared, "Charlie Brucato, the 1932 basketball captain, is among those who doesn't [sic] have to worry too much about being left off the squad, and what's more important, his coach needn't worry that Charlie will get an elongated head when he reads this, if he does. Charlie took more backslapping last fall than any little athlete around this burg and, despite it all, is about as conceited as a rabbit at a wolves' convention."[55] He clearly had heeded the words of the Sicilian proverb his father had communicated to him.

55 "Baseball Brevities," *Milford Daily News*, April 9, 1932.

Captain "Rube" Kurlansky, Bill Bellantuonio, and sophomore lefty Arthur Kenney were selected as the team's pitchers. Sammy returned at third base, Charlie at short, and Camel was behind the plate. Bernie Marcus was in center, and Tate would earn a position as the team's left fielder. Anticipation for the team's success was high, but there was a deeper issue lurking. The *Daily News* reported, "Just how much the current Depression will affect... Milford baseball... is a problem worrying everyone who has anything to do with supplying the wherewithal for the support."[56]

The season began with a 6-1 win over Wellesley where Kurlansky allowed only five hits. Tate had three hits and Sammy had two in the victory. They next beat Natick 6-3 with Kenney pitching. In the third game, they routed Clinton 11-3 behind Kurlansky's pitching and hard hitting by Camel with a double and a home run, Charlie with a single and a triple, and Bernie Marcus with a homer. Attleboro was dispatched next 13-5 with Bernie leading the team with two doubles.

Marcus continued his hot streak with another home run in a 6-4 win over Framingham. Kurlansky shut out Dedham 11-0 in a game played in drizzly conditions. Charlie had two hits and Camel had a double and triple in the win. Tate, who had been hitting well and playing great defense, was unable to play against Dedham due to a leg injury. In the next game, Bellantuonio pitched a three hit shutout in an 8-0 victory over Franklin. "In the seventh, Brucato ushered in the festivities with a home run over the left field fence."[57] Charlie added a single and Camel collected four hits in the game.

"Charlie Brucato seems to have hit his stride again.... His home run in Franklin, they tell us, was a gem,"[58] commented one reporter. On May 11, Camel homered and Kurlansky pitched Milford High to a 10-3 win over Walpole at Town Park. The day after the game, the front page headline and lead story in the *Milford Daily News* and every

---

56 "Baseball Brevities," *Milford Daily News*, April 11, 1932.
57 "Bellantuonio Shuts Out Franklin as H. S. Romps 8-0," *Milford Daily News*, May 10, 1932.
58 "Baseball Brevities," *Milford Daily News*, May 11, 1932.

newspaper in the country was the same. The Lindberg baby had been found dead. It was another blow to a nation already reeling from the economic crisis.

Watching the high school baseball team was a welcome diversion for the townspeople. They flocked to Town Park to see every home game. A bittersweet commentary in the newspaper said, "Milford may not be able to give its people bread, but it certainly does supply them with games. The big crowd at yesterday's contest between the high school and Walpole was made up considerably of gentlemen who had nothing else to do.... While a man who is unemployed is not expected to buy a ticket, it is to be hoped that those who still can pay for their amusements do the right thing by the clubs putting on the show for them."[59] The players did not realize at the time how vital their role was not only in the integration of town but also in instilling a sense of pride in its people. Years later, their contributions to the community would be recognized and praised.

Wins against Marlboro (9-0), Brockton (3-2), and Dedham (6-4), followed with virtually every Milford hitter contributing. In the Dedham game, Sammy had four hits, Camel two doubles, and Charlie a double and a single. Norwood fell next in a 9-4 game where Kurlansky struck out twelve. Tate had recovered from his injury and returned to the lineup. They next beat Framingham 9-1. Charlie led the way with three hits, and Sammy, Bernie, Camel, and Lutfy each got two. Milford then beat Marlboro 13-2 and swept the Town Series by beating St. Mary's 7-1 and 7-4.

In the first game of the series, Kenney struck out twenty and Charlie had three hits. In between the two games with their crosstown rival, Rube Kurlansky pitched a no-hitter against Clinton in a 7-0 win. Camel had four hits including a home run and Charlie was 3-5 with a home run of his own. Both round trippers were tremendous blasts that cleared the centerfield fence at Clinton in almost the same spot. Milford dispatched Brockton 6-0 for its eighteenth consecutive win in

59 "Baseball Brevities," *Milford Daily News*, May 12, 1932.

a game where Charlie had a home run and a single and Camel had three hits including a home run.

It is said that all good things must come to an end. In Milford's case, Norwood did them 3-2 and the streak, regrettably, was over. The *Milford Daily News* report of the game began, "Gentlemen, the party is over. The string of victory, prettily threaded through eighteen ball games, was abruptly snapped yesterday afternoon... as a huge delegation of Milford rooters, watched, hoped, and wept."[60] They had reeled off eighteen straight wins including three shutouts and a no-hitter by Rube Kurlansky.

Going into the final three games, Tate was leading the team in hitting at .429 in the fourteen games he played while Camel, Charlie, and Sammy were hitting .399, .378, and .342, respectively, in the full nineteen games. Charlie, Sammy, and Tate were leading the team in stolen bases and Charlie and Camel were leading the team in slugging percentage. They rattled off wins against Marlboro, Cambridge Latin, and Attleboro, securing both the Midland League Championship and the mythical State Championship. Charlie had a total of five hits in nine at bats in those games and finished the year with an average of .391.

In the Cambridge Latin game, before 6,500 spectators at Town Park, Kenny shut out the visitors, yielded a mere three hits and struck out nineteen in the 8-0 triumph. "If the 'city slickers' had any delusions about the quality of horsehide played in the 'wilds,' they were dispelled yesterday afternoon.

"Charlie Brucato shone as brilliantly on the offensive side of the ledger as did Kenny on the defensive. His rousing single in the very first frame gave notice that the famed "Muggsy" Kelley could be hit; his double in the sixth, which went into Spruce Street, and which was prevented from becoming a home run by the ground rules, served notice that Kelley could be hit hard and his deep double to left in the seventh proved that the other two blows were no flukes. Charlie made three safe

60 "Milford High's Victory String Cut By Norwood," *Milford Daily News*, June 9, 1932.

blows in four trips to the plate, scored three runs himself, and drove in two more."[61]

On June 13, a reception for the ball club was held at the State Theatre where attorney William J. Moore presented a silver loving cup to Milford High principal Thomas J. Quirk in recognition of the team's work. William D. Leary, editor and publisher, also bestowed on the team the Milford Daily News Cup "as a token of victory in the local scholastic series with St. Mary's."

The *Daily News* later reported, "Charles Brucato, one of the best athletes ever to wear the colors of Milford High, was elected captain of the 1933 baseball team at a meeting of the lettermen at close of the game with Attleboro yesterday."[62] "Another unassuming lad will captain the Milford High School club of 1933 on the diamond.... Charlie Brucato is what coaches dream and pray for. He's capable, has a natural bent for athletics and an excellent competitive temperament. He very rarely makes mistakes and still more rarely repeats them. The big grin is always decorating his face and he doesn't believe in having slumps."[63]

After the season, negotiations began to bring the Greater Boston All-Scholastic High School team to Milford to play against the Milford High players. Since the school year had ended, it was decided that Milford High School could not authorize the game. The Ford Motor Company agreed to sponsor the team and provide uniforms. Though the squad was composed of the same players as the high school team, it was called the Milford Fords. The All-Scholastic team was assembled by Boston sportswriter Doc Mooney. On June 27, before six thousand sun-drenched spectators at Town Park, Milford defeated the All-Scholastics 12-5. Charlie had two hits in five at bats and made a spectacular play in the field.

"Some insist that the 1932 team was the strongest ever produced at Milford High. For certain the team piled up a magnificent record of

61 "Kenny Whiffs 19 As Milford High Wins, 8-0," *Milford Daily News*, June 15, 1932.
62 "Charlie Brucato Is Chosen Ball Captain," *Milford Daily News*, June 20, 1932.
63 "Baseball Brevities," *Milford Daily News*, June 19, 1932.

21-1...and won the mythical State Championship by walloping Cambridge Latin...."[64] "'We drew 6,500 fans to the baseball game at Town Park against Cambridge Latin,' (Tate) Bodio said. 'And we had six thousand for the game with the All Scholastics. All of a sudden, the city newspapers were turning out a lot of stories about Milford athletics.'"[65]

Fifty-eight years later, another Milford High baseball team would win the Division I State Championship with a spotless record of 24-0 to stake its claim to the title of best team in the history of the school. The cleanup hitter on that team was Charles J. (C. J.) Brucato III, my son and Charlie's namesake and grandson.

AS SUMMER BEGAN, PRESIDENT HERBERT HOOVER, WHOSE term was plagued with the never-ending Depression, was seeking another four years in the White House. In the Democratic Party, Governor Franklin Delano Roosevelt was gaining momentum to be Hoover's opponent in November. Charlie spent this summer playing for the Junior Legion team. He and Arthur Kenney were among the few on the team with experience. Tate, Sammy, Camel, and Sooey played that summer for either the Milford Fords, which was reorganized and had added players after the All-Scholastic game, or the Milford Athletic Association (AA). The *Milford Daily News* covered each of the teams on its sports pages.

It was an odd year for the Legion team with no official regular season games. Apparently, they qualified for the state tournament because they were state champs the previous summer. To prepare, the team played a slew of exhibition games against area Legion teams, the Milford Fords and local "all-star" teams from nearby towns. Notwithstanding the fact that the games were exhibitions, the loyal fans of Powers Post turned out in large numbers to watch them.

Charlie captained the team and was clearly its best player. In a 16-3

---

64 Jones, "Greater Milford Area Sports."
65 Hamwey, "League of Nations."

win against Walpole at Town Park, he got two hits and "gave a fielding exhibition handling eleven chances without an error and participating in a double play."[66] He had four hits against Dedham and two more against the Upton Juniors.

In the first series of the State Tournament, they lost to Jamaica Plain twice but were awarded the series victory after their protest about an ineligible player was granted. In the second game, a 16- 2 loss, "Charlie Brucato put up a great battle all the way, snaring three base blows and trying for everything this side of Boston."[67]

In the next series, they swept Walpole 6-5 and 7-2. Charlie had five hits in ten at bats including a home run which traveled down the left field embankment at Town Park. They then swept old rival Brockton. It was the fourth straight year they eliminated them from the tournament. Kenney struck out nineteen in the first game, which Milford won 2-1, and Charlie had two hits including a triple. In the second game, they trounced Brockton 12-1 and Charlie had three hits and three stolen bases.

The final series against Springfield Milford was swept by scores of 5-0 and 10-7. Charlie got two of his team's three hits in the first game and two more in the next game. The season had ended on a sour note. They had been eliminated from the tournament and would not go to the regionals. Charlie had fourteen hits in twenty-six at bats in the tournament games.

Three weeks later, a sportswriter reported, "Charlie Brucato is home after several weeks of much needed rest at the home of his brother John Brucato in Stamford, CT."[68] Though football season was on the horizon, the Milford Fords and the Milford AA were still playing baseball. Charlie was asked to play for the Milford AA, where Sooey was playing, and he agreed. He played three games and had seven hits in fourteen at

---

66 "Local Legionnaires Massacre Walpole's Legion Club 16-3," *Milford Daily News*, July 7, 1932.

67 "Milford Loses Game 16-2 But Wins Protest," *Milford Daily News*, August 3, 1932.

68 "Baseball Brevities," *Milford Daily News*, September 7, 1932.

Stamford Police Officer John Brucato (Brother John)

bats. His brother finally got to see him play. "In the bleachers Saturday was Officer John Brucato of Stamford, CT watching his brother play baseball for the first time.... For his brother's benefit, he slapped three hits including a triple and fielded perfectly."[69]

Brother John was now a police officer in Stamford and had two children of his own. To say that he was proud of his younger brother is an understatement. Brother Charles and Brother John had developed a bond that would never be broken. Giuseppe was almost as proud of Charlie's accomplishments as Brother John. He loved the fact that people in town would congratulate him and tell him how great an athlete his son was.

---

69 "Baseball Brevities," *Milford Daily News*, September 12, 1932.

Years later Ninfa told me a funny story about her father's pride. Charlie McCarthy, Edgar Bergen's famed ventriloquist dummy partner, was popular at the time and there was a carnival or fair in Milford where dolls of the dummy were being sold. Said Ninfa, "Pa and I were at the fair, and he didn't understand English all that well. He turned to me and said, 'Nee, did you hear that? People are yelling Charlie Brucato over and over.' I listened, and what I heard was a hawker yelling Charlie McCarthy and holding up the doll. I said, 'Pa, the guy is yelling Charlie McCarthy, not Charlie Brucato.'"

IN THE FALL, THE YANKEES WERE PLAYING THE CUBS IN THE World Series and the Hoover-Roosevelt presidential race was nearing an end. Charlie entered his senior year at Milford High in September. It would be his final season on the gridiron for his hometown team. In the *Milford Daily News*, there was unbridled optimism "for what promises to be the greatest [season] in its [Milford's] history."[70] The newspaper was not wrong. Sammy, Tate, and Camel joined Charlie and Captain Doc Lombardi in an outstanding backfield. The opening game against Attleboro, which Milford won 13-0, was an introduction for what would become a dominant defense.

In the second game against Clinton, Charlie scored two touchdowns in a 20-0 rout. "Charlie Brucato, who weaves as neatly as a loom but much more interestingly, chalked up the most spectacular feats of the game.... His thirty-five-yard sprint on a cleverly handled crisscross accounted for one touchdown, and he scored another after getting the ball in position by another classy excursion through the opposition for thirty yards."[71]

Charlie had another touchdown in the next game against Marlboro which Milford won 27-0. In that game, Charlie, Camel, Tate, Sammy, and Captain Doc Lombardi amassed a total of 263 yards on the ground. In the next game against Franklin, the backfield accounted for 260 yards on

---

70 "Gridiron Gossip," *Milford Daily News*, September 24, 1932.
71 "Milford Jogs Over Clinton for 20-0 Win," *Milford Daily News*, October 3, 1932.

running plays, and each of them scored a touchdown in a 32-0 win. They then faced Natick and rolled over that squad by a score of 19-0 with Charlie scoring all three touchdowns, two of which were on passes from Camel.

Coming into the Brockton game, Milford was undefeated at 5-0, untied and unscored upon. Brockton was much heavier and proved to be the better team by defeating them 33-6 for their first and only loss of the season. Camel and Charlie played well on defense and the backfield had another good game, but Brockton's weight advantage was too much to overcome.

Up next was North Attleboro where Milford squeaked out a 14-0 victory. In the game, "Brucato, usually Milford's premier ground grabber, had a hard fight to get by the No. [sic] Attleboro linemen as they drove through on plays to that side [right]. Charlie made a couple of smart gains through sheer speed and canny footwork, but his yardage total reached its low for the season. Defensively, however, Brucato's game was flawless as the Kohinoor diamond. His tackling was fiercer than a tiger's mother-in-law, and he intercepted two passes to start Milford on its touchdown parades."[72]

The biggest news, however, was Roosevelt's landslide victory over Hoover. FDR would become the thirty-second president of the United States. He would be faced with the unenviable task of getting the country out of the Depression, which had crippled it for over four years.

On Armistice Day, Milford traveled to Framingham and won 7-0. The lone touchdown was set up by Charlie's thirty-nine-yard sideline sprint and a nineteen-yard pass he caught from Camel. At that point in the season, "Charlie Brucato, who heads for a goal line as naturally as a compass needle nose to the north, is leading the high school's point scoring so far this season.... Milford's shifty carrier has collected fifty-six of his team's 144 points. This total represents nine touchdowns and two points after touchdown..... 'Camel' Comolli, alias Henry is next with forty-five points to his credit."[73]

---

72   "Belated Spirt Gives Milford 14-0 Victory," *Milford Daily News*, November 7, 1932.
73   "Gridiron Gossip," *Milford Daily News*, November 12, 1932.

The team finished the season 9-1 after beating Walpole 20-3 and Wellesley 20-6. In each game, Charlie registered a touchdown bringing his total to eleven for the season. Milford was once again Midland League champions, registered seven shutouts, and outscored their opponents 184-46. Thirty-three of the forty-six points the team allowed were scored by Brockton. In the other nine games combined, Milford allowed only thirteen points.

At the end of the season, "Charlie Brucato, Milford High's best bet in a broken field for the past few seasons, was given honorable mention on the all-scholastic team selected by the Boston Advertiser the other day.... Brucato had a grand finale of a season piling one finished performance on top of another to climax his schoolboy career.... There wasn't a smarter, steadier, or cleaner football player in the vicinity than this shifty lad, and it's gratifying to see him gain some measure of recognition."[74]

ROOSEVELT WAS SWORN IN ON SATURDAY, MARCH 4, 1933. IN his inaugural speech, he told the nation that "the only thing we have to fear is fear itself." The first New Deal would begin immediately thereafter. In April, Coach Riopel held tryouts for the 1933 Milford High School baseball team. Before them was the unpleasant task of following arguably the best team ever at the school, and there were enormous holes to fill on the roster. Captain Rube Kurlansky, who shared mound duties with Arthur Kenney, had graduated along with Bill Bellantuonio, leaving a large gap on the pitching staff. Half of the infield was gone with first baseman Charlie Rae graduating and third baseman slugger Sammy Tomaso dropping out of school. Two-thirds of the outfield was also gone with the graduation of right fielder Hite Lutfy and hard-hitting center fielder Bernie Marcus. The starters returning were shortstop Captain Charlie Brucato, second baseman Al Cook, power hitting catcher Camel Comolli, fleet outfielder Tate Bodio, and pitcher Art Kenney.

---

74 "Gridiron Gossip," *Milford Daily News*, November 28, 1932.

1933 MILFORD HIGH BASEBALL TEAM

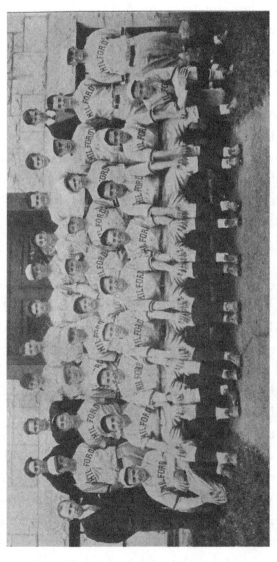

Top row, left to right: John Arcudi, Donald Mann, William Burns, Albert Cummings, Reynaldo Consoletti,
Frank Ghiringhelli, Lewis Luchini, Richard Siegal, Blaine Libbey, Robert McGinnis.
Center row: Principal Frank C. Berry, Joseph Cornacchia, Harvey Marcus, John Doyle, Mario Bruno, Francis Bodio,
Joseph Milani, Ernest Roberti, Francis Fitzpatrick, George Porter, Eben Reynolds, Coach Albert "Hop" Riopel.
Front row: Arthur Sabatinelli, Harold Marcus, Arthur Kenney, Alfred Cook, Charles Brucato,
Henry Bodio, Henry Comolli, Joseph Blascio, Albert Bonetti.

The season got off to a terrible start. Milford High lost to Wellesley 10-6 and Attleboro 9-6 in the first two games. To make matters worse, Tate turned in his uniform after an uncharacteristic run-in with Coach Riopel, who had benched him during the Attleboro game. They then beat Framingham 6-2 in the third game behind the hitting of Charlie and Camel in a game which was ultimately forfeited by Framingham for some unspecified reason. Tate rejoined the team for the Brockton game and turned in a spectacular catch that resulted in a double play as Milford won 9-4. Arthur Kenney pitched an outstanding game against Marlboro in a 15-1 win.

Milford beat Walpole 7-1 in the next in a game where "Brucato, Bodio, and Comolli were riding them high and handsome."[75] Charlie stroked two doubles and a triple, and Tate and Camel also tripled. Art Kenney was the star in the win against Norwood 4-3 by striking out fourteen and giving up only four hits. Framingham fell next 7-2 with Kenney getting the win and Camel supplying the hitting.

Milford avenged its early loss to Attleboro 6-4 as Camel and pitcher Sunny Cornacchia belted long home runs. They then swept the Town Series against St. Mary's. Art Kenny pitched a three hit shutout and hit a home run and a triple in the first game Milford won by a margin of 9-0. In the second game, Kenney and Cornacchia shared the pitching duties and Milford emerged with an 8-1 triumph. Charlie had three hits and Camel had two.

Norwood was the next victim. Milford beat them 8-5 in a game where Charlie had a triple and single and handled ten chances with one error. It was sweet revenge against the one team that had defeated them last year. Milford once again defeated Marlboro 7-6 as Camel starred with a home run and a double, and Tate also contributed with a double. Kenney pitched Milford to its thirteenth straight win by blanking Brockton 12-0. Camel had three hits and another home run and Tate had a double and single.

---

75   "Capt. Charles Brucato Heads Attack with Two Doubles and A Triple," *Milford Daily News*, May 17, 1933.

The squad's fourteenth consecutive win came at the hands of Natick 12-0. Cornacchia pitched the shutout, and Charlie was the hitting star, going three for three with two long home runs and a single. Tate also hit a home run. In the final regular season game, Milford beat Cambridge Latin 11-7. Charlie led the attack with a double and a home run while Tate had a double.

After losing its first two games, Milford had reeled off fifteen straight wins to finish the season at 15-2 and again win the Midland League Championship. They then lost to the Boston All-Star team 6-4 in a charity game. Charlie finished the season (excluding the charity game) leading the team in batting average (.409), hits (twenty-nine), and runs (twenty-three) followed by Camel's .386 average, twenty-seven hits, and twenty-one runs. Charlie also had three home runs, three triples, and a number of stolen bases.

With the end of the season, another chapter had closed for Charlie and Tate. Their high school athletic careers were over. They would be missed. Robert E. McGinnis, a junior at Milford High wrote, "The prospects for a banner year with the 1934 [baseball] club are bright with the exception of two noticeable gaps left by the graduation of two fine ball players. Captain Charlie Brucato combines great hitting power with extraordinary fielding and the result is an All-Scholastic shortstop. His diminutive classmate, Henry 'Tate' Bodio, cannot be omitted, for good things come in small packages, and such is the case with Tate, for he could play the whole outfield single handed, and his hitting would also make up for the other two players."[76]

On June 28, 1933, Tate and Charlie received their diplomas at the Milford High commencement. They were not only athletes at the school but contributors in other areas of school life. Tate won the coveted Gallagher Medal which went to the athlete who had earned three letters and had the highest scholastic average. Charlie was treasurer of the Class of 1933 and editor of the yearbook. Though still shy and quiet, he had emerged as a leader amongst his peers as well as a contributor

76   Robert E McGinnis, 1933 Oak Lily and Ivy Yearbook, p. 57.

outside the sports arena. In later years, he was prouder of these accomplishments than he was about his athletic prowess.

That Charlie finished twelve years of schooling and graduated from high school was a major accomplishment for the son of Sicilian immigrant parents, especially when one considers that English was his second language. Few of his childhood friends from the Plains got the opportunity to do this, and some who had the opportunity and started their educations never finished. Many of these unfortunate kids had to leave school and work to help their families get by during the Depression.

"'I cried the last day of school,' Bodio said. 'I knew I wouldn't be with that group again. That's how emotional it was as we went our own ways.'"[77]

The day after graduation, a sportswriter paid tribute to the careers of both Tate and Charlie in a farewell note. Of Charlie, he wrote, "Brucato was probably one of the greatest all around athletes ever turned out of the high school.... He amassed a total of seven letters: three in baseball, three in football, and one in basketball.... In football, he has been the kingpin for at least the past two seasons.... His broken field running and defensive play on the gridiron was foxy and reliable.... In baseball, he was a great ground covering shortstop and an irrepressible long- and short-range hitter...and a good sport to boot."[78]

Charlie's picture in the 1933 Oak Lily and Ivy (yearbook) was captioned, "Charles 'Flash' Brucato," but no one knows where the nickname "Flash" came from, and it never stuck. His ambition was to play professional baseball. In the class prophecy, it was predicted that he would be a coach at Notre Dame. The poem describing him in the yearbook read,

"In fine, we thought that he was everything
To make us wish that we were in his place."
—Edwin Arlington Robinson

---

77 Hamwey, "League of Nations."4
78 "Baseball Brevities," *Milford Daily News*, June 29, 1933.

Another chapter in Charlie's life had come to a close, and he looked forward to the next. Like Tate, leaving high school was bittersweet for him. Years later, he was elected with the first group of inductees to the Milford High School Hall of Fame.

Charlie had become a local hero, but he was unfazed and remained the same shy, quiet, and modest individual he had always been. Celebrity was the last thing on his mind. His family and paisanos, on the other hand, regarded his accomplishments and humility with an awesome sense of pride.

In the summer, with no Junior Legion eligibility, Charlie joined Tate, Sooey, and Sammy on the Milford AA team in the Blackstone Valley League. The league was one of the best semiprofessional baseball leagues in the country. Many major leaguers started careers there. Among them were Gabby Hartnett, Hank Greenberg, and Wes Farrell. The Milford team would be league champs from 1933 through 1935, and Charlie was one of the stars, earning MVP honors.

It was in the Blackstone Valley League where Charlie was tabbed with the nickname that he would carry with him to the grave and the one which I would be labeled with. In a letter to his grandson C. J. many years later, Charlie told the story.

Bronko Nagurski played football for the [University of Minnesota] and the Chicago Bears. He was considered the strongest and most powerful runner of all time. More importantly, the nickname tabbed on your father and grandpa, namely "Bronkie" and "Bronc," stemmed from Bronko Nagurski.

The name became attached to me in a semipro baseball game by the late Angelo Ferrario, a first baseman. In a close baseball game, I was rounding third and heading for home. I dipped my shoulder and literally ran through the catcher who dropped the ball. Angelo said, "Fellows we have another Bronko Nagurski on our team." The nickname stuck from that day on.

When your dad was born, I said to Grandma Connie, "That's 'little Bronkie.'"

BEFORE HE GRADUATED FROM HIGH SCHOOL, HOLY CROSS, Hop Riopel's alma mater, was interested in Charlie for both their baseball and football teams. Unfortunately, his decision not to enroll in college preparatory courses came back to haunt him. He did not have enough credits to qualify for entrance at Holy Cross. Charlie was also being pursued to play professional baseball, and he probably would have, but the admission officials at Holy Cross told him that he would have a full scholarship if he went to prep school and obtained the necessary credits. Dean Academy in nearby Franklin was a school which had just what he was looking for. He was offered a full athletic scholarship there which he quickly accepted.

CHAPTER FOUR

LEAVING HOME TO GET AN EDUCATION

IN SEPTEMBER, AT THE TENDER AGE OF SEVENTEEN, CHARlie left home for the first time in his life to pursue a postsecondary education at Dean Academy. Many years later, he told me about what would become a seminal event in his life. As he told it, his first few days at the school did not go well. He said he was homesick and missed his family and friends even though he was less than ten miles away from Milford.

It was clear he was ill-prepared to be on his own. Brother John and his two sisters had always coddled and taken care of him. He had always been shy and introverted even after gaining accolades and publicity for his athletic prowess. He had been comfortable living in the closely knit Sicilian community in the Plains. Making new acquaintances and fitting in at an unfamiliar place terrified him.

After only a few days at Dean, he was despondent and had decided that the school was not for him, so he packed his bags and headed home. When he arrived at the apartment on Mount Pleasant Street, he was greeted by his father who was surprised to see him with all his luggage.

"Pa, I don't want to stay in school," he said in Sicilian. "I have decided to come home."

Giuseppe frowned and looked him in the eye. "If you are leaving school to come home, you better find somewhere else to live. You can't stay here. Get out."

He was shocked. His father was stern, but he never imagined Giuseppe would be angry and react as he did. He got the point. There would be no quitting by a Brucato. He quickly grabbed his bags and headed back for Dean.

It turned out to be an excellent decision both athletically and socially. Playing halfback for legendary Coach "Dirty" Dan Sullivan, Charlie was a star at Dean as soon as he hit the field. He continued to be fast and elusive with the football in his hands, galloping on many long runs. But Sullivan, who called him "Brouccardi," also used him in several other roles. Charlie became a kicker, passer, and pass catcher. Faithful Milford fans traveled to the games to watch their favorite son compete and he did not let them down.

At that time, in January of 1934, the Gold Reserve Act was passed, ordering the surrender of all gold to the United States Treasury. President Roosevelt raised the price of gold from $20.67 per ounce to $35.00. Both steps were taken to help speed the end of the Depression. The hit movie *It Happened One Night* starring Clark Gable and Claudette Colbert was released in February. In March, a notorious gangster, John Dillinger, escaped from jail, joined his gang, and they robbed the First National Bank in Mason City, Iowa. In April, gangsters Clyde Barrow and Bonnie Parker killed two highway patrolmen in Grapevine, Texas. In May, Texas Rangers ambushed and killed them in Louisiana.

During that spring, Charlie played second base for Dean and was voted team captain. He had an exceptional baseball season as he displayed his prowess as a fielder, speed on the basepaths, and incredible hitting. Nearly fifty years later, he would be inducted into the Dean Athletic Hall of Fame for his exploits on the gridiron and baseball diamond. By the end of May, he had completed the required course work at Dean, and he was accepted to the College of the Holy Cross in Worcester, Massachusetts, with a full athletic scholarship.

When he finished at Dean, Charlie returned home, reunited with his friends, and continued playing baseball for the Milford AA. Late in the summer, after completing another outstanding baseball season in the Blackstone Valley League, Charlie anxiously awaited his first year in college. Before he headed off to Worcester, a Jesuit priest from Holy Cross visited him in Milford.

"I couldn't believe it," he would tell me several years later,. "The priest picked me up, took me to New York, and bought me all the clothes I would need for college. I guess the people at the school knew that my father was poor, and they wanted me to dress the way other kids dressed. It was a wonderful gesture, and I appreciated it very much."

NONE OF THE ITALIAN BOYS FROM CHARLIE'S NEIGHBORhood had ever been to college, and he did not know what to expect. He would, however, have two familiar faces on campus and on the playing fields at Holy Cross. High school coach Hop Riopel had accepted a coaching position at the college and left-handed pitcher Arthur Kenney, Charlie's teammate at Milford High, received a baseball scholarship to Holy Cross. Though Riopel was an outstanding coach, it is more likely than not that he rode the coat tails of two of his star players to a coaching position at his alma mater.

When he arrived at "the Cross," as he always referred to it, Charlie was assigned to a dormitory room with five other football players. They were not eligible for varsity ball until their sophomore year, so they were on the freshman team. "We'd go to mass every morning, then to our classes, then to football practice. When I got back to the dorm each day, I would be exhausted but knew I had to study. My roommates had other ideas. They wanted to have fun. When the other guys saw me trying to study, they would say, 'You don't have to study, the profs know we are athletes, they won't fail us.' I did not believe them. Rather than argue with them, I decided that I would go to bed early, wake up at dawn, and study before Mass. That way I got my sleep and studies in.

It was a good thing I did. At the end of the first semester, four of my roommates flunked out."

In October, the St. Louis Cardinals beat the Detroit Tigers four games to three to win the World Series. That same month, FBI agents shot and killed "Pretty Boy" Floyd followed in November by the mortal wounding of bank robber "Baby Face" Nelson in a gunfight where one federal agent was killed and another mortally wounded. It had not been a good year for gangsters.

While playing freshman football, Charlie met Paul Bartolomeo, a highly rated halfback from Philadelphia. Paul was a fellow Italian and a serious student as well as an excellent athlete. He was at Holy Cross to get a quality education, and the two of them clicked almost immediately. Charlie, who was now five-foot-eight and 175 pounds, was bigger than Bartolomeo, and he was also a halfback. This created competition for playing time. They both had excellent seasons in the fall and were expected to be varsity players next year. In baseball, it was more competition between the two. Both were second basemen. Though they were rivals at the same position in both football and baseball, they became great friends.

AS 1935 BEGAN, RICHARD HAUPTMAN, WHO WAS ACCUSED OF kidnapping and killing the Lindbergh baby, was brought to trial. He was convicted in February. Around the same time, Adolf Hitler reinstated Nazi Germany's air force, which violated the 1919 Treaty of Versailles. It was becoming clear in Europe that hostilities were imminent.

In the spring, Charlie and Paul played on the freshman baseball team. Hop was their coach. Charlie won the second based position and had an outstanding season. Great things were expected of him the next year when he would get an opportunity to play for the varsity. One of the highlights for him that spring was the varsity's game against the Boston Braves at Fitton Field. Babe Ruth was finishing his career with that team. To say that the Holy Cross players were excited is an understatement. Babe didn't let them down. He was his own larger than life self, chatting with each of them and frolicking around the field before the game to the delight of the fans. Charlie said, "Babe was past his prime and not in very good shape. That didn't matter to us. Meeting him was one of the biggest thrills of my life." It was also the last season that Ruth played in the Major League.

Charlie made it through freshman year and returned home for the summer where he once again played in the Blackstone Valley League. His team won the championship, and he was the League MVP.

As the year went on, Hitler continued to violate the Treaty by beginning a conscription for the German Army along with other aggressive actions to ready his country for war. In August, FDR signed the Social Security Act. It was a harbinger of the future.

LATE IN THE SUMMER, CHARLIE RETURNED TO HOLY CROSS for his first varsity football season. At that time, the Crusaders were a national power. After preseason camp and when the students returned for the fall semester, Charlie and Paul Bartolomeo put in a request with the administration that they be roommates that was approved. It was an excellent decision for both. As one article in the Worcester Telegram (date and writer unknown) reported, "Milford, nearby, was visited frequently by Bartolomeo, who lived in Philadelphia and could not make frequent trips home. They [Charlie and Paul] were in each other's company whenever they had free time, and they worked together in their study periods in their rooms.... Brucato is a good student, and Bartolomeo is on the honor roll.... They are constantly in each other's company despite their rivalry."

When the football season began, the two sophomore halfbacks would no longer have to compete for playing time. Head Coach and Holy Cross legend Dr. Eddie Anderson put Charlie at right halfback and Paul at left halfback. Though upperclassman Nick Morris was the star at halfback, both Charlie and Bartolomeo saw a lot of action and

1935 HOLY CROSS FOOTBALL TEAM

Charlie in second row, Number 11

Charlie at Fitton Field

were more than capable players. In the game against Maine that year, Charlie had a touchdown and a thirty-yard scamper.

Against St. Anselms, they saw their first significant action in what the yearbook termed the "all Italian backfield of Canini, Brucato, Bartholomeo, and Massey."[79] "Before the contest had cut its first teeth, Massey ran forty-three yards off tackle, then Bartolomeo went over from the five spot. In the second session, Brucato, the Milford speed vendor, pivoted like a finely trained splicer in a machine and scampered from tree to tree in a mythical forest with St. Anselms in futile pursuit."[80] In a 79-0 rout of Bates, Bartolomeo and Charlie again starred.

The team finished the season with a win against archrival Boston

79   *1936 Purple Patcher*, P. 371.
80   *1936 Purple Patcher*, P. 371.

College. Their record was 9-0-1, the first undefeated team in the school's history. They were crowned Eastern Champions.

IN THE SPRING OF 1936, CHARLIE STARTED HIS COLLEGE baseball career under legendary ex-Major Leaguer Jack Barry, who was an exceptional baseball coach. Charlie loved playing for Barry.

Often, he would marvel, "You know that fella was the third baseman in Connie Mack's $100,000.00 infield."

"Barry's success was due to his absolute insistence that you play the game by the book. It meant that you worked on every detail of the game no matter how minute. It meant that your shoes and your uniform were neat and clean. It meant that you never stopped hustling."[81] When he became a coach, Charlie set down the same standards for his players.

Charlie won the second base job for the Crusaders, pairing with shortstop Joe "Specks" Kelley to create a formidable double play combination, much to the delight of Coach Barry, who wanted a team that was strong up the middle defensively. Charlie had played against Kelley, who was from Jamaica Plain, when they were in high school.

Before 8,500 fans at Fitton Field, the Crusaders' first game was played against the Boston Red Sox, who were returning from spring training. Though they lost 2-1, "Charley Brucato, the Milford will-o-wisp starting his first game, was the recipient of much favorable praise for his work. He made two catches of the sensational type and was the seasoned pivot man in the (three) double plays executed which caused a clever cartoonist well known in Worcester to remark, 'Yep, Jack Barry is still the coach of the ball team.'"[82]

Charlie described one of the "sensational" catches in a less flattering way. "Jimmy Foxx [who later would be inducted into Baseball's Hall of Fame] hit the highest pop-up I had ever seen. I ran to get under it, but

---

81   Rev. Raymond F. X. Cahill, S. J., *The Quiet Crusader*, 1976, P. 24 (quoting Jack "Pookey" Brennan).

82   *1936 Purple Patcher*, P. 384.

it was so high, I was spinning around trying to get a bead on the ball. I was still spinning as the ball came down and I fell on my ass. The ball ended up in my glove as I was lying on my back. When I got up, I was really embarrassed.

"The next inning, I came up and hit a single. As I was standing on first base, Foxx came over to me, patted me on the ass, and said, 'Nice catch kid.'" Charlie set a record in that game by handling fifteen chances without an error. It was a great opening act for the young sophomore. He and his teammates had fun both before and after the game mingling with Foxx, Joe Cronin, and the other Red Sox players.

Charlie said that there were some interesting characters on the Holy Cross baseball team that year. Nick Morris, who starred on the football team, was the first baseman. "During drills in the preseason, Nick sat back as his competition for the position made a strong showing," Charlie recalled. "I went over to him one day and said, 'Nick, aren't you worried that guy is going to take your position?' Nick looked at me with a smile and said, 'Don't worry about me. I'll put his dick in my watch pocket. When the season begins, I'll be the starter.' He was one cocky son of a bitch, and he was tough as nails. Sure enough, Nick won the starting job and had a great year."

Another character was Wilfred "Lefty" Lefebvre. Lefty was a fierce competitor and one of Charlie's classmates who would go on to play for the Red Sox. Charlie liked to tell a story about Lefebvre's fire. "We were in a tight game, and Lefty was in trouble with men on base. I called time-out and walked over to the mound with the ball in my hand and was about to offer him some encouragement. Before I could open my mouth, Lefty glared at me and said, 'Give me the fucking baseball and get back to your position.' I did and he got out of the jam."

After losing to the Red Sox, the Crusaders won eight in a row and then finished the season at 18-2. They were named the Eastern Intercollegiate Champions. Charlie emerged not only as a great defensive player but an exceptional hitter. He moved from the bottom of the batting order to the top. In an article following the Boston University game, a 16-1 win, a student writer for the Holy Cross newspaper said, "The work of Charlie Brucato has been just about good enough to make us forget the great work of Eddie Moriarty last year. The change in which he and Nick Morris swapped places in the lineup benefitted both players as they went out to pace the team in hitting in the BU slaughter."[83]

In a game against Harvard, Charlie started a double play, got two hits, and knocked in two runs. Against Boston College in a thirteen-inning game, he had two doubles and scored the winning run as the Crusaders beat their arch-rivals 7-6 to sweep the annual series. By the end of the season, Charlie had hit over .300 with power, played excellent defense, and used his great speed on the basepaths.

———————

AFTER THE COLLEGE SEASON WAS OVER, CHARLIE SPENT THE summer playing for Bourne in the prestigious Cape Cod Baseball League. He had a great summer and was selected to the all-star team. The best story of that summer involved his cousin Sammy Tomaso. During the season, Bourne needed another player because one of the team members either got hurt or had to leave. Charlie told the coach that one of his teammates in Milford would be a great fit. He raved about what a great ballplayer Sammy was, and the coach put him on the team sight unseen.

Charlie recalled many years later, "Sammy arrives, and he has this thick moustache [mooostache as Charlie pronounced it]. The coach takes one look at him and then glares at me. He was not pleased to have put Sammy on the team without seeing him. I had to admit that he did not look like a ballplayer, and when I suggested he shave it off, he refused, as I knew he would. Sammy was stubborn that way.

"So, the season goes on, and the coach won't put Sammy on the field. I keep telling him that Sammy is a great player and pleading with him to let him play. He continues to keep Sammy on the bench. One day, we

83 Jim Collier, "Purple Pennings," *The Tomahawk*, April 28, 1936.

were in a ballgame and needed a relief pitcher. Unfortunately, we didn't have anyone left to come in. I went up to the coach and said, 'Sammy can pitch,' even though I knew he wasn't a pitcher.

"The coach had no choice but to put Sammy in, and he not only finishes the game, but he also gets a couple of hits. After that game, the coach started to play him, and Sammy became one of our best players and even made the all-star team. At the end of the season, the coach came over to me and said, 'Boy was I wrong about Tomaso. He may not look like a ballplayer, but he's as good as anyone in this league.'"

IN THE FALL OF 1936, CHARLIE BEGAN HIS SECOND SEASON on the Holy Cross football team. Prospects were high with a number of veterans returning and highly touted sophomore fullback Bill Osmanski joining the team. "Osmanski was a great football player," Charlie said. "I was a step faster, but he was bigger and stronger. If he liked you, he would run around you. If he didn't, he'd run over you." The captain of the team was senior Bob Curley, a hard-nosed lineman who would become one of Charlie's closest lifelong friends.

To open the season, they beat the Providence College Friars 21-6. Charlie had a touchdown in the game. They then beat an excellent Dartmouth team 7-0 in a hard-fought game where Osmanski scored the only touchdown. They continued their winning ways beating Manhattan 13-7 and highly regarded Carnegie Tech 7-0. Charlie scored another touchdown in the Manhattan game and Osmanski had the lone one against Carnegie Tech. They next traveled to Philadelphia where they suffered defeat at the hands of Temple 3-0 in a defensive battle.

Colgate was the next opponent, and they had defeated a strong Army team the previous week. Before a crowd of nearly twenty-five thousand at Fitton Field, the Crusaders prevailed by a score of 20-13. When Colgate coach Andy Kerr was asked whether Holy Cross could beat Army, he responded, ". . . The way they played today, Holy Cross

Charlie running through line at Holy Cross

is better than Army."[84] Though Charlie did not know it at the time, it would be the last college football game he would ever play.

On a fake kick play, from the Crusaders thirty yard line, Charlie took a handoff from Osmanski and headed up field. Jake Brody, a *Worcester Telegram and Gazette* reporter, described what happened next. "Once he had the ball, Charlie was out there all alone like the last lamb chop on the platter.... He cut wide around his own left end and sprinted for the Holy Cross sideline.... So he was still traveling to his left when the Colgate tackler, coming up fast, crashed into him with full momentum.... Brucato, going slightly sideways, went down on his left shoulder... climbed to his feet, but his left arm hung limply, and he was wobbling like the Spanish government."[85]

He was taken to St. Vincent's Hospital where he was diagnosed with a badly dislocated left shoulder. It took three attempts by doctors to get the shoulder back in place. Brody reported, "The last time, the pain was so great that Charlie had to be given a second shot of anesthetic while the men in white labored to get him properly reassembled."[86] Giuseppe visited him that night in the hospital and said that Charlie complained of pain all over his body. Charlie's season was over, and he hoped he would be ready when baseball season started.

Holy Cross finished the season by winning the next two games and then losing to Boston College. Osmanski was voted All-American. He would later go on to play professional football for the Chicago Bears.

———

WHEN SPRING OF 1937 CAME AROUND, CHARLIE HAD RECOVered from his shoulder injury, and he was ready for the baseball season. He had been lucky that the injury was to his non-throwing shoulder. There were a lot of holes to fill with the graduation of star players, including Nick Morris, Joe Cusick, and Bob Daughters. The Crusaders

———

84 Jack West, "Purple Pennings," *The Tomahawk*, November 10, 1936.
85 Jake Broudy, "Sports Talk," *Worcester Telegram & Gazette*, (date and page unknown).
86 Broudy, "Sports Talk."

Charlie hitting at Holy Cross

opened at Fitton Field against the Boston Red Sox again. They lost 5-0, but it was another great experience for Charlie and his teammates. In another exhibition game against the Boston Bees, Charlie had a long home run and a single. Holy Cross then went to New York, tied Princeton 5-5, and crushed Columbia 12-3. In the Columbia game, Charlie picked up another two hits.

By mid-season, Charlie was hitting .316 and the team had beaten Harvard and Colgate. They finished the season with a record of 16-2-1, and Charlie was elected captain of the 1938 team.

IN THE CAPE COD BASEBALL LEAGUE THAT SUMMER, CHARLIE again played for Bourne and had another excellent season. In one game against Orleans, while being watched by a Detroit Tigers scout, he hit a home run, double, and two singles. When the scout approached him, Charlie told him that he intended to finish his studies and would then look to further himself in the baseball world. Charlie's season ended abruptly when he broke his left ankle.

He was running out a hit and tripped over first base. That not only ended his Cape League season, but it also prevented him from playing football in the fall. To honor him and help with his medical expenses, a game between the Cape Cod League All-Stars and the Milford AA was held at Town Park in Milford on September 19, 1937. The fans were treated with an excellent game that ended in a 7-7 tie in the tenth inning when rains prevented further play.

DUE TO HIS ANKLE INJURY AND THE EFFECTS OF HIS SHOULDER injury in the Colgate game during his junior year, Charlie was not able to play football in his senior year. Though football was his second sport, missing his final year on the team was frustrating. Even without playing that year, he had left an indelible mark on the gridiron. He looked forward to baseball and his graduation from Holy Cross.

Charlie jumping for baseball at Holy Cross

It would be a mistake to think that Charlie's college experience was limited to sports and study. He truly enjoyed the entire college experience, meeting new and different friends he would have for life and having the fun that college kids have. There were the card games after lights out when he would sneak into other rooms and play late into the night and early morning. One story he told involved a card game in a dormitory room where four or five of his friends had been playing poker. One of the Jesuits, doing a random bed check, knocked on the door. Having no other avenue of escape, he and his buddies opened a window and walked onto a narrow ledge and hid until the priest left.

SPRING FINALLY ARRIVED, AND CHARLIE'S ANKLE HAD healed so he could start his third varsity baseball season at Holy Cross without any limitations. The 1938 *Purple Patcher* (the Holy Cross yearbook) season recap stated, "The second sack was crowned once again with that great sportsman Captain Charlie Brucato. Charlie is noted for his prowess on the field and his keen eye at bat, a truly great leader for the Crusader nine and a remarkable player to watch in action."[87]

With his great play and baseball acumen, Charlie had gained the confidence of Coach Barry as he assumed captaincy of the Crusaders. "Jack was a very private guy, but my senior year when I was captain, I got a little closer to him," Charlie said. "I think that I was one of his favorites. He never showered with us, but one day when I was showering alone, he came in naked and turned on the spigot opposite me. I couldn't help but stare at the huge scar on one of his legs. He noticed this and said dryly, 'That's a souvenir from when Ty Cobb spiked me.'"

One of the best stories of his days playing for Barry occurred during a close game. "We were tied in the late innings of a ball game, and I made an error causing the go ahead run to score. As I approached the dugout at the end of the inning, Hop Riopel, who was my coach at Milford High and now Jack Barry's assistant coach, glared at me and

87 1938 *Purple Patcher*

barked, 'Brucato, you are a foul ball!' I was angry to begin with, but this pissed me off even more, and I snapped right back at him, 'Your ass!' I then went into the dugout and sat down. Jack saw the whole thing but didn't say a word.

"In the next inning, I got up with a man on and hit a ball over the left field fence for a home run to win the game. As I passed by Jack on my way into the dugout, he said, 'That's how I like to see my ballplayers respond,' making sure Hop heard him. Hop just stood there. Jack was just that type of guy. He didn't like anyone getting on his players for a physical error, and he made sure Hop knew it."

Holy Cross won fifteen games and lost five. They started the season by beating the Red Sox 3-2 before seven thousand fans at Fitton Field. They then suffered the worst loss of Charlie's varsity baseball career when Brown beat them 14-8 in the first regular season game. In the next game, they trounced Fordham 12-4 with Charlie contributing a sacrifice bunt and two hits to the cause. The Holy Cross nine beat Dartmouth 4-2 behind the pitching of Art Kenney. Charlie crushed a long triple in the game. They then beat Springfield 9-5 and avenged the earlier loss to Brown by beating them 5-2 in Providence. Charlie was off to his best start ever, hitting .545 after three games and leading the team in RBI.

The team lost to Providence College 10-3, defeated Colgate 13-3, Yale 9-4, and Villanova 5-4 before losing to Rhode Island State. They then went on to shut out Providence 3-0, New Hampshire 3-0, then beat Colgate 14-1 and Harvard 8-1. In the game against New Hampshire, Charlie clouted a long triple to drive in two runs in the ninth inning. Before the Harvard game, a large delegation of Milford fans honored Charlie, Arthur Kenney, and Hop Riopel along with Harvard's Harold Curtiss, all Milfordians, with a presentation at home plate.

Charlie's Holy Cross career ended with a flourish against Boston College. He was the pivot man in two double plays and started another one. At the plate, he hit a two-run homer, double, and drove in four runs as Holy Cross won 9-3. According to the *Worcester Telegram and*

Charlie and Giuseppe at Holy Cross

Gazette, "Brucato's homer was the first hit on Fitton Field by a HC player this season.... His two hits enabled him to finish the campaign with a .395 batting average and twenty-two runs batted in.... Both are high marks for several seasons among HC players."[88]

During the season, Charlie was portrayed in a cartoon by Art Brewster titled "Purple Captain." In it, he is shown swinging a bat with the notation, "Charlie 'Chick' Brucato! Brilliant Second Baseman and Captain of the Holy Cross nine!" His image is surrounded by four caricatures showing him running with a football with the note, "He's a great man with a football;" taking advice from a coach, with the note, "Charlie is a Milford boy and received his early training under Hop Riopel, present HC freshman coach;" facing a devil with "Injury Jynx" embossed on the devil's chest with the note, "He likes to follow Charlie;" and sitting

88 "Diamond Dust," *Worcester Telegram & Gazette,* (date and page unknown).

at a table eating with the note, "He's quite a man at the plate—specially if it's spaghetti! p.s. He's Italian."[89]

In the 1938 *Purple Patcher*, he was described as

> The Plainsman from Milford...the prized protegee of 'Hop' Riopel...'Charlie' deserves a place among the immortal athletes of Packachoag.... For two years, he was one of our star halfbacks... small...fast...elusive.... We saw the purple-jerseyed '11' romp for many a yard.... In junior year, the ball carrier on that deceptive 'fake kick' play, 'Charlie' delighted the Purple rooters with repeated gains through Dartmouth, Manhattan, and Carnegie...a shoulder injury that year brought to a close his activities on the gridiron.... But baseball was his real forte.... Spring of senior year found him captain of the nine...again busy on Fitton Field, giving consistent performances at second base which brought pleasant warmth to the heart of 'Jack' Barry.... Quiet and unassuming...his words were given consideration at the Hot Stove meetings.... He was a regular caller at the rooms with the battle cry of 'Suits.'...Ambition is to be a major leaguer...and 'Charlie' was always a hard worker.[90]

Charlie graduated later in the spring and was voted "best athlete" by his classmates. It was a fitting end to another illustrious chapter in his life. In 1985, he was elected to the Holy Cross Hall of Fame for his exploits on the gridiron and baseball diamond.

---

89 Art Brewster, "Purple Captain," *Worcester Telegram & Gazette*, (date and page unknown).
90 *1938 Purple Patcher*

CHAPTER FIVE

STARTING A CAREER

A S SUMMER OF 1938 BEGAN, HEAVYWEIGHT CHAMPION
Joe Louis knocked out Max Schmeling in the first round of their
rematch at Yankee Stadium and the winds of war were continuing to blow.
After graduating from Holy Cross, Charlie signed a professional baseball
contract with Connie Mack's Philadelphia Athletics and was assigned to
Fredericksburg, a Class D team in the Eastern Shore League. He did not
stay there long. In fourteen games, he had fifty-two at bats and twenty
hits, including three doubles and a home run, for a .385 batting average.

He was immediately moved up to Williamsport, a Class A team in
the Eastern League and a step away from the major leagues. There he
joined one of his high school teammates, Hank Comolli, who was the
catcher on the team. Charlie became the starting second baseman and
continued with his excellent play.

Several days after he arrived, manager Marty McManus called him
to his office.

"Look, Charlie, I know you are a good player and could help this
team, but I got instructions from the 'big club' to play Dario Lodigiani
at second base. They sent him down here to get at bats."

CHARLIE'S WILLIAMSPORT TEAM

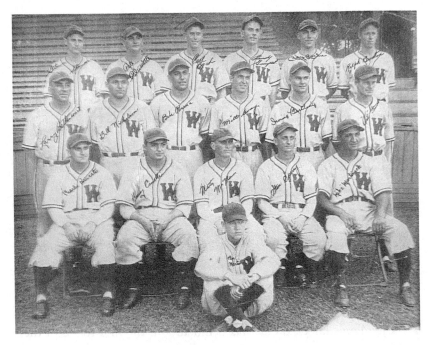

Charlie: front row, first from left;
Hank "Camel" Comolli: front row, second from left.

Charlie was not happy. As a twenty-two-year-old college graduate who had excelled on every team he played on, including this one, he simply was not going to sit on the bench and wait his turn. Minor league baseball was a grind and there was no way to make it to the big leagues sitting on the bench. He told McManus that he was going home, and he packed his bags and returned to Milford.

In later years, he said he never regretted his decision. He never really liked the idea of being away from home and riding buses and trains and hanging around ball parks with men who had different backgrounds and mindsets. The big leagues in the '30s and '40s were not like they are today. The travel was exhausting, and the pay was meager. In addition, many pro baseball players at the time were uneducated, hard drinking roughnecks with whom Charlie had little in common. Though he loved baseball, he knew that there was more to life than being what he often termed "a jockstrap."

Sports had come very easy to Charlie. He was always the fastest runner, best hitter, and most accomplished player on each team on which he played. Success in sports, he would often say, "was no big deal." Intelligence and culture were the qualities what he respected most. He wanted to pursue a career in education and coaching.

On September 21, 1938, a massive hurricane hit southern New England. Named "the Great New England Hurricane of 1938," it was one of the most destructive and powerful storms ever recorded. "The hurricane was of unprecedented force and left the town [Milford] paralyzed. Roads were washed away, and trees blocked railroad tracks."[91] Buildings, businesses, and houses were destroyed. Schools and businesses were forced to close. Residents spent weeks cleaning up the mess. At the time, Charlie was living with Giuseppe and Ninfa at the Liberto two family home at 94 Hayward Street, a few doors down from their former residence on Mt. Pleasant Street.

On November 30, Giuseppe filed his naturalization papers in the United States District Court of Massachusetts in Boston. He listed himself on the petition as "Joseph Failacci AKA Joseph Brucato" and requested that he be known as Joseph Brucato when he became a citizen of the United States. The petition was granted, and the now the fifty-nine-year-old Sicilian immigrant could proudly call himself an American.

AS 1939 BEGAN, JOE LOUIS REMAINED THE HEAVYWEIGHT champion of the world. In April, Ted Williams took his first at bat for the Red Sox in Massachusetts in an exhibition game. This historic event, which is immortalized in a black and white photograph, took place at Charlie's favorite venue—Fitton Field on the campus of the

91 Deborah Eastman, Anne Lamontagne, and Marilyn Lovell, *Images of America: Milford* (Charlestown, SC: Arcadia Publishing, 2014), 107.

College of the Holy Cross. On April 30, Lou Gehrig played his 2,130th consecutive and final game for the New York Yankees, setting a record that would stand for nearly sixty years.

Charlie's first opportunity to coach also came in the summer of 1939 when he took a job as a twenty-three-year-old player-manager of the New Waterford Dodgers, a Class C professional baseball team in the Cape Breton Island Colliery League. He followed in the steps of his good friend and Crusader teammate Nick Morris, who held the position a year earlier. Tate Bodio and Sooey DeGaetano had played for Morris that year and would be returning. Charlie signed his cousin Sammy Tomaso and Holy Cross teammate Wally Bracken to play on the team, so he was surrounded by players he knew very well.

When he got to Cape Breton Island, Charlie's first task was to evaluate his players and make roster decisions. He immediately traded the second baseman because that was the position he was going to play. "He had the prettiest girlfriend of all the players," Charlie would chuckle. "And when he was gone, she became my girl. Her name was Effie McMullen."

Charlie told many stories about his time in the Colliery League. Two of his best involved a twenty-one-year-old pitcher named Edward Rivers. He was a strapping six-foot, 182-pound right hander nicknamed "Chief" because he was, as Charlie put it, "a full-blooded Indian [Native American]." The Chief was pitching one day and was tagged for a double. Facing the next batter, he went into a full wind-up rather than pitching out of the stretch to keep the runner on second close to the base. The runner was so surprised by this that he didn't even try to steal third.

"I called time-out and went to the mound," related Charlie. "'Look, Chief, you should know you don't go into a wind-up with a man on second. Just take your stretch.' On the very next pitch, he winds up again, and this time the runner does steal third standing up. I was fuming and returned to the mound and screamed at him. 'What the hell is the matter with you, Chief? I just told you to pitch from the stretch so the guy on second wouldn't steal.' He looked at me and said, 'Yeah, yeah, but it's this way. I can pitch better with a man on third. When he's on second, I can't see him, and it bothers me. But when he's on third, I can see him perfectly and I don't worry, so I let him steal.'"

Another story involving Rivers ultimately cost him his position on the team. Chief was having difficulty on the mound, and Charlie learned that he was out late every night with his lady friend. "I called him into my office and told him that he was spending too much time shacking up with his girl and it was affecting his pitching. I told him if he didn't improve, I was going to ship him out.

"The next evening, I was hanging around in town when Tate rushed over. 'Charlie, Chief Rivers' girlfriend is in the drug store looking for you, and she's pretty angry.' I walked into the drug store to meet her. She approached me and said, 'I want to speak to you, but not here. I'll meet you in the alley outside.'

"I was very uncomfortable going into the alley, thinking she might have a knife or a gun. Fortunately, she did not, but she was very angry. 'My boyfriend said you called me a whore, and he should stop seeing me,' she said. I looked her in the eye and calmly stated, 'I don't know what you are talking about. I never said anything to Chief about you at all. I don't even know you.'

"She was not convinced, but at least she had calmed down enough to simply warn me never to talk about her like that again. I was relieved. The stupid son of a bitch ran right to her after I had spoken with him. I traded Chief the next day."

Charlie had a great time playing and coaching the New Waterford Dodgers. His team finished in second place with a record of 31-25. He led the team with a .323 batting average and was narrowly edged out for the League batting title. He also led the team in hits (seventy-one), home runs (two) and was second in doubles (ten) and triples (five). His summer romance with Effie kept him occupied when he was not playing. She begged him to stay after the season.

His buddies also played well for him. Sooey hit .303 and even pitched a game. Tate hit .295 and Wally Bracken hit .263. Sammy slipped a bit at

CHARLIE'S 1939 NEW WATERFORD DODGERS

Charlie, front row, second from left; Tate Bodio, front row, fourth from left;
Sooey DeGaetano, second row, second from left; Chief Rivers, back row, second from left;
Sammy Tomaso, back row, third from left.

the plate with an average of .224, but he hit in the clutch, and he made only two errors at third base during the entire season.

At the end of the season, Charlie decided that his professional baseball career was over.

"I know that I would have been a good hitter at the major league level," he would say, "but I don't think I had a 'big league' throwing arm. And playing in the minor leagues was horseshit. The travel and hotels were no fun. Most of the players were uneducated and crude. Some of the guys were drinkers, skirt chasers, and fighters."

In any event, he was unwilling to toil in the minors for the period needed to get the seasoning the teams then required. He also learned on Cape Breton Island that he enjoyed coaching. Now twenty-three, he returned home and got a job as physical education director for the

Milford school system. He would continue to play baseball in the Black-stone Valley Baseball League for a few more years, but his focus was now on education and coaching.

Charlie had achieved things he could have never imagined because of his athletic prowess. He had gained respectability and even admiration from those who usually looked down upon those from the other side of the tracks. He had earned a scholarship and graduated from one of the best Catholic colleges in the nation. He had achieved exalted status from coaches, sportswriters, and fans throughout the Northeast. These accomplishments were remarkable for the son of Sicilian immigrants. Throughout it all, he remained the same quiet, modest, and humble kid from Mt. Pleasant and Hayward Streets in the Plains.

———————

WHILE CHARLIE WAS IN NOVA SCOTIA PLAYING AND COACH-ing baseball, much was happening both in the United States and overseas. Germany, under Adolf Hitler, was beginning its quest for world domination. Italy had invaded Albania. The Spanish Civil War had ended, and Francisco Franco had assumed power in Madrid. At that point, the United States was still unaffected, but that would soon change. The New York World's Fair had opened. *The Wizard of Oz* was released, and Frank Sinatra made his recording debut.

On September 1, 1939, Adolf Hitler ordered the extermination of the mentally ill in his country and his Nazi German Army invaded Poland. Britain and France immediately declared war on Germany and World War II began. President Roosevelt advocated neutrality. As school opened later that month, Charlie began his career in education as the physical education director of the Milford Public Schools. Since Molly had her own family, now only he and Ninfa were living with Giuseppe. Brother John was a police officer and was still living at 45 Beckley Avenue in Stamford with Jeanette and their four children.

In October, Jimmy Stewart was the star in Frank Capra's *Mr. Smith Goes to Washington* and Joe DiMaggio was voted Most Valuable Player in the American League. On Armistice Day, Kate Smith sang *God Bless America* for the first time. Five days later, Al Capone was freed from Alcatraz Prison. The continuing story for the entire year, however, was World War II.

Charlie undertook his job in the Milford Public Schools with enthusiasm. He still yearned to be a head coach, and he viewed physical education as a steppingstone toward that goal. Working with the kids in PE class gave him the added benefit of learning who were the athletes in town when he did get a coaching job.

In the fall of 1940, he was appointed head football coach at Milford High School. At twenty-four, he was not much older than the boys he would coach. Unfortunately, the team he inherited was inexperienced and not very good. Charlie installed the Notre Dame system, but the team had problems implementing it. To make matters worse, Town Park was in such poor shape that no games could be scheduled there, and the team would have to play all its games on their opponents' fields.

They lost the opening game to Clinton 25-7 before defeating Marlboro 12-6 as Ben Zachilli and John Espanet emerged as reliable ball carriers. They then fell to Natick 13-0. "Irked by lack of charge, drive, and lift with which the Milford line carried out its assignments last Saturday against Natick High, Coach Charley Brucato has been using sweatshop methods with his linemen this week."[92] The tactic was not successful. They lost the final four games losing to Norwood 19-0, Hudson 7-0, Framingham 18-7, and Maynard 6-0. The team finished with a record of one win and six losses. For someone accustomed to winning, the lack of success of the first high school team he ever coached was disheartening.

Showing maturity beyond his years, Charlie chose to focus on the positive in his report of the season in the school yearbook.

> From an educational standpoint alone, the advantages gained from playing the sport are numerous. The football athlete faces a daily

---

92 "Seeks to Put Lift in Milford High Line," *Milford Daily News*, October 26, 1940.

examination on the field of play and unless the player's mental lesson is perfect, his individual physical capacities go to waste.

Those participating in the sport must be willing to submit to the most rigid discipline. Only by such discipline can errors be minimized if not eliminated. Every man cannot run with the ball, nor can every man be allowed to choose the particular territory he prefers to defend. It is a game of individual sacrifice for the general good of the team.

There is still another form of discipline which is of equal value if not greater value to the football player. It is the intensive discipline of the individual over himself. First, he must learn the simple rule of self-control. Displays of temper do no good and generally interfere with the playing ability of the angered individual.

It takes time for boys to begin to know themselves, their capacity to stand physical fatigue and to absorb bodily punishment. Many so-called 'quitters' are boys who haven't given themselves a fair chance to make use of the possibilities within themselves.

To the graduating members of the 1940 football team, I extend my congratulations to each of you for your untiring efforts in the performance of your duties to the best of your ability.

Charles J. Brucato, Coach[93]

Written over eighty years ago, this narrative is as relevant now as it was then. Charlie's philosophy is eerily similar to that of New England Patriots head coach Bill Belichick, who is arguably the best professional football coach in history.

In terms of wins and losses, Charlie's first season of coaching was not what he would have liked, but he had begun to build a program and more than that, he built courage, character, and discipline in young men who would desperately need these qualities in the very near future.

---

93   1941 *Oak Lily and Ivy*, Football Section.

THE NEWS DURING THE WINTER OF 1940 AND SPRING OF 1941 was dominated by stories about the war. In June of 1941, Britain was being pounded by Nazi bombs, and it was becoming almost inevitable that the United States would soon be entering the war. The draft for soldiers was instituted, battleships were being built, and the major automobile manufacturers were beginning to build airplanes. The theme of graduating senior Alexandria Satkiewicz's address to her Milford High classmates was "National Defense—A Safeguard for Democracy."

When the school year ended, Charlie traveled to Vermont where he played and managed the Montpelier baseball team in the Northern League. It was another notch on his coaching belt. Since it was becoming clearer that the United States would be joining the war, he must have known that it would be his last season of baseball for a long time.

As summer turned to fall, Charlie returned from Vermont and began his second stint as head football coach at Milford High. This team was even worse than his first. They did not win a game and finished with a record of 0-7. Its best games were against Norwood and Framingham.

After its 13-6 loss to Norwood, *Daily News* columnist Frank Bergstrom wrote, "A fighting Milford High football team conceded little chance of taking Norwood in pregame dope, outplayed Norwood for two periods only to find itself overcome by the power of its opponent."[94] In its loss to Framingham 13-6, Milford stunned 6,500 fans by outplaying its rivals. Versatile back Red Oates, freshman halfback Dick Consigli, and senior captain Joe Pessotti were standouts the entire year.

The yearbook titled its season review, "M.H.S. Football Team is Plucky, But Also Very Unlucky," and reported, "When it became evident that the season would not be termed a success, Coach Brucato wisely aimed for higher stakes.... The undergraduates were used more often and gained valuable experience. The whole school and the town are aiming for a successful campaign next year."[95] It was not to be.

---

94 *Milford Daily News*, October 27, 1941.
95 1942 *Oak, Lily and Ivy*, 72.

CHAPTER SIX

———

WORLD WAR II

"**B** Y EARLY 1941, IN A SERIES OF CAMPAIGNS AND TREA-
ties, Germany conquered or controlled much of continental
Europe and formed the Axis alliance with Italy and Japan (along with
other countries later on). Following the onset of campaigns in North
Africa and East Africa and the fall of France in mid-1940, the war
continued primarily between the European Axis powers and the British
Empire, with war in the Balkans, the aerial Battle of Britain, the Blitz of
the United Kingdom, and the Battle of the Atlantic. On June 22, 1941,
Germany led the European Axis powers in an invasion of the Soviet
Union, opening the Eastern Front."[96]

Japan, seeking to dominate Asia, had been at war with China, but it
had reached a stalemate in 1940. In early 1941, the United States began
negotiations with Japan to end their strained relations and end the
war with China. The negotiations failed, and the United States entered
secret discussions with Britain and the Netherlands for joint defense
of their territories in the event of an invasion by Japan.

In December, tensions between the United States and Japan escalated.

———

96 "World War II," Wikipedia, https://en.wikipedia.org/wiki/World_War_II.

After denying it had territorial ambitions in East Asia or elsewhere,[97] United States leaders felt an early move by Japan was not expected.[98] They were wrong. On December 7, Japanese planes bombed Pearl Harbor, destroyed most of the Pacific Fleet, and killed thousands of military and civilian personnel.

The United States had been drawn into World War II. Faced with formidable enemies on opposite ends of the world, American men and women from every city and town were being drafted into the army or enlisting in other branches of the United States military. The war in the Pacific would preoccupy military personnel and resources long before the United States would join its European allies to fight Nazi Germany on the Western front.

After the Pearl Harbor invasion, American men and women from every city and town began enlisting in all branches of the United States Military Service. Many of those who didn't enlist were drafted into the army. Charlie did not wait to be drafted into the army. Instead, he chose to enlist in the United States Marine Corps. Many years later, in an interview with Luke Tobin, one of his grandchildren who was writing a school paper, Charlie said:

> As soon as I found out what was going on in Europe, I tried to get into the military as soon as I could. At first, I tried to enlist in the air force, but they rejected me because of a problem I had with my ear. I had some scarred tissue in my ear that I had not known before. To get into the air force, you had to be in perfect physical shape. Though I was in top physical condition, the air force was very strict about injuries, even old ones. So the air force was my first choice. I didn't want to go into the army because most everyone there was drafted in and really didn't want to be there. I wanted to be with real soldiers that wanted to fight for their country. So, I enlisted in the marines.

97 "Japan 'Hedges' in Reply to United States," *Milford Daily News*, December 5, 1941.
98 "Early Move by Japan Not Expected," *Milford Daily News*, December 6, 1941.

On April 6, 1942, he began basic training ("boot camp") at Parris Island, South Carolina, and on August first, he completed it. It is doubtful that he knew beforehand that marine training was the most difficult and physically demanding of all branches in the military. Being in great shape and accustomed to pressure from playing athletics at a high level made it much easier for Charlie, both physically and emotionally, than most of the recruits.

When he was at boot camp, the war intensified in both Europe and the Pacific. Japanese forces began the last phase of the Battle of Bataan, an all-out assault on the United States and Filipino troops on the Bataan Peninsula. The peninsula ultimately fell, and American and Filipino forces (some seventy-five thousand soldiers) surrendered to the Japanese 14th Army under General Masaharu Homma. Following the surrender, American and Filipino prisoners of war were forced by the Japanese to march from San Fernando to Capas (some sixty-five miles) in what was termed "the Bataan Death March." During the march, some fifteen thousand soldiers were tortured and killed. Those who completed the journey were malnourished and subjected to severe physical abuse. One who survived the Death March was Milford's own "Spike" Moran, who spent his last years living in the house next door to Charlie. Understandably, they would become best friends.

April also saw the beginning of the Holocaust, as construction of the Nazi German extermination camp Treblinka II began in occupied Poland near the village of Treblinka. Between July 23, 1942, and October 1943, around 850,000 people were killed here, more than 800,000 of whom were Jews.[99]

After boot camp, Charlie was encouraged to enter officer candidate school (OCS) because as a college graduate, he met one qualification. He decided to do this, and in October, he began training in Quantico, Virginia. Anyone who has completed OCS will tell you that it is extremely difficult intellectually. The course is highly technical, covering not only leadership but advanced map reading, tactics,

99 "1942," *Wikipedia*, https://en.wikipedia.org/wiki/1942.

weaponry, forward observing, and mathematical courses in fire direction to name a few.

"It was much harder than college for me," Charlie said. "There were times I thought I would never make it."

On December 2, 1942, he completed OCS and was commissioned as a second lieutenant 1542 infantry officer. From there, he had two more months of formal officer training, which ended on February 10, 1943. With this intense training coupled with his background as a school district director of physical education, as well as a coach and teacher, Charlie was well prepared to be a leader of men.

He was assigned the position of platoon leader in the Headquarters Company of the Third Battalion, Twenty-Fifth Regiment, Fourth Marine Division. He was part of an infantry battalion of nine hundred men divided into five companies, led by thirty-seven officers whose mission was "locate, close with, and destroy the enemy with fire power and maneuver." His battalion carried the nicknames "Three Deuce Five" and "Cold Steel Warriors." The commander was Colonel Justice Marion "Jumping Joe" Chambers, who was arguably the toughest, most relentless commander in the marines. He would prepare his troops for battle in the Pacific by training them hard under the worst possible conditions he could create.

The Third Battalion would play significant roles in the battles of Kwajalein, Tinian, Saipan, and Iwo Jima, and because of their specialized training, they would receive many of the most dangerous combat assignments. From May 1 through August 24, 1943, they trained at New River, North Carolina, which would later become Camp Lejeune. While boot camp was physically and mentally demanding, over the next eighteen months, the rigors of military training in preparation for war in the Pacific made Parris Island look like a summer camp.

At New River, Chambers set up three permanent areas that he did not call camps. He required his men to sleep in foxholes and not in the barracks. He set up the training areas on islands in swamps inhabited by snakes and stinging insects. The colonel kept the three installations

Second Lieutenant Charles J. Brucato, USMC

Lt. Brucato at camp

two miles apart and ensured that they were organized for defense with barbed wire, booby traps, and anything else he could think of. The men trained day and night, and Jumping Joe made sure that every night, one camp attacked another. Since Charlie was an officer in Headquarters Company, he came to know Chambers personally because the colonel was also in that company.

Chambers explained the reasons he made the training so difficult. "What I was trying to do, simply, was to make the men's lives so damn miserable in training that when they got into combat, the only thing they had to worry about was the enemy." He told his officers that if they didn't like what he was doing, they should put in for transfers.[100] The Third trained day and night while other units were still getting organized. Jumping Joe's methods were as unorthodox as they were brutal.

---

100 Col. Justice Marion Chambers, *Third Battalion, Twenty-Fifth Marines: An Oral History*, (n.p.: n.d.) 7.

Word spread fast, and soon, commanding officers from neighboring regiments would ask Colonel Chambers if they could visit his installations and observe his methods. He was always more than happy to oblige them. He knew that he was preparing his men for a much different war than previous ones. They would be fighting the Japanese, a relentless enemy of men who valued dying with honor more than survival. Having observed his methods first-hand, many of his fellow commanding officers would later speak up in his defense during the numerous occasions he found himself in the doghouse.

He was an outstanding marine, but Chambers, like General George S. Patton, had little use for red tape and military decisions that made no sense to him. Perhaps not as insubordinate as Patton, he was just as hot-tempered, fiery, and outspoken. He would advocate for what was in the best interest of his men regardless of the ramifications. He led by example and was probably more aware than most about the importance of mental conditioning for combat soldiers. "Joe Chambers was determined that the Third Battalion was going to go through as much morale-breaking, nerve-wracking drudgery and downright misery as he could possibly devise without actually calling out the artillery to fire on them in training. He succeeded."[101]

The men of the Third would take a good deal of razzing from fellow marines in other units. They were always dirty and sloppy, spending little time doing marching drills or laundry. They were probably the least tidy outfit in the corps. Their reputation would change once the fighting started. Eventually, they became known as the roughest, toughest fighting marines in the Pacific. Charlie could not have known at that time that he was about to become one of the few surviving officers of one of the most respected, storied, and decorated marine battalions that fought in World War II.

Charlie never talked about the rigors of his training, but he was a tough bastard in his own right. He would have wanted to be prepared for war by a man like Joe Chambers because the colonel would improve

101 Arthur Hill, *Marine Corp Gazette*, November 1945, 27.

his chances of survival. It is clear Charlie's reputation for toughness as a football and baseball coach after the war stemmed in large part from Chambers' influence. He was as relentless training his athletes as the colonel was training his men, and the results would be the same. Players on Charlie's future teams would put the team first and follow his every command without question. They would practice until they got it right. They were always more disciplined than their opponents, and this is why his teams were so successful.

On August 24, 1943, the East Coast echelon of the Fourth Marine Division sailed aboard the USS *Neville* to San Diego, California, to begin training at Camp Pendleton. A much larger and better equipped military installation on the Pacific Ocean, here the marines could engage in the amphibious landing training for the beachhead assaults they would face when they got into the fighting. Chambers made sure that all men he trained were quartered together in the companies he formed, knowing the men would grow closer and develop trust in one another. He was prepared to resist any attempts by superiors to reorganize his units and change his command assignments.

The colonel knew the politics within the corps and was certainly not one of the favorite sons of the high command. He was a reserve officer and not a "lifer." When his battalion entered the harbor and docked, Chambers insisted that they unload their cargo with speed and efficiency. He wanted his men to look good so that he looked good. As his men did their assigned work, he spotted a group of officers standing on the pier. He recognized and knew most of them, including Lieutenant Colonel Hewin O. Hammond whom he heard was in line to get the Third Battalion.

Later, Chambers explained, "I went down on the dock and went over to this group. After we all shook hands, I stuck my right hand in Hammond's face and said, 'Forget it, you're not about to get this battalion!' He kind of stammered a denial, and I knew in the back of my head he was hoping for just that."[102]

---

102 Chambers, *Third Battalion*, 17.

Chambers left the pier, and he and his men boarded a train for Camp Pendleton. When they arrived, they immediately hiked to the battalion's training area which was an hour away in a place called Pulgas Canyon.

The Third would train at Camp Pendleton for the next four months before heading off to war. It was obvious that the flat, wet, swampy ground of New River was much better suited for jungle warfare preparation than the dry, hard, mountainous terrain of southern California. Regardless, each company trained realistically with a lot of live firing.

As the colonel recalled, "Why we didn't have casualties on that, I'll never know. We were shooting up a lot of live ammo that was hitting awfully close to the guys."[103]

According to his military record, Charlie was promoted to first lieutenant on October 31. Chambers placed him in charge of a mortar platoon. The platoon's mission was to provide light artillery and machine gun support on call. During the war, Charlie and his men would fight all their battles in proximity of the colonel.

The remainder of the Fourth Division trained in the vicinity of the beaches and canyons of Camp Pendleton during the last few months of 1943. Assault units did combat drills, ship-to-shore movement, demolition, and pillbox clearing, and the Fourth completed its first division level amphibious landing exercises on the Aliso Canyon beaches on December 14 and 15. Their final rehearsals were held on January 2 and 3, 1944, under live supporting fire. "Within days of their training, the Fourth Marine Division, now fully equipped and numbering 17,086 men, was combat loaded aboard Task Force Fifty-Three in San Diego Harbor. The Fourth was no longer in training. It was a fully operational marine corps amphibious division, off to war in the Central Pacific, as part of the Fifth Amphibious Corps. In all of World War II, the Fourth Marine Division would have the distinction of being the only Marine Division that was mounted out and staged into combat directly following training in the continental United States."[104]

103 Chambers, *Third Battalion*, 18.
104 Carolyn A. Tyson, *A Chronology of the United States Marine Corps*, vol. 2, *1935-1946* (self-pub., 2014), 49.

Charlie never talked about the war unless he was being interviewed for a story, so it has taken years of research, piecing together timelines, reading memoirs, and collecting anecdotes to get to the truth of what he and his fellow marines endured in the ferocious fighting against the Japanese for the control of tiny islands. The physical elements of the battleground were just as deadly as enemy artillery and bullets. These marines could never have imagined what they were in for.

There have been countless documentaries and major motion pictures describing the heroics of the fighting men of the Pacific, thousands of whom died on those islands. None, however, could possibly describe the extent of the hell and horror the soldiers would endure. Knowing what Charlie lived through and how those experiences impacted him was important because those experiences had everything to do with how he lived his life thereafter.

———————

WHEN GRANDSON LUKE TOBIN ASKED CHARLIE HOW IT FELT to go to war, he responded, "Everyone in the marines was going to be shipped off to either Europe or the Pacific. That's why you had to volunteer to be in the marines. Obviously, I was scared to be going off to fight—everyone was—we knew we had to do it, so we had to stay calm because we knew we were doing the right thing. We had all been in boot camp for six months before active duty, so we were supposed to be prepared for anything that could happen, but none of us were mentally ready. But yes, I was very scared."

It was a 4,400-mile voyage from San Diego to the Marshall Islands, which would be the first military objective assigned to the Fourth. On January 11, 1944, the Third Battalion with attached units boarded the USS *Biddle* for the long journey. Chambers was a scrounger, always looking for additional ammunition, supplies, weapons, and explosives to take into battle. While on the West Coast, he made arrangements with Colonel Roosevelt for the "extra things" he needed. They were loaded on board along with a platoon of engineers from the Twentieth Marines A Company.

The Third left port on January 13, with 1,300 men, many more than there were bunks for. This put the colonel back in the doghouse with the men, but he was used to that and clearly didn't care. During the journey, all men of the Chambers's battalion were required to do physical drills so they wouldn't get comfortable or soft.

The Marshall Islands included thirty-two atolls. Kwajalein, which was one of those, would be the objective for the US Army while the marines would be responsible for securing the two tiny islands of Roi and Namur at the northwestern tip of the atoll. The US Navy was in charge of the entire operation and would soften up the islands with heavy bombardment from gunships prior to amphibious troop landings. Chambers believed the whole plan of attack was fouled up with too many different units doing too many different things. With only one stop off in Maui to refuel and rendezvous with the army support units, his men would be attacking all the way from the United States.

There was one thing Chambers knew for sure: the "Japs" would be situated in heavily fortified emplacements with well-hidden gun and artillery positions, allowing them to kill as many enemy soldiers as possible before they were overcome. When it was time for the Third to move to its objective, there were not enough landing crafts to transport the men. He managed to scrounge up eight LVTs (landing vehicles tracked), a few LCMs (landing craft medium), and some LCPVs (landing craft personnel vehicles). The men were transported to a small island called Albert and moved quickly to Abraham Island where there was no enemy resistance.

Chambers had his entire battalion in place by nightfall when the naval ships started shelling Roi and Namur. In its first taste of war, Charlie's platoon, with four eighty-one-mm and six sixty-mm mortars, contributed to the barrage. As it turned out, the Third was only needed as a reserve unit for the remainder of the campaign in the Marshalls and spent fourteen days with next to nothing to do but make raids on food stores from other units once their rations were depleted. The colonel condoned pilfering and would often run interference for his men to get what they needed. In his oral history, Chambers revealed that he taught his men that any military material they could get their hands on, regardless of what unit it belonged to, was fair game.

Charlie explained his first experience in the war to his grandson. "We landed on the Marshall Islands. There wasn't much defense by the Japanese other than some random mortar fire, so we took those islands easily without a man being shot or killed." While the Third would leave the Marshall Islands with few casualties, they would not leave without incident.

Chambers explained, "After about two weeks, our boys began to come down with amoebic dysentery. There had been a lot of bodies buried around the atoll, and if we dug down two or three feet, we hit water. This coupled with all the flies created a real health hazard that became serious. If it had not been for sulfa quinidine, I'm certain that we would have had very heavy casualties. People would have died. When we were finally evacuated, we had 187 stretcher cases. The rest, including myself, were heavily infected. We were pretty bad."[105] Whether Charlie developed the illness is unknown. If he had, he never talked about it.

———

THE SICKLY MEN OF THE THIRD LEFT THE ATOLL ON FEBRU-ary 29 aboard the USS *Haywood* and reached the beautiful Hawaiian island of Maui on March 8 for a much-needed rest. The natives of Maui loved the Fourth Marines and treated them with kindness, courtesy, and hospitality. The officers hung out at the Maui Grand Hotel where they could get a great meal and drinks of their choice. Leave among the soldiers was rotated between training regimes. Maui would become the Fourth Division's second home. What Charlie did talk about in later years was the beauty of Hawaii and his admiration for the natives.

The Third was the last to arrive in Maui and had to be quarantined for three weeks. They would only get a month or so of rest and relaxation

———

105 Chambers, *Third Battalion,* 59.

before having to ship out again. The army rangers had built an obstacle course on the west side of the island. The colonel had his men train there whenever they could. They were the only marine unit using the course for training.

On May 12, 1944, the Third boarded the USS *Leonard Wood*, a coast guard ship that would transport them to Saipan. The plan was that they would remain on Saipan after it was captured. Prior to the marines leaving, the mayor of Maui, Eddie Tam, circulated a petition which was signed by most men, women, and children living on the island. The petition read, "Bring our Marines back to us!"—which Admiral Nimitz approved to the amazement of the troops.

There would be marine reunions on Maui for years after the war.[106] A monument on the island near Haiku dedicated to the Fourth Marine Division reads, "Maui's Own." When Charlie returned to Maui many years later to reunite with his marine brothers, he was joined by his wife, whom he had met at home before the war. The photos and personal notes exchanged by him with his buddies reveal that this could have been one of the happiest occasions of his life.

When the ship left for Saipan, Chambers was made the designated commander of all troops on board. He was not happy about this. Most of the brass from the Fourth Division was on the same transport, which meant he would have to tone it down a bit. Before the long journey, the *Leonard Wood* went to Pearl Harbor's Ford Island for three days to fuel and get supplies. This gave the marines some liberty to have a few beers and play some ball.

During the months of training, Charlie regularly corresponded with his family, sometimes sending them photos of him in uniform assuring them he was all right. Before he left for war, one of his friends introduced him to Connie Oliva, a young, pretty teacher, and she agreed to write to him. The letters he wrote to and received from Connie Oliva are what elevated his spirits. Like all soldiers away from home, Charlie looked forward to mail call. As time went on during the war, the letters

106 Chambers, *Third Battalion*, 66.

with Connie became more intimate, and a close relationship between the two began to blossom.

———————

ON MAY 29, 1944, THE MARINES BEGAN THE 3,200-MILE VOY-age to the Mariana Islands, which included the Japanese strongholds of Saipan and Tinian. When they arrived, they would be merely 1,500 miles from Tokyo. Everyone anticipated that the fighting on those islands would be ferocious. The Japanese knew that if they lost control of these islands, the United States would be able to use them to attack targets on the Japanese mainland with long range bombers.

Saipan was the most critical linchpin to the Japanese defenses of the Central Pacific, as it was headquarters to their Pacific fleet, the Thir-ty-First Army, and Northern Mariana Defense Force. It was defended by Japan's Forty-Third Division, Forty-Seventh Mixed Brigade consist-ing of an infantry regiment, tank regiment, anti-aircraft regiment, two regiments of engineers, and two transportation companies. They had twenty-three thousand combat troops, substantial naval forces, and other units with seven thousand more men. There was also a civilian population of twenty thousand on that island.

The Japanese defensive positions would prove to be well-hidden. There were numerous underground caves along with hundreds of heavily for-tified high ground artillery installations.[107] Intelligence, received by the marines, greatly miscalculated the strength and numbers of the Japanese forces on Saipan, and an operation that they anticipated to last seven days went on for twenty-seven. There were nearly 166,000 US troops sup-ported by eight hundred ships from the Fifth Fleet deployed to the Mar-ianas. The Japanese knew they were vastly outnumbered, but with the home field advantage, they were confident they could defend their island.

The marines were a tough bunch, but they were scared. Charlie and his fellow marines were especially frightened because they were well

———————

107 Carl W. Hoffman, *Saipan: The Beginning of the End* (Ann Arbor, MI: University of Mich-igan Press, 1950), 12.

informed by their commander on the Japanese war mentality. Chambers had already been in the fight at Tulagi prior to training his men, and he had shared his experiences with them. Influenced by an ancient Samurai moral code called *bushido*, which arose from Zen-Buddhism, Confucianism, and Shintoism, Japanese military personnel adhered strictly to the role of service to their master and country. Surrendering to the enemy was not an option. Suicide was honorable and murdering fellow countrymen who violated the code was acceptable. Fighting men with this mindset would be brutal.

Exhausted and needing sleep, the fighting marines could never really rest in their foxholes at night. The cover of darkness provided Japanese soldiers the opportunity to make their self-sacrificing banzai attacks which involved close contact and even hand to hand fighting. These attacks would result in the deaths of thousands of Japanese and marines throughout the war in the Central Pacific.

The bushido code was also imposed on Japanese civilians who were fed propaganda portraying Americans as a barbaric enemy who would torture, rape, and kill them. This was not only untrue but ironic. During the Japanese invasion of Chinese Manchuria, prior to the bombing of Pearl Harbor, Japanese soldiers raped civilians and executed thousands of Chinese men, women, and children. That and the Bataan Death March where Japanese soldiers tortured, beat, and killed an estimated five thousand to eighteen thousand Filipino and five hundred to six hundred fifty American POWs showed that the enemy was both ruthless and ferocious.

Knowing this and the fact that Japanese soldiers were willing and even desired to die in battle produced a high level of fear, apprehension, and anxiety in the men who were about to encounter them. It would be difficult for them to enjoy the traditional steak and eggs breakfast the navy fed them prior to battle and even more difficult to hold down whatever they did eat.

For the invasion of Saipan on June 15, the First and Second Battalions were designated for assault while the Third was in reserve. Prior to the landing of combat forces, tons of naval gunfire and bombs dropped by fighter planes rained on the small island. "How can any living thing there survive this pounding?" rationalized many of the troops. Unfortunately, the bombing would have little to no impact on the Japanese defenders.

After boarding their LVTs, the men huddled together, some smoking nervously, some praying silently, others shaking in fear, and many vomiting. They realized that some of them would not survive. The amphibious vehicles sped toward the island. As soon as they landed at the shore, the men jumped out and charged onto beach, the Japanese opened fire with machine guns, artillery, and mortars.

The Third Battalion went in on the second wave of LVTs and attempted to land in combat formation on the beach area designated as "Yellow 3" even though they were in reserve. The enemy hit the beaches and approaching LVTs with such a vicious artillery bombardment that the landing turned chaotic. Hundreds of marines whose landing craft made it to the beach were in front of the colonel's transport while others were behind him.

"The landing was vigorously opposed. The opposition consisted primarily of artillery and mortar fire from weapons placed in well defiladed positions and previously registered to cover the beach areas, as well as fire from small arms, automatic weapons and anti-boat guns sited to cover the approaches to the immediate landing. Units of the Twenty-Fifth Marines on the right flank were receiving such enfilade fire they were forced to debark at the beach."[108] Charlie and his mortar platoon, hunkered down in their slow moving LCVT, were headed directly into this fire storm.

In one of the few stories he shared about the war, Charlie said, "We had no chance, so I looked to my right and spotted a large formation of rocks at the end of the beach. I told the navy coxswain driving the craft that I wanted him to veer off to the right and head for rocks at the end of the beach.

108 John C. Chapin, *The Fourth Marine Division in World War II* (1945; repr. Washington, DC: United States Marine Corps, History and Museums Division, 1974), 20.

"The coxswain said to me, 'I can't. I have my orders sir!' I got right in his face and told him, 'Son, I'm in command here!' I could tell my boys were happy when he followed my order and broke formation and turned for the rocks. Of course, I had no idea if we were headed for an ambush. As it turned out, we were able to unload and take cover. We waited for things to calm down and then made our way back to the unit."

Charlie was proud of the fact that he had saved his men from almost certain death, and they certainly appreciated it.

There was no way of knowing that he landed his men at the extremities of Agingan Point, just out of reach of the enemy guns, which were pounding the First Battalion. He and his men were no more than 150 yards from Chambers, but between them were hundreds of dead or maimed soldiers and burning landing crafts. "No words can convey the fury of battle, but the men of the division who were there that day will remember the smoking wrecks of LVTs, the blasted pillboxes, the dead Japanese and marine bodies, the reek of high explosives in the air, the searing flash of a flamethrower in action, the high pitched 'wheeng' of Jap bullets and freight train roar of Jap shells 'zeroed in.'"[109]

As soon as Colonel Chambers made it to the beach, he received word to turn over one of his companies to the First Battalion, which was taking on heavy fire near Agingan Point. He was not happy to learn that Major Joe Strunk, commander of the First Battalion, had already taken several of his men from I, L, and Headquarters Companies.

During the first few days of fighting, Chambers kept the men close to a railroad bed near Aslito Airfield, which was heavily fortified with "big guns." The colonel knew he had to act and called up Lieutenant Brucato's mortar platoon to get an observer on a ridge close by where they could accurately put mortar rounds on those guns. Charlie's men did exactly what he ordered.

Because Chambers committed his reserve without authority, he radioed regimental headquarters to explain what he did. The officer he

109 Chapin, *Fourth Marine Division,* 20.

spoke to at headquarters was complimentary and approved what he had done. The Third was now in assault mode and, over the coming days, would play a key role in the fight. Casualties would be heavy. Before nightfall on June 17, Chambers managed to get his entire battalion back together. That night, Charlie's mortar platoon and the battalion artillery laid a relentless barrage on the gun positions protecting the airfield. The next day, the Third secured Aslito Airfield, taking little resistance while still waiting for the other US regiments to get to their assigned positions.

Chambers knew he had to take charge, because the 165th Army Regiment was especially disorganized and fought with different tactics. He could not trust that they would be in the right position on his left flank. He was also concerned about the movement and positioning of the rest of the Twenty-Fifth Regiment which was behind but reporting otherwise. Colonel Batchelder had moved regimental command closer to the fight.

Aware of the issues, Batchelder radioed Chambers for a meeting. Both Jumping Joe and "Batch" had a keen understanding of how ground troops had to be deployed to fight the Imperial Japanese Army who counted on tactical errors to inflict the greatest number of casualties. There could be no voids in the lines of troop movement, and the regular reporting of battalion and divisional locations was critical.

When the two colonels met, Batch informed Jumping Joe that he had a special mission for the Third—Hill 500. This was a strategic target believed to be a Japanese brigade headquarters, from which the Japanese had repelled three days of attacks by battalions of the Twenty-Fourth Regiment and the Twenty-Third Marines. Colonel Batchelder was confident that Joe Chambers would get the job done and Chambers was happy to oblige. Chambers also learned from Batch that another division, the Twenty-Seventh Army, would be added to the ground forces and moved to the left flank of the Fourth Division.

Chambers knew that the enemy was slowing the movement of US forces by keeping them pinned down in the myriad gullies, draws, and rough terrain of the island. He immediately moved his battalion to the reverse slope of some high ground located about 1,500 yards southwest of Hill 500. There, they had a clear view of the terrain they needed to negotiate for the attack. "On the afternoon of June 19, I gathered all my senior noncoms and all my officers, and we sat up on the edge of this hill and looked over the objective. We drank some beer, and right then and there I planned out the attack for Hill 500."[110]

That night, Charlie's mortars and the Third's heavy artillery shelled the hill with great accuracy. Chambers feared that the Japs would have his attacking troops in a kill zone before they reached the base of the hill. The Fourteenth Marines were to provide the pre-assault artillery support, so he instructed them to get their hands on as much smoke ordinance as possible. The men had never used smoke before but followed the order. At eleven a.m., the Fourteenth smoked the hell out of Hill 500 while the Thirds, I, L, and K Companies advanced to the base of that hill. They were backed up by the Second Battalion.

As the smoke cleared, the assault groups reassembled while the Fourteenth unleashed a second smoke barrage. When the smoke from that salvo cleared, it took less than two hours for the Third to capture the hill under great enemy resistance. The Third suffered forty-nine casualties and nine dead. After the battle, the division planning officer, who was an observer, wrote Chambers a note saying that the assault on Hill 500 was the best planned, best executed, battalion attack he had ever seen.

After Hill 500, the fighting became intense, and more Japanese supply caves and ammunition dumps were uncovered. At three p.m. on June 22, the Japs blew up a large ammo dump close to where Colonel Chambers and several of his men were standing. Jumping Joe was blown high in the air, knocked out cold, and sustained a concussion. He was evacuated to a medical tent where he woke up the next morning, put on his clothes, stole a jeep, and returned to his battalion. He learned that, in his absence, L Company had moved further north to Mt. Tapochau,

110 Chambers, *Third Battalion*, 91.

another Japanese stronghold. While positioned there, the company was attacked at night and lost more men and officers.

That same day, the Twenty-Seventh Army Division was ordered to relieve the exhausted, depleted Third battalion, which had pulled back to Hill 500. The Third spent the next eight days resting and regrouping while dug in on the southern slope. On the night of June 27, Japanese soldiers infiltrated their position and set up a machine gun fifty yards from the nearest foxhole. The desperate enemy executed a surprise banzai attack. Two marines were killed. Another two marines paired in their foxhole, grabbed their rifles, started shooting, and killed all the Japs around the machine gun.

Over the next fifteen minutes, the marines fought the advancing enemy mostly in hand-to-hand combat, using shovels, gun butts, or anything else handy. The fight was over as quickly as it started. Charlie was in one of those foxholes and was involved in hand-to-hand combat, but he never talked about this. (I think that he repressed a lot of memories because they were so painful.) While the Japs managed to kill eleven marines, the Third marines, who now called themselves "Chambers's Raiders," killed 112 Japanese soldiers.

"Actually, they weren't really raiders. The raiders as separate units had been disbanded. They were just a battalion of the Fourth Marine Division. But they were a cocky, self-sure lot and the 'Old Man' Lieutenant Colonel J.M. Chambers had been a captain with Edson's Raiders on Tulagi. So, in the weeks of training between Namur and Saipan, they had dubbed themselves 'Chambers's Raiders.' And on Saipan they had made the title stick—so well, in fact, Lieutenant Colonel Evans Carlson, who was with them a good bit of the time until he was hit, called them the equal of any battalion he'd ever seen."[111]

The references made to "Chambers's Raiders" did not sit well with Major General Clifton Cates, commander of the Fourth Marine Division. In fact, it "pissed him off." Cates wanted it made clear that this great fighting organization was an ordinary rifle battalion of the

111 "War on Japan's Doorstep," *Leatherneck Magazine*, November 1964, 3.

Fighting Fourth and not one of the marine raider battalions which had won fame in the first year of the war against Japan.

This, of course, was not completely true. There was nothing ordinary about Jumping Joe Chambers's Third Division. Through their deeds and heroics under his training and leadership, they became the elite fighting battalion of the Fourth Division. While it would be unfair to dismiss the courage and valor of the countless marines who fought in the Central Pacific, many who never returned home, it is important to note that it is the Third which contributed to defining the identity of their brothers who accomplished as much, if not more, than any other marine unit called raiders.

By July 1, the Third would return to action. Colonel Rogers, who Chambers had no use for, ordered him to move the Third to a new assembly area about a mile or two from Hill 500 and to do so immediately. Jumping Joe had no intention of putting his men on the road at night, so he waited until morning. He was insubordinate, certainly, but there is no telling how many lives he saved by following his instincts.

Because the Twenty-Seventh Army kept exposing the marine divisions' flanks by not moving, the Third was again called in from reserve to attack, and by July 3 were involved in heavy fighting for control of Hill 721. The Twenty-Third Marines were losing men and ground there. By the end of America's Independence Day, the Third was subjected to a heavy mortar barrage which killed a large number of marines. While Chambers began to reorganize his battalion, he took inventory. "My combat troops now consisted of only 315 men and six officers out of 630 men and twenty-eight officers. My Headquarters Company, which included all my staff, communicators, mortars, and whatnot, had 153 men and ten officers. This was all that was left of the Third Battalion, Twenty-Fifth Marines. We had 468 men out of a total of 1,050 that had landed on Saipan" [112]

The Third had another nine days left on the island and would be afforded a short rest before the invasion of Tinian. They suffered more

---

112 Chambers, *Third Battalion*, 114.

than 50 percent casualties. Charlie was fortunate to be one of the ten surviving officers of Headquarters Company. He certainly did not want to reconcile with the inner demon that asks to know, "Why did I not die?"

The rest of the Third's days on Saipan were spent cleaning up. They witnessed with horror the murder of hundreds of civilians killed by Japanese troops while they tried to surrender. They also watched hundreds of Japanese women jump to their deaths from ocean cliffs while holding their children. Some witnessed people getting into huddles and detonating explosives that would disintegrate their bodies. It is hard to imagine how the American soldiers processed this atrocity.

Colonel Chambers helped put it into focus when he said, "It is hard for me to describe the fog of war. You are moving, almost subconsciously, through another world. Things are happening all around you. You see them, are aware of them, but they don't hit you in a sharp manner. They are just things happening around you. You concentrated only on getting the job done. Sherman was right about war. The best way to get a war over is to kill off a bunch of the enemy and make things terrible for them in the process. You can only hope that they will surrender or die."[113]

TINIAN WAS ONLY THREE MILES FROM SAIPAN. THE LANDings there were scheduled for July 24, 1944. During their short nine days of rest between battles, the Third got back some of their wounded men but would be far from full strength. After reorganizing, Chambers had only three assault companies, and they were all short several men. Knowing that his battalion was assigned an assault role for Tinian, the loss of so many good marines on Saipan weighed heavily on him.

Fortunately, the island of Tinian was much smaller and not all as well defended. There were only nine thousand soldiers from the Japanese Fiftieth Infantry Regiment defending Tinian. Not only would the

113 Chambers, *Third Battalion*, 125.

US military forces have better than thirty thousand assault troops, but they would be also supported by naval artillery and fighter planes.

At Tinian, napalm incendiary bombs would be used for the first time against fixed Japanese positions. Additionally, during the attack on Saipan, a battalion of corps artillery had managed to neutralize Tinian airfields and destroy military targets. There were also daily plane strikes and naval bombardments which proved effective in damaging Japanese defenses and weaponry.

It was clear from the start that the Tinian operation would be much different than the long, exhausting, bloody war fought on Saipan. "The terrain of Tinian was more favorable than Saipan's; it was flatter and had a better developed road net. Thus, the marine tanks were able to operate much more effectively. Moreover, close tactical support was furnished from the start by army P-47s operating from the captured Aslito airfields on Saipan."[114] There were also another eleven divisions of shore-based artillery on Saipan which were staged to reach every grid on the small island of Tinian.

The only issue the advancing US forces would have on Tinian was the geographical disorientation caused by the thousands of acres of sugar cane fields they would have to cross to get from one road network to another. Having surveyed the terrain, Colonel Chambers knew that the landing on Tinian would be unorthodox. "Normally a battalion is supposed to have a five-hundred-yard beach to land on. We were going to put two battalions across a beach that was only two hundred yards wide." He further lamented, "You couldn't even call Beach White 2, where the Third was to land, much of a beach because there were sections of coral rock hung over the water. In that, we spotted mines in the water and had to assume the beaches were mined as well."[115]

The Japanese defenders had little resistance to offer as they had been pounded by everything the marines, navy, and army had for days before the US's arrival. The boys of the Third took care of the mines and two

---

114 Chapin, *Fourth Marine Division*, 34.
115 Chambers, *Third Battalion*, 133.

forty-seven mm guns the Japs had to defend the beach, but a number of LVTs were blown up by mines before they were all cleared. Most of the attack forces were ashore and dug in before nightfall with minimal casualties sustained, but Joe knew that the Japs would make their banzai attacks as soon as they believed the marines were settled in for the night.

At midnight, all hell broke loose. Japs came pouring in from all directions and hit the Third's K Company hard. Another Jap unit ran right into L Company. When they realized what they were up against, the Japs retreated, only to be cut to pieces by the thirty-seven mm set up on K Company's left flank. By daybreak, the entire perimeter around K Company was littered with five hundred dead Japanese soldiers.

The Fourth Marine Division's lines were fully intact, and another 750 enemy were dead. The Japanese force was reduced to 6,800. US headquarters command had no idea that they had literally broken the Japanese defenses on Tinian after one night of battle. These were the elite troops of the Japanese Fiftieth Infantry who may have been capable of mounting a stiffer defense had it not been for nonstop air and artillery strikes called in on their positions. It would only take another eight days to capture the island, mostly because the effectiveness of the pinpoint air and artillery strikes that destroyed nearly all the Japanese defensive positions which lacked the cover and underground caves that protected them on Saipan.

On the morning of July 25, Colonel Chambers was given orders to attack and seize a plateau called Mount Maga. With little resistance, he had all his men on the plateau by early evening. The next objective was Mount Lasso where he would request smoke for the high ground as they approached. The Third also had flank support from Colonel Mustain's First Battalion and the Twenty-Third Regiment which Chambers had less confidence in because it always seemed to be lagging behind them. The Third faced little resistance on route to their objective and the Mustain's First had almost reached the top of Mount Lasso.

The men dug in for the night. The next morning, Chambers sent out patrols to survey the surrounding area. They found plenty of enemy emplacements, but no Japs. The Third was sent seven officers and fifty-five men as replacements which he sent over to L Company under the command of Lieutenant John Hallabrin. Charlie would become good friends with John, and they remained close after the war. While Charlie was a baseball and football star at Holy Cross, John was an All-American football player at Ohio State.

The Third jumped off on the attack at 9:45 a.m. with the replacements led by Hallabrin, who later told Chambers, "Colonel, I was used to the old outfit. I got up with my runners and started forward. I got about fifty feet, turned around, and there wasn't a soul with me." Jumping Joe asked him what he did. "I went back and kicked more ass in five minutes than I ever kicked on a football field in my entire life. After that, they moved when I moved."[116] The Third met little resistance, so Chambers concluded that there were not many enemy troops left in the north.

A short time later, the weather on the island changed. Torrential rains kept the men soaked, and their foxholes became bathtubs. On the morning of July 28, they began moving from the high ground back to the cane fields, taking prisoners along the way. Chambers did not like traversing this area as it was perfect for an enemy ambush. He moved the men to a small cane railroad, and they camped there for the night.

On the morning of July 29, Chambers received new orders. With the First and Second Battalions on their flanks, the Third attacked upon a road where they met heavy resistance from dug in Japs and took heavy casualties. It was hard to stay oriented in the sugar cane fields. Before nightfall, the Third was better organized but still soaked and miserable from the nonstop rain. By July 30, after seven days on the attack, the marines were relieved for the first time. The colonel made sure his exhausted men were not subjected to any more fighting, and on August 2, 1944, nine days after landing on Tinian, it was declared secured.

For the marines, one of the most difficult aspects of finishing the battle was convincing civilians and enemy soldiers to surrender. As it

116 Chambers, *Third Battalion,* 145-146.

was in Saipan, most chose suicide. Except for a small complement of prisoners, the entire Japanese Fiftieth Infantry had been destroyed. In many ways, the Marianas campaign signaled the beginning of the end for Japan. In addition to losing the islands of Saipan, Tinian, and Guam, the Japanese also suffered a crushing defeat at sea.

In the epic battle of the Philippine Sea, the Japanese lost three fleet aircraft carriers and 480 aircraft. After the battle, Prince Higashikuni, commander in chief of home defense headquarters, said, "The war was lost when the Marianas were taken away from Japan and when we heard the B-29s were coming out."

Charlie told grandson Luke Tobin, "After that [the Marshalls], we took Tinian and Saipan which were two of the heaviest battles of the war and where my division had heavy casualties. All of our forces were still very strong after taking the first few islands. But next came Iwo Jima...."

WHAT WAS LEFT OF THE THIRD WAS GETTING READY TO HEAD back to Maui. Having just spent thirty-seven days in hell, they were now on their way back to the beauty and serenity of their home away from home. The fog of war would be temporarily lifted. There was so much to process and when rest and relaxation was over, these now battle-hardened marines were headed for a bloodbath of unimaginable ferocity. At Iwo Jima, the Third would descend to an even lower depth of hell.

When the fighting in the Marianas had ended, "The Fourth Marine Division had suffered ten thousand casualties, which was more than half the division. The Third Battalion casualties would be much worse." "We had a total of nine hundred men going in, and after it was over, twenty-four officers and 658 men killed or wounded." [117] An army ship, the *Adabelle Lykes*, which was a small C-1 transport, would take the Third, landing teams one and two, plus regimental headquarters back to Maui. There were so few marines left the ship was more than adequate.

---

117 Chambers, *Third Battalion*, 59.

On August 5, 1944, the ship began the seventeen-day voyage. On route, Colonel Batchelder informed Chambers that he was recommending his three battalion commanders for both the Navy Cross and Distinguished Service Medals. The citations were drawn up, approved, and sent to the Board of Awards. Unfortunately, there was a Colonel Schubert on that board who did not like Joe Chambers or any of the Fourth Division leaders. When General Cates took over the Fourth, he removed Shubert from the division leadership. Navy Cross and Distinguished Service Medals had been downgraded to what Jumping Joe referred to as "lousy Legion of Merit citations." It is hard to believe that grudges and jealousy among the marine brass ran that deep but apparently the same was prevalent among all branches of the US Military where competition for rank was fierce.

Colonel Chambers put it all into perspective. "I've always felt that I got more than I deserved, but it burned me up when they started cutting in on my officers and men. There wasn't, however, a damned thing I could do about it. I believed most guys on the Board of Awards were officers who couldn't cut it in combat. I think they resented seeing anyone else receive awards for valor."[118]

The *Adabelle Lykes* arrived in Maui on August 22, 1944. The entire Fourth Division was given a chance for rest and rehabilitation before training would resume. Marines were offered three-day liberty to spend on Oahu, but most chose to stay in Maui. During the first few weeks of what would be close to five months there, Colonel Chambers spent a good deal of time restaffing and reorganizing the Third. Because of the heavy losses suffered in the Marianas, he was forced to make several changes in leadership.

During this time, a good number of his men who were wounded in the Marianas returned to active duty. There were also some three thousand replacement marines on Maui. They would be the men Colonel Chambers would pick from to backfill his depleted companies and bring the Third back to full strength. By mid-September, the

118 Chambers, *Third Battalion*, 163.

reorganization was complete. The marines were rested and ready to begin training.

Chambers had a new concern when the troops began training. He soon realized that his officers were driving the men harder than even he thought they should. Having learned from their experiences in the Marshall and Marianna Islands, the leaders wanted to make sure the new men of the Third were trained as they were by Jumping Joe. The colonel was afraid the troops would become overtrained. It was ironic that the leaders he had trained had become as tough on their men as he had been on them.

Colonel Chambers worked diligently as he prepared his troops for the next objective, still unknown to him. The team leaders would take an active role in the planning. Among other things, Charlie's platoon was augmented by an additional two mortars, which would allow for two in support of each company or six in general support. The Third continued to train hard while acclimating their new members to the methods and codes of honor shared by all members of the fighting Third. They trained with great intensity, incorporating all lessons learned from past experiences.

It wasn't until November that Chambers began to get a hint on their next objective. It would be Iwo Jima, which was part of the Bonin, or Volcano Islands midway between the Marianas and Japan. The island was about six miles long and shaped like a pork chop. On the southwestern tip of the narrow end of the island was Mount Suribachi, some five hundred feet above sea level. As the aerial photos of the island became accessible to Chambers, he grew more concerned, knowing that this terrain of volcanic ash with no cover gave tremendous advantages to a desperate enemy.

Since it was clear that the Japanese could not realistically defeat the overwhelming American military forces that outnumbered them better than ten to one, the objective of the Japanese defenders would be to kill as many Americans as they could. Chambers was especially concerned about the geography on Iwo Jima. There were quarries on the right flank of the landing beaches which would likely be heavily fortified with well dug in Japanese troops. All the Japanese soldiers would have their weapons zeroed in on the beach where approaching marines would have no cover. The Japanese artillery would likewise have its cannons registered in on the shoreline.

General Cates was aware of the circumstances his troops would be facing. He knew the marines would take a massive number of casualties in the process of securing the island. He understood that it would take courageous marines like those under the command of Colonel Joe Chambers to forge onward while under relentless bombardment. The Third Battalion would play the key role in the battle of Iwo Jima. It would also lose an inordinate number of brave marines.

———————————

THE PLANNING FOR THE IWO JIMA CAMPAIGN TOOK TWO months, with most of the deliberation taking place on Maui where General Cates and his staff set the plan of attack. Colonel Chambers spent hours viewing aerial photos of the terrain. He was especially focused on the rock quarries, where, with a magnifying glass, he could see Japanese soldiers moving up to position themselves there.

Chambers concluded, "Hell, if they could go up the face of the quarry, I knew damn well that they must also have a way of getting in from the back. These quarries were on the right flank of what turned out to be the landing beaches."[119]

It was decided that the Twenty-Third and Twenty-Fifth Regiments would land in assault while the Twenty-Fourth would be kept in reserve. It was obvious that General Cates would be counting on Jumping Joe and the Third to assume what was arguably the most important and dangerous role of the assault forces. Colonel Chambers was told this after the war.

At a staff meeting in Maui, Cates approached Pat Lannigan, who commanded the Twenty-Fifth, and said, "Now Pat. I am going to put

119 Chambers, *Third Battalion*, 178.

you on the right flank, and I want you to put Chambers on your right flank. If any battalion can get up on those quarries on the first day, it will be the Third Battalion."[120]

Every operation was required to have a flank battalion for amphibious landings. The flank troops were always in a vulnerable position, but on Iwo, the right flank was especially vulnerable because the Japanese had every grid on the landing beaches sighted in with mortars, heavy artillery, and machine guns. Prior to the loading of some eighteen vessels that would head for Iwo, Colonel Chambers did what he always did. He set plans in motion to collect as much unauthorized equipment as he could to use in the battle. The acquisition of a bulldozer and M-4 army tank he traded for cases of whiskey would turn out to be his best haul of the war.

Two days after Christmas, many of the assault troops were transported by LSTs to Saipan where they would train for the Iwo assault. On January 16, 1945, Chambers and the rest of his assault team boarded the USS *Sandborn* and sailed with a convoy to the Marianas where the staging for the Iwo assault would take place.

Iwo Jima had three airfields. Two were complete and a third was still under construction. Losing the island would make it impossible for the Japanese to defend its mainland, so the defenses they set up on Iwo were their most intricate. "In addition to the island's many natural caves, which the Japanese defenders pressed into service as underground shelters, they also added coastal gun emplacements. The defensive positions consisted of 240 light and heavy antiaircraft weapons, at least 434 blockhouses, covered artillery positions and pillboxes. They also had twelve light and twelve heavy tanks, huge mortars, and rocket launchers, some of which could fire eight-inch projectiles weighing two hundred pounds."[121]

The Japanese defenses were so formidable that the sixty-two days of American warplane bombings staged from Saipan had little impact. The concurrent shelling of Iwo from naval ships, consisting of twenty-three

120 Chambers, *Third Battalion,* 179.
121 Whitman S. Bartley, *Iwo Jima: Amphibious Epic* (Washington, DC: Historical Branch, G-3 Division Headquarters, US Marine Corps, 1954), 13

thousand rounds of five- to sixteen-inch shells, (ironically, one round for each of the twenty-three thousand Japanese troops entrenched on the island) also had little impact. Japanese Lieutenant General Tadamichi Kuribayashi had his troops dug deeply into the black volcanic soil and rocky base of Iwo, making the surface shelling loud and terrifying but not deadly.

Colonel Chambers spoke about this in his oral history, saying, "General Kuribayashi advocated a defense in depth and aimed to make it as tough as he could for the attacker. There were no defense lines along the beaches. He had learned what other Japanese commanders had not: that the naval gunfire and airstrikes would be overwhelming, making a beachline defense impractical. We later found out that he had ordered his troops to kill ten marines before being killed himself. For a while, it would appear that they were meeting their quota!"[122]

In Chambers's view, the Japanese general made one costly error. On February 18, a day before the assault, a naval underwater demolition team escorted by several LCIs (landing craft infantry) were dispersed to the beaches to search for mines and obstacles. As they approached the beaches, Kuribayashi must have thought this to be part of the invasion. He ordered his guns to open fire. All the LCIs were either destroyed or badly damaged and many sailors were killed, but by opening fire, several Japanese gun placements were revealed in the quarries. Having been given the coordinates, gun crews from the USS *New York* fired fourteen-inch guns into the face of the quarries until all the enemy guns were destroyed. Had it not been for the Japanese general's miscalculation, those quarry guns would have killed countless more marines.

By eight thirty on the morning of February 19, the first three waves of assault troops, loaded on LVTs, headed for the island under clear skies and moderate seas. The Third Battalion's objective was to get to the high ground on the right flank. They would land on Blue Beach 1, behind the First Battalion. Jumping Joe had his companies land in columns, with I Company in front.

---

122 Chambers, *Third Battalion*, 180.

Charlie fifth from the left in second row from top.

The colonel was in the second wave and the rest of the battalion in the third wave. Charlie's mortar platoon was in the dreaded fourth wave with the artillery units. (From past landings, the marines had learned that the Japs would allow the first three waves onto the beach with little resistance but when the fourth wave landed, they would unleash all of their weaponry with an endless ferocity.)

While the first two waves met little resistance, once the smoke cleared from the supporting naval gun fire, the Japanese "opened up with every weapon they had, and soon, a solid sheet of fire was pouring down on the beaches and incoming waves. It was the heaviest enemy mortar and artillery fire yet seen in any operation. Boats were hit; they broached and clogged the beaches. Personnel casualties mounted rapidly. Vehicles ashore found the sandy volcanic ash and first terrace nearly impassable. Even tanks were bogged down. Every move was under direct observation of the Japanese on top of the cliff line near the quarries on the right flank and Mount Suribachi on the left."[123]

This is exactly what Charlie and his mortar men saw unfold in front of them. Unlike his deviation maneuver which got him and his men safely to shore on Saipan, here there was no such option. Many years later, he would describe the scene to sportswriter John Gearan.

"'We were all scared,' Brucato said. 'We were in the so-called fourth wave at Iwo Jima. I was in an amphibious tank [LVT] when we were struck by a shell. I was toppled over into the water. I was hit but more concerned with the *bang* I got in the shoulder than I was with the actual shrapnel wounds. I couldn't swim but was able to wade with others slowly to the beach,' he explained. Brucato went on to say that this was the start of the worst twenty-five days of his life. For the next twenty-four hours, he was pinned down, dug into the sand, and immobilized by enemy gunfire that was nonstop. 'The only way we could move was to crawl inland, but we had to wait for air attacks to loosen things up.'"[124]

---

123 Chapin, *Fourth Marine Division*, 44.
124 John Gearan, "HC Feats Nothing Next to Real Game," *Worcester Telegram*, May 19, 1985.

Charlie's wounds would eventually be treated, but he would never leave the battle. In fact, for the remainder of the days on Iwo Jima he and all the other marines would never be safe from enemy bullets, shells, and Japanese banzai suicide attacks. He and the other marines who were pinned down and could not move far inland were amidst hundreds of dead marines and body parts, all from Twenty-Fifth, First, Second, and Third Battalions. The enemy was never visible to the attacking marines as the Japs were hidden underground or in well camouflaged pillboxes and block houses. They could always see the approaching marines, who were forced to gain ground crawling five to ten yards at a time.

With all the enemy fire still concentrated on the beach, Colonel Chambers was able to move about three hundred yards inland (halfway to the quarries) but was aware of the mounting casualties of the Third, especially K Company, where all seven officers were dead or wounded at day's end. He knew that I Company was not too far ahead, so Jumping Joe and the men, mostly from Headquarters Company (including Charlie), took cover in a massive bomb crater.

Chambers reflected, "From where I was, I could see I Company's walking wounded moving back down to the beach. Lieutenant John Hallabrin, the I Company executive officer who was wounded in Saipan, was coming down the terrace with blood spurting out of his left shoulder. I was over on the edge of the second terrace, and he saw me looking at him. A big grin came over his face, and he pointed at his shoulder. 'Hey Colonel! Look! Stateside!' He made it too." [125] The rule was that to be shipped back home, a marine had to be wounded in battle a second time or have a wound so severe that he could not function as a soldier.

While the Third Battalion remained pinned down by enemy fire, the Fifth Division, with two attacking battalions, managed to capture Airfield 1. The Twenty-Eighth Regiment of the Fifth Marines then headed for the capture of Mount Suribachi. Unfortunately, during the capture of Airfield 1, "Manila John" Basilone, Medal of Honor recipient, was killed by a mortar shell while leading his machine gun patrol. Basilone, who

125 Chambers, *Third Battalion*, 198.

was asked to sell war bonds for the US after his heroics earlier in the war on Guadalcanal, wanted to get back in the fight and had finally received approval to return to his combat unit prior to the Iwo Jima campaign.

Colonel Chambers knew that he had to take the quarries by nightfall. "The victory on Iwo Jima depended upon the ability of the pitifully exposed and riddled Third Battalion to take that ground."[126] Jumping Joe called headquarters for air support which he wanted to commence at six p.m. while his troops moved toward the quarries under the command of Jim Headly who gathered up about 150 men for the assault.

"When the artillery barrage started, Colonel Chambers gave the order for his men to advance. He did so by getting on the radio and saying, 'Get the hell up there before the Japs get wise and grab the ground for themselves.' And under one of the most vicious and terrifying artillery, mortar, and rocket barrages in the history of modern warfare, those men moved across the open sand and took the ground. There was no cover, no concealment. They were in the open, plainly visible to the Japanese defenders, like targets in a shooting gallery.... Many of those soldiers didn't make it, but when night fell on D-Day, the Third Battalion dug in on top of the quarries, prepared to resist any attempt by the enemy to retake the area. Historians have agreed that this was one of the bloodiest engagements of the Pacific war which occurred almost before the battle was well underway."[127]

It was what one might call the beginning of the end of the war against Japan, but in drawing that conclusion, hundreds of marines who fought with the same bravery and resolve, losing their lives in the process, would not be properly honored. "In the end, it was the strength of Captain James Headly and Lieutenant Colonel 'Jumping Joe' Chambers who led the survivors of the Third Battalion onto the top of the cliffs. The battalion paid an exorbitant price for this achievement, losing twenty-two officers and five hundred troops by nightfall."[128]

---

126 Hill, *Marine Corp Gazette*, 28.

127 Hill, *Marine Corp Gazette*, 34.

128 Col. Joseph H. Alexander, *Closing In: Marines in the Seizure of Iwo Jima* (Washington, DC: History and Museums Division, Headquarters, US Marine Corps, 1994), 8.

As the days went by and the painful, inch-by-inch progress of the divisions fighting on the bloody rock became more and more heartbreaking, the history of the Third Battalion was enriched by hundreds of examples of unselfish bravery and devotion to duty. It became commonplace for marines to expose themselves to fire so as to tempt Jap snipers to give away their positions.

As many marine observers have noted, heroism was not the exception but the rule. It was no longer surprising; it was just what it was. Colonel Headly put things into focus in his reflections.

"They died so fast that the whole business of heroes and death is a little mixed up in my mind. You'd see a man do something almost unbelievable and a minute later you'd see him die. It's pretty hard to pick out any outstanding man or men."[129] The battle of Iwo Jima would be recorded in American military history as one of the most epic battles of the United States Marine Corps, and any historian could argue that there were few military conflicts which better identified self-sacrifice for God, country, and brotherhood.

The first morning after the battle began, Chambers and his men were still in the bomb crater. His reflections articulate what he and his marines believed substantiated their purpose while defining what was important about America.

"We hadn't had any grub since the previous morning aboard ship when Corporal Dallas Conrad opened up a can of c-rations. There were my people, Abe Bryan (my radioman), an Italian boy from the intelligence section, and some Black kids from the Pioneers. Conrad took a spoonful of food, ate it, and handed the can with a spoon to the marine beside him. He took a bite and passed it on. That can went around the entire group. Catholics, a Jew, some Blacks, an Italian, a Pole, an Irishman, a West Virginia hillbilly, and a Florida cracker. None of us cared a damn about who we were eating after. We were hungry marines in combat. Nothing else mattered at that moment."[130]

---

129 Hill, *Marine Corp Gazette,* 34.
130 Chambers, *Third Battalion,* 208.

They were a special breed of combat soldiers who would eventually return to a country where there was no experience like the war to inspire people from all races to put aside their institutionalized prejudice so that all Americans thereafter could enjoy the promise of equality. This had to be a conundrum for the thousands of American soldiers who returned home with the memories of war which taught them so much more about the value and sanctity of human life than the history that preceded them. Their war experience would greatly change how they looked at other Americans and how they treated them. Charlie was deeply affected by this experience as will be evident from his post-war life.

The slaughter of marines continued for hours on the three-thousand-yard-wide beach. Two marine combat veterans who witnessed the carnage could not help but express what you might call begrudging admiration for the Japanese artillery gunners. "'It was one of the worst bloodlettings of the war,' said Major Karch of the Fourteenth Marines. 'They rolled those artillery barrages up and down the beach—I just didn't see how anybody could live through such heavy fire barrages,' said Lieutenant Colonel Joseph Stewart. 'The Japanese were superb artillerymen.... Somebody was getting hit every time they fired.'"[131]

Because of the heavy casualties sustained by the marines in the first few hours of battle, by late in the afternoon on that dreadful first day, General Cates took three battalions from the Twenty-Fourth Marines out of reserve and sent them to shore in more waves of LVTs. Many of the reserve units suffered heavier casualties while crossing the beach than the initial assault forces because General Kuribayashi's nonstop artillery bombardment intensified, dialed in from all points of the island, especially Mount Suribachi.

Lieutenant Michael Kelleher, USNR, the Third Battalion surgeon, was sent to the beach to take over the Twenty-Fifth Marine's aid station because the surgeon there had been severely wounded. Kelleher was a veteran of the three previous assault landings and was appalled by the

131 Alexander, *Closing In*, 2.

carnage on Blue Beach as he approached. "Such a sight on that beach! Wrecked boats; bogged-down jeeps, tractors, and tanks; burning vehicles; casualties scattered all over."[132]

With the marines taking control of Airfield 1 and the quarries, their main objective would be to continue to gain ground and repel the nocturnal attacks of the enemy. By the end of day two, Colonel Chambers had most of what was left of the Third back together, but with the Second Battalion losing most of their officers, Chambers had no choice but to place his executive officer, James Taul, in command of the Second, and he did so without authorization from headquarters. On the morning of February 21, Jumping Joe set out to reconnect with Colonel "Musty" Mustain, commander of the First Battalion. Just before he reached him, Musty was killed by a Japanese mortar barrage.

This left Colonel Chambers as the only surviving battalion commander of the Twenty-Fifth Regiment. The fighting in the so-called "Meat Grinder," where the Third continued to operate, remained fierce, and casualties continued to mount. On the morning of February 22, Chambers received orders to attack a heavily fortified enemy high ground called Charlie-Dog Ridge. He had Charlie and his mortar platoon pound the ridgeline with eighty-one-mm shells. The colonel could not attack until he had the remaining elements of the Third in place.

They were behind, so when a rocket platoon showed up just before dark with 124 rockets that needed to be disarmed for the night, rather than do that, the rocket platoon commander asked if he could fire on the ridge. Jumping Joe recalled, "We had been putting mortars and naval gunfire on that damned ridge all day long and hadn't seen any Japs. When the smoke cleared from the rocket barrage, we could see any number of nips stumbling around in plain sight."[133]

His boys, without orders, cut loose with everything they had and killed a large number of enemy soldiers. It was too late to finish the

132 Alexander, *Closing In*, 6-7.
133 Chambers, *Third Battalion*, 216.

attack on Charlie-Dog Ridge, but as Jumping Joe was standing there getting ready to move out, he was hit. He went down and later learned that the bullet had entered his right shoulder, gone through his lung, knocked out a bunch of ribs and exited out his back. In his oral history, he noted, "The corpsman probably saved my life, because I had a sucking wound, and he packed the exit wound to keep my breathing from filling my lungs with blood."[134] That would be the end of the war for Colonel Chambers, but the remainder of the Third Marines would continue fighting on Iwo for twenty-four more days.

On February 23, the American flag was raised on top of Mount Suribachi. The iconic photo capturing this is one of the most famous of the war. Charlie was in the area when the flag went up. He said later, "I was shocked. The island was far from being taken and there was a battle ongoing. I thought to myself, *What the hell are those crazy bastards doing?* We were dug in, and my boys kept poking their heads up to see what was going on. I had to keep telling them to get the hell down. There were Jap snipers everywhere killing anyone they could take a clean shot at."

A day or so later, while Charlie was dug in with his platoon, he was told that he had a visitor. "I thought to myself, *who would be crazy enough to want to visit?*" Charlie recounted later. "The island was not captured, and there was still a lot of shooting going on. Before I knew it, Jack Davoren, a friend from Milford, appeared with a bundle of treats—salami, bread, and other Italian delicacies. Jack was a naval officer, and when he learned that I was on Iwo, he left his ship and boated over just to see me and make sure I was okay. I couldn't believe it. He had risked his life to do this, and I will never forget it." Davoren would enter the world of politics after the war and ultimately be elected to the position of secretary of state in the Commonwealth of Massachusetts.

With all the heavy artillery now destroyed or captured by the Twenty-Eighth Marines, the number of casualties the marines would take thereafter would be reduced. The Twenty-Fifth was now in reserve in

134 Chambers, *Third Battalion,* 217.

the vicinity of Charlie-Dog Ridge, which was finally taken after more bloody fighting. It was now up to thirty-two-year-old Reserve Officer Jim Headly, with only three years in the Corps, to take command of the Third. "But he had what it took to lead. He had been molded in the Chambers crucible and believed in the marine corps's doctrine that the only reason for risking men's lives in combat was to kill the enemy and take ground. And the officers and men who fought under his leadership drove ahead the same way they would have done with Chambers at the helm. And the manner in which Headly led them to final victory is known to every man in the Fourth Marine Division."[135]

From February 26, savage fighting would rage on for the next seven days, much of it in close hand-to-hand combat. The Japanese line of defense was developed around strategic strongholds: Hill 382, Charlie-Dog Ridge, the Amphitheatre, Turkey Knob, and Minimi Village. In looking at a scaled map of the island, one realizes that all these defenses were in an area of no more than four thousand square yards. There were thousands of marines and Japanese soldiers concentrated in this relatively small area. That is why it was called a "meat grinder."

Another significant problem for the American troops was that the Japanese defensive positions had hundreds of tunnels, caves, pillboxes, and backdoors. This gives a better perspective as to why the flamethrower became a key weapon for the marines. There would be no Japanese soldiers surrendering. Using the flamethrowers, they burned the enemy out of hiding. It is hard to imagine the stench of decaying bodies combined with the smoke, fire, burning flesh of torched Japanese soldiers, and the sulfur from the smoldering volcanic terrain. If this wasn't hell like no other, it would be interesting to know what was. It wasn't until the afternoon of March 3 that Hill 382 was secured by the marines.

The capture of Turkey Knob was even much more challenging. "No amount of shelling, demolition, flamethrowers, or riflemen could dent the enemy's fanatical resistance. Time and again, advances would be

135 Hill, *Marine Corps Gazette*, 35.

MARINE CORPS OFFICERS AFTER IWO JIMA

Bare chested Charlie second row, fourth from the left.

made at the cost of heavy casualties, only to find at the end of the day the position reached was untenable. After days of bloody battering, the remaining Japanese defenders were isolated." [136]

The exhausted remaining marines of the Twenty-Fifth were finally relieved by the Twenty-Third Marines on March 3. Charlie survived the meat grinder, but the Fourth Division had lost 6,591 men and were now at 50 percent combat efficiency. By March 9, the Fourth had lost another 1,500 men. The battle of Iwo Jima would not officially end until March 15. The Third Battalion was nine hundred men strong when they landed on Iwo. A month later, 750 were dead, wounded, or missing. When it was over, the heroics of the Third Battalion would hold a special place in marine corps history.

"Cut off from hope and doomed to inevitable annihilation, the Third fought ahead, inspired by a smiling Lieutenant Colonel who never allowed himself to think of defeat. It could be told in figures. The

136 Chapin, *Fourth Marine Division*, 51.

men of the Third were recommended for eighteen navy Crosses, six Legions of Merit, fifty Silver Stars, 150 Bronze Stars, countless Purple Hearts, and numerous other awards. In the operations report, the story is told in cold, precise military language. But, in one way or another, it had to be told. For its written in blood on the ugly black sands of Futatsune Beach: in bone and flesh and in names on white crosses in the crowded cemetery above the beach. And it's etched with a sharp-pointed knife into the hearts of those who lived to fight again. They won't forget."[137] For the Fourth Division, 9,090 casualties, including 1,731 killed in action, were recorded in the battle of Iwo Jima. In recognition of its contributions and sacrifices in four major campaigns, the Fourth received two Presidential Citations, one each for Saipan-Tinian and Iwo Jima, and a navy unit Commendation for Iwo Jima.

Charlie described his experiences on Iwo to his grandson Luke Tobin.

Well, we knew going in that Iwo was going to be very well defended because that was the last major island we had to take. So, everyone was scared. While we were storming the beach, I was coming in on an amphibious tank while all the mortar fire was happening. A shell hit the side of the tank and knocked the twelve of us down from where we were. When I got up, I saw that I had gotten hit in the left shoulder by a piece of shrapnel. For the rest of the battle, I had to fight with throbbing pain in my shoulder, which made hand-to-hand fighting very difficult.

We landed and there were thousands of Japanese all along the beach firing at us. We were all firing blindly into the crowd of Japanese soldiers. When you are a kid playing war, you think how great it would be to just run around killing everybody, but we were just trying to keep from being shot. We didn't care if we hit anything or not. There were twelve of us in my platoon, of which five were killed, and after a few minutes of fighting at Iwo Jima, we were all separated. Nobody knew where their platoon was or was supposed

---

137 Hill, *Marine Corps Gazette*, 37.

to be. It was just thousands of American boys shooting at anyone with dark skin. After digging foxholes through all the mortar fire, artillery fire, and rifle fire, we just dug down as deep as we could and listened to all the explosions. It was probably the scariest thing I have ever gone through.

When they got close enough it was even worse because that was when you would have to get involved in hand-to-hand fighting. That was easily the scariest kind because you never knew when anyone was coming at you until the last minute, and they were all around you. That is the point where you just didn't think that you would get out alive.

Colonel Justice Marion Chambers received the Silver Star for his heroics at Tulagi, a Legion of Merit Award, and in 1950 was awarded the Congressional Medal of Honor for his leadership on Iwo Jima where he survived a near fatal bullet wound.

Charlie received a Purple Heart for the shrapnel wound he received on Iwo Jima. He also received a Fourth Division Citation, which read in part:

> For excellent performance of duties in connection with operations against the enemy on Saipan and Tinian, Mariana Islands, from June 15 to 1 August 1944. Serving as platoon leader, eighty-one-mm mortar platoon, Headquarters Company, Third Battalion, Twenty-Fifth Marines, by cool and capable direction, and in an efficient manner, First Lieutenant Brucato directed his platoon, causing it to deliver accurate and effective fire in the face of heavy enemy artillery and mortar fire and under the difficult conditions of front-line combat.... During the initial phase of the Iwo Jima operation, he kept his guns in action under the most adverse conditions of combat, on numerous occasions exposing himself to heavy enemy fire in order to better direct the fire of his guns, During the final stage of the battle, when the mortar platoon was no longer

required to function, he disbanded his platoon and formed a rifle platoon which joined the front line positions....

C.B. Cates, Major General, USMC,
Commanding Fourth Marine Division

On Nov 14, 1972, at a Fourth Division reunion in Maui, Colonel Chambers wrote a personal note to Charlie, which read,

Charlie,

It was great to see you after all these years. We went through too much together to fail to meet. After sweating out our training and then hitting Kwajalein, Saipan, Tinian, and Iwo Jima, we shared too much past to let it pass. You were a fine officer and a dependable part of the brothers.

My best,
J.M. (Joe) Chambers, USMC, (Ret.)

After Iwo, the Fourth began the long trip back to Maui to once again rest and reorganize for combat. It was rumored that they would be training for what could be the worst battle yet—the final battle on the Japanese mainland. Operation Coronet was expected to be the second stage of an attack on the Japanese mainland that was planned to land on Honshu's Tokyo plain in March 1946.

The war in Europe ended with Germany's surrender on May 8, 1945, so the entire focus of the United States Military was on the invasion of Japan. After the Fourth was rested and resupplied, they began training as they did in preparation of all other battles. It's hard to imagine what the surviving members of the Fourth were thinking having just experienced the horrors of Iwo Jima.

The invasion of Japan was not to be. "By July 1945, the Allies' Manhattan Project had produced two types of atomic bombs: 'Fat Man,' a plutonium implosion-type nuclear weapon, and 'Little Boy,' an enriched uranium gun-type fission weapon. The 509th Composite Group of the United States Army Air Forces was trained and equipped with the specialized Silverplate version of the Boeing B-29 Superfortress and deployed to Tinian in the Mariana Islands. The Allies called for the unconditional surrender of the Imperial Japanese Armed Forces in the Potsdam Declaration on 26 July 1945, the alternative being 'prompt and utter destruction.' The Japanese government ignored the ultimatum." [138]

On August 6, 1945, Little Boy was dropped on Hiroshima, and three days later, Fat Man was dropped on Nagasaki. The Japanese surrendered on August 15, 1945, and the war in the Central Pacific was over. Many years later, Charlie said, "I cannot tell you how happy I was that those atomic bombs were dropped. I truly believe this saved my life."

After two years, three months, and thirteen days of active duty which included sixty-three days of battle on four islands and five months at sea, the fighting Fourth was going home. There is a picture of jubilant marines hoisting beers at Camp Maui, which was taken after the marines learned the Japanese surrendered. It includes officers from the three battalions of the Twenty-Fifth Marines. Of the fourteen officers in the picture, only Charlie, Executive Officer Jim Taul, and surgeon Mike Kelleher represented the Third battalion. The rest of the men were from the First and Second Battalions.

On August 14, 1945, the Fourth Division was selected as the first marine division to be sent back home, and on November 28, 1945, the Fourth Marine Division was officially deactivated. Charlie was discharged from the marine corps on February 5, 1946 after nearly four years of active duty. He was one of the few marine officers to survive four Pacific Island campaigns against the Imperial Japanese Army. Ninety five percent were killed in action.

He told his grandson, "I was very happy to leave the war behind and in the past. Some guys enjoy the danger and adventure in war, but not me." Charlie did leave the war with a sense of enormous pride. He told sportswriter Frank Gearan, ". . . I can never compare anything to the feeling of pride I have about fighting beside such courageous marines."

---

138 "Atomic bombings of Hiroshima and Nagasaki," Wikipedia, https://en.wikipedia.org/wiki/Atomic_bombings_of_Hiroshima_and_Nagasaki.

CHAPTER SEVEN

COMING HOME

I N JANUARY OF 1946, CHARLIE RETURNED TO MILFORD. HIS arrival was announced in an article on the front page of the January 4, 1946, edition of the *Milford Daily News*. He was obviously eager to put the war behind him and get back to a sense of normalcy. Giuseppe and Ninfa were living together in a small apartment at 94 Hayward Street. Molly and Tope now had two daughters of their own, Jeanne Marie and Barbara, and were living in an apartment next door at 92 Hayward Street. They had not moved very far from where they lived before the war.

Ninfa was now thirty-two years old and looked very much like her mother. She was no taller than five-foot-two, had a chubby frame, dark hair, and sympathetic brown eyes. Her round face always featured a smile. She was truly unique in every way. Unlike her father, she was a warm and happy person who exuded tenderness and love. She never married and had devoted her life to Giuseppe, preparing meals for him, making sure his clothes were clean, and keeping their small apartment spotless. She was another mother to Molly's two daughters, and they worshipped her.

Molly was thirty-four, petite and attractive with brown hair and eyes. Though quiet and reserved like Charlie, she, too, radiated warmth. Even with two young daughters, she was still working at the shop while Ninfa took care of her children. Giuseppe had not changed. Quiet and somber, he continued to work at Draper Corporation. In his leisure time he enjoyed reading the Italian newspaper which was available at one of the stores in the Plains.

Giuseppe, Molly, Tope, and Ninfa rarely ventured outside the enclave on Hayward Street. Nearly all their social interactions were with their relatives who lived less than a block away. None of them had a driver's license so they had no need of a car. If they had to go to work or leave the neighborhood for other things they would walk, take a cab or bus, or ride with a cousin who had a car.

When he arrived at the apartment, Charlie was welcomed home as a returning hero, but that was nothing new for him. Ninfa and Molly had always treated him that way. They could not be prouder of all his accomplishments, and they always had revered him. Any time he entered their small apartments, they would immediately stop what they were doing and attend to his every need.

"Charlie, what can I get for you?"

"Are you hungry?"

"Can I make you something to eat?"

"Can I get you a soda or something?"

In later years, my siblings and I received the same treatment from them. Molly and Ninfa had an unusual way of showing their affection for members of the family. When they saw us, they would comment to each other, "Look at Bronkie. He is so handsome," or "Look at Marilyn. She's such a doll." We were right there when they said these things and would turn red with embarrassment. If we ever had a problem with anyone and told them, they would say things like "the rat" or "he (lor) she is no good." They were two of the most loyal and wonderful people I have ever known.

Milford had changed dramatically from the time Giuseppe first arrived. Many of the Italian immigrants had gained United States citizenship. Some had purchased homes. Their children had become "Americanized," having been exposed to life outside their enclaves in the schools and on the playing fields. The fact that the Italian Americans had fought for the country in World War II against not only the Germans and Japanese but also against Italy was confirmation for the people uptown that they were loyal to the "stars and stripes."

The war had brought people in town closer together, and the railroad tracks in Milford were no longer the great divider that they once were. Most Italian families now owned a car, though others like Giuseppe would never buy or even drive one. I don't think he even had a license. They were able to conduct their business uptown. Those who did not speak English were taking courses at the high school to learn the language.

Charlie moved in with Giuseppe and Ninfa and returned to work at Milford High School. Physically, he appeared to be the same man he was when he left to serve his country, strong and very fit, but he was more serious, less patient, and there was a tenseness about him. The war had taken its toll on him. Seeing friends maimed and killed in battle and a fanatical enemy that chose suicide over capture had made him vigilant and protective of himself and those around him. This would define him in the future.

He resumed his positions as physical education director and football coach and was also appointed head baseball coach. Unlike his father and sisters, he owned his own car, a boxy Hudson. It did not take him long to visit Connie Oliva, his wartime pen pal. Even though they had not dated or even spent much time together, they had developed a strong loving relationship through their letters.

Coming from a small, isolated family, Charlie was overwhelmed when he met Connie's family. In addition to her mother Angelina, she had four sisters—Mary, who was older, Josephine (Jessie), Marguerite, and Eleanor—and two brothers—Joseph and Anthony ("Babe"), both of whom were younger. All but Mary lived at 89 East Main Street. Also living there with them was Angelina's mother, Concetta.

Concetta D. Oliva circa 1940

As if this were not enough, Connie's family also included uncles and aunts, most of whom lived with their families in different houses on the property. Angelina was one of six children born to Antonio and Concetta Mastroianni. Her siblings—Frank, Giuseppe (Joseph), Raffaele, and Nicholas, and her sister Mary (Lena)—were all married with children.

The Mastroianni-Oliva family property encompassed nearly half of a city block on East Main Street bordered on one side by Plain Street. Beside the house at 89 East Main Street was a patch of grass and a thirty-foot-high, sixty-foot-long wooden billboard with periodically changing advertisements pasted on it. Adjacent to the billboard along East Main Street was a group of attached one story structures which extended to Plain Street. The structures were a small shoe shop, an abandoned garage with an inverted roof, a grocery store, and a small house with the address 83 East Main Street. Frank and his family lived in that house.

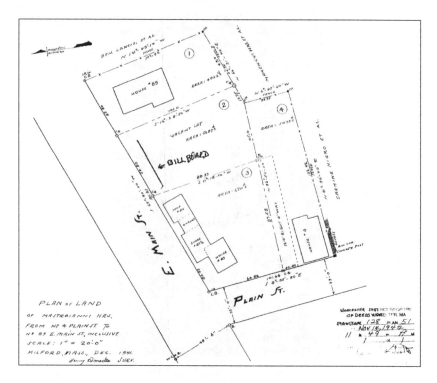

Behind the small house was a patch of grass and a two-family home which fronted on Plain Street. Raffaele's family resided there on the first floor, and Joseph, his wife, and his daughter resided on the second floor. Behind the billboard was a large yard which was shared by all the families. The family had a self-contained enclave of their own. It was communal living to say the least.

Communal living began when the Mastroianni family immigrated to the United States and settled in Milford. The family patriarch, Antonio, purchased a large farm in the most rural area of the Plains near the granite quarries. To finance the purchase, he took a mortgage loan from a finance company operated by a paisano. The interest on the loan was usurious, and Antonio required that his sons and Angelina's husband work and turn over all their earnings to him so that he could pay it and run the household.

Antonio, Frank, Raffaele, and Angelina's husband Nicola Oliva worked as stonecutters in the granite quarries. Joseph, who was a deaf

MASTROIANNI FAMILY CIRCA 1927

Back row, left to right: Rafael, Antonio, Nicholas Frank, Joseph, Nicola Oliva.
Front row: Mary (Lena), Rafael's wife Elizabeth with son, Antonio's wife Concetta,
Frank's wife Clara with son, Mary Oliva with Josephine Oliva in front of her,
Angelina Mastroianni Oliva holding son Joseph, and Concetta Oliva
leaning over in foreground.

mute, worked as a cobbler. Antonio's wife Concetta and Angelina did the cooking and maintained the household. The only son of Antonio who didn't work was Nicholas, who graduated from high school and college. They all lived in the large farmhouse even after they were married, and Antonio made the decisions for everyone.

Though in a traditional Italian family the eldest son is chosen to become the next patriarch, Antonio had picked Nicholas to succeed him. This did not sit well with Frank, the oldest son, who felt he had been passed over. Nicholas (who the Olivas always referred to as "Uncle Nick") ultimately went to medical school and became a surgeon. His education was paid for by Antonio with the earnings of his other sons.

According to Connie, life on the farm was wonderful. Though each of them had chores, Connie, her siblings and cousins always had someone to play with. The family did everything together. Connie tells of the time when Uncle Nick set up an operating room at the farmhouse and removed the tonsils of each of the children. Her sister Jessie was the one child who escaped by running into the woods and hiding.

Among the traditions of life in the family commune was Sunday dinner, which started at noon and lasted until nightfall. Angelina and her mother would rise early to make the gravy, which began with putting tomato paste and tomatoes in a large pan and simmering it. Then they put olive oil in a frying pan and fried sliced onions. Once the onions were done, they would pour them into the simmering gravy. The next step was making meatballs and frying them with sausage and garlic. When they were semi cooked, they would be placed in the gravy along with their drippings. A little homemade red wine would be added, and the gravy would continue to simmer.

The women would next make homemade macaroni and prepare either roast beef, chicken, or pork for the course after macaroni. The meal ended with a serving of salad made with the lettuce and vegetables raised on the farm. In addition to the Mastroianni and Oliva families, there were often guests invited to the feast. Many times, there were over forty people to feed including children.

Things were not always idyllic with the Mastroianni-Oliva clan. Connie's father Nicola Oliva was a frail man, and working in the quarries led to his premature death from stone cutters disease.

She was in college at the time and was devastated. Antonio also died around the same time. Shortly thereafter, Angelina moved her family from the farm to the property on East Main Street, one of the busiest streets in town in the heart of the Plains. Antonio had purchased this property prior to his death.

The Olivas took up residence at 89 East Main Street, Angelina's two brothers, Joseph and Raffaele, moved their families to the two-family residence on the property, and Frank, who had been living at 83 East

STONECUTTERS AT MILFORD QUARRY

Second row: Frank Mastroianni (second from left), Rafael Mastroianni (third from left), Antonio Mastroianni (eighth from left).

Main Street, moved his family to a home on the other side of town. Before his death, Antonio deeded the farm property and the East Main Street and Plain Street properties to his seven children.

Though the three houses, cobbler shop, vacant store on East Main Street, and the farm property were owned by the six Mastroianni children, Uncle Nick, who had become a successful Milford surgeon, exercised dominion over all of them in the fashion of his father. Angelina and her children adored the doctor.

When Charlie got over the initial shock of the size of Connie's family, he was undeterred.

Connie said, "We had fallen in love by mail, but I had a lot of anxiety about his coming home, thinking, *what if we don't like each other in person?*" She needn't have worried. Not long after their first date, Charlie proposed, and Connie happily accepted.

My sister Marilyn said, "Mom told me that when he came home after the war was over, he was quite handsome, and he was like a rock—so strong and muscular. Dad told her that he had a 'pocket full of cash,' and he was going to take her to buy an engagement ring. Soon thereafter, they took a train into New York City with Angelina as their chaperone. They picked out the ring together. It was quite large for the time: .75 carat, platinum setting."

Their engagement did have some bumps along the road. Connie was also teaching at Milford High School. One incident she related involved a day Charlie told her he would pick her up at school and take her home. Later, he decided that he wanted to be with "the boys," so he sent his buddy Bruno Zacchill to do this. He had not told Connie and when Bruno arrived, she was livid. She could not believe her fiancé would send another man to take her home, especially without letting her know. When Charlie saw Connie later, she read him the riot act and followed that up by giving him the silent treatment. It would be a theme that played out over and over for the rest of their lives together.

In fairness, Charlie had no ill intent. He had never had a deep relationship with a woman. All his past relationships were casual. It became clear to me that he never comprehended the dynamics of the man-woman relationship. Since his mother died when he was a baby, he had no model to follow. He also was used to being independent, and as a thirty-year-old bachelor, he was very set in his ways. Connie would always say that he was "a man's man."

———————

A FEW MONTHS AFTER HE RETURNED FROM THE SERVICE, Charlie welcomed fifty-five candidates to tryouts for his first Milford High School baseball team. One of the candidates was Connie's younger brother Anthony "Babe" Oliva. Though he was a junior, he had not previously played any high school sports. Angelina, an immigrant from Calabria, was a stern, no-nonsense woman whose husband had died before the war, leaving her to manage seven children alone. She allowed Babe and his brother Joe to go to high school, but playing sports there was another matter. They had to work to help support the family after school. To Angelina, playing sports was frivolous. She had not let Joe play, and she was not going to let Babe play either.

Charlie knew Babe was a good ballplayer because he had seen him perform on the playgrounds. He wanted him on the team. He also knew that Angelina was not going to let it happen. One day when he was courting Connie, Charlie approached Angelina, who spoke broken English and didn't understand the unique Sicilian language that he spoke. Somehow, he was able to convince his future mother-in-law to allow Babe to play.

Charlie would develop a warm relationship with Angelina over the years, even though she always said he was a stubborn Sicilian. Babe earned a position on the team as its starting third baseman. The 1946 team would launch Milford's second golden era of baseball under the leadership of one of the stars of the first.

The baseball season started very late for some reason. They did not play their first game until May 1 and were trounced by Maynard 22-13. They then reeled off six straight wins before losing again. They finished

SEVEN PLAYERS ON 1946 MILFORD BASEBALL TEAM

Antonio "Babe" Oliva, fifth from left.

the season with ten wins and three losses which included taking the Town Series against St. Mary's two games to one. The early games were played at Town Park but midway through the season, the town completed construction of a new field. Named in honor of Milford's first man killed in World War II, Fino Field became the home field of both Milford High and St. Mary's.

To this day, the field is considered one of the best baseball parks in the state. Unlike Town Park, Fino was located on the Plains side of the tracks. Built in a swampy area which had been painstakingly filled in, it was fenced in on all sides. It was used exclusively for football and baseball games. Practices on the field were not permitted. As a result, except for the infield clay, the entire playing surface consisted of lush green grass.

Home plate was located in the corner of the field near the railroad tracks behind St. Mary's Church. The distance from home plate to the left field fence was about 325 feet while the right field foul pole was well over 350 feet and the centerfield fence was in excess of 450 feet from the plate. In later years, home plate was relocated to where left field had been. The distance from home to left was increased to about 350 feet, to right 375 feet, and to center over 550 feet. There were bleachers in the outfield for football games and bleachers around the diamond for baseball. In addition to the high schools, Fino would become the home of the American Legion team as well as Milford's team in the Blackstone Valley League.

As if teaching, coaching, and getting ready for his wedding were not enough, during the 1946 high school baseball season, Charlie played for the Soda Shoppe, which was Milford's semipro Blackstone Valley team. He was not able to play all the games until the high school season ended, and when he did play, his defensive positions were in the outfield or first base rather than his natural positions, second base and shortstop.

CONNIE AND CHARLIE DID NOT HAVE A LONG ENGAGEMENT. They were married on June 22, 1946, a mere six months after he returned from the war. A photograph of the couple, Connie in a white gown and Charlie in a tuxedo and black bow tie, appeared on the front page of the June 28, 1946, edition of the *Milford Daily News*. He was thirty and she would be twenty-seven in September. The war, which improbably bonded them together, had also robbed them of precious time with each other. They felt an urgency to make up for the lost years.

Charlie selected Brother John as his best man and Sooey DeGaetano and Tate Bodio as his ushers. With her father deceased, Connie chose Uncle Nick to give the bride away. Giuseppe and Brother John could not have been prouder. Before the ceremony, the Oliva family gathered at 89 East Main Street for photographs.

BRUCATO WEDDING PARTY

Men, from left to right: Sooey DeGaetano, Tate Bodio,
Dr. Nicholas Mastroianni (Uncle Nick), Charlie, Brother John.
Women: Connie's two friends, Connie, Connie's sister Marguerite.

Left to right: Charlie, Giuseppe, Brother John.

WEDDING PHOTO IN FRONT OF BILLBOARD AT 89 EAST MAIN

Left to right: Angelina Oliva, Connie, Connie's friend.

THE OLIVA FAMILY ON WEDDING DAY

Left to right: Josephine "Jesse" Zacchilli, Babe Oliva, Connie, Joe Oliva,
Angelina, Marguerite, Mary Oliva Zacchilli, Connie's friend.
(Missing from photo: Eleanor Oliva.)

They were quite a couple. Connie was attractive and petite with brown hair and brown eyes. She was happy, vivacious, and outgoing. Charlie had short dark hair, brown eyes, and a rock-hard physique. He was quiet, reserved, and introverted. She was devoted to her huge family, which was a big part of her life. His family was small in comparison, and he was independent, liked to hang out with his friends, play poker, and go to the racetrack.

There were also a lot of similarities between the two of them. Both were children of Italian immigrant parents. Both had college degrees, which was rare for men with Charlie's ethnic background but rarer still for women. Connie had a bachelor of arts from Boston University and a master's degree in Italian from Wellesley College. They both were educators. They both had special talents. Charlie was an exceptional athlete, and Connie was a gifted linguist, fluent in Italian, French, and Latin.

Their differences were evident early on. They were living with Angelina at the time. One evening shortly after their marriage, Charlie went out and did not come home until after dawn. Connie was frantic. In her family, the men never went out. They were either working, doing chores, or spending time with relatives. Connie went to her mother for comfort and advice. She did not get what she was looking for. Angelina was an old-fashioned Italian woman. To her, the husband was the king of the castle, and she supported Charlie, much to Connie's dismay.

When Charlie returned in the morning, he said that he had been playing poker all night, as if this were a normal thing for a married man. Connie screamed at him. He did not back down. She gave him the "silent treatment" for several days. Both were strong willed individuals and often butted heads, but they were loyal partners their entire lives.

———

DURING THE SUMMER OF 1946 CHARLIE SPENT TWO WEEKS of service in the marine corps reserves. When he returned to Milford, he rejoined Sooey, Tate, and Sammy to resume playing in the Blackstone Valley League. He made history on July 14, 1946. The *Milford*

Daily News reported, "Charlie Brucato playing first base clouted the first home run ever hit at Fino Field in the seventh inning with one man on. It was a line smash that cleared the left field barrier with plenty to spare."[139]

The year 1946 was the first full year after the war, and it was unique for several reasons. During the year, the newspaper was filled with stories of returning veterans and weddings. Everyone was elated that the war was over and anxious to return to normalcy as soon as possible—but this was only part of the story of the time. Strikes against major companies dominated the national news. There were food shortages in various parts of the country. Relations with Russia were deteriorating as the Soviets began to flex their muscles and move to expand their domain under Stalin.

Early in the fall, Connie learned that she was pregnant. She and Charlie had wasted no time starting a family. Her sisters Jessie, who was married to Aldo Zacchilli, and Mary, who was married to Aldo's brother Dewey, were also pregnant.

––––––––

IN SEPTEMBER, CHARLIE RESUMED HIS POSITION AS HEAD football coach at Milford High School. Before the players arrived for tryouts, he did an inventory of the equipment. He was appalled at the condition of the helmets, pads, cleats, and uniforms so he went to the office of the principal, David I. Davoren, who was a good friend.

"Dave, the football equipment is in very bad shape. Can you give me some money so I can buy new gear?" asked Charlie.

Dave said, "I'm sorry, Charlie, we don't have any money in the budget for that. You are going to have to get by with what you have."

Charlie looked at him and said, "If we put our boys in that shitty equipment, somebody is going to get hurt."

Dave would not budge.

---

139 "Brucato Homers as Milford Drubs Douglas Nine, 8-1," *Milford Daily News*, July 15, 1946.

Charlie was angry and said, "Then they'll be no football this fall," and walked out of his office.

As I look back on life with my father, I understand why he took such a difficult position with his boss. The war had taught him that life was fragile. Rather than harden him, his experiences coupled with his Sicilian mindset had made him fearful of perceived dangers and protective of those for whom he was responsible. As tough and hard-nosed as he was, he was not going to allow his players to be hurt because of faulty equipment.

When the day for tryouts arrived, Charlie greeted the team and told the boys that there would be no high school football team this year. To say they were upset is an understatement. Charlie had to field calls from enraged parents, all of whom he told to speak with the principal about the situation.

A few days later, Dave called Charlie into his office and said, "Buy the damn equipment. I'll find the money somewhere."

After tryouts, Charlie picked his starting lineup, and now brother-in-law Babe Oliva, in his first season of football, earned a position at tackle and as the team's place kicker. Led by Cocaptain Bob Consigli, an excellent pass receiver and defensive standout, Cocaptain Buddy Bibbo, a three-year starter at center, and triple-threat back Al Consigli, the team finished with a record of five wins, four losses, and one tie. They beat crosstown rival St. Mary's 21-0 in the final game. In a summary of the season, the school yearbook said, "For the first time in many years, the 1946 football team presented a formidable opposition to rival schools."[140]

Charlie's coaching style embodied elements of his mentors, Colonel Joe Chambers and Jack Barry, his baseball coach at Holy Cross. Charlie demanded that his players be physically fit, well disciplined, thoughtful, and clear in their understanding that individuals perform their roles in the best interest of the team. His expectations were always clear. He held his players to the highest standards of sportsmanship, and he did not tolerate acts of showboating. When a player did not

140 1947 *Oak Lily and Ivy*, 72.

Caricature of the 1947 Milford High football team.

perform according to his expectations, he better have had an answer. Charlie would be relentless in demanding an explanation for anything he deemed a mental error.

Like Chambers, he drove his players to the maximum extent of their physical and mental limits. They would practice a play over and over until the execution was perfect. He accepted no excuses. The games were never as brutal as his practices. Now everyone was calling him "the Bronc" and for good reason. His toughness and no-nonsense attitude, coupled with the fact that everyone knew that he was a wartime marine officer, inspired fear but also respect.

Like Barry, he insisted that his players "looked like ballplayers" and played the game by the book. If your uniform were sloppy or if you did not hustle or if you didn't give it everything you had, you could not play for him regardless of your talent. He was a stickler for detail and "knowing the situation." Missing a sign in a baseball game or going offsides in a football game meant that you were not concentrating, and you would incur his wrath. But he never dressed down a player publicly and never "showed his players up." Rather, he would take the offending player aside, clench his teeth, and growl his criticism or coaching point at him in a voice no one else could hear. There is a litany of stories his players have recounted about him through the years.

In November, Jessie and Aldo had their first child, a baby boy, and named him Peter. A few weeks later, Mary and Dewey had a baby girl and named her Maryellen. Uncle Nick delivered both children. The post war baby boom was well underway.

When he was not coaching, Charlie was less intense, and he tried to adapt to life in the Mastroianni-Oliva commune. It was not easy. Connie's family was always close by. Charlie was an extremely private man, and he was not used to everyone being involved in each other's lives. He did like needling Connie's sisters, each of whom were as attractive as her. He also liked to tease Angelina.

He became great friends with Connie's brother Joe, who shared his interest in the horses, and brother-in-law Aldo Zacchilli, who was

Aldo Zacchilli holding son Peter circa 1950.

quick witted and always fun to be around. Both Joe and Aldo were combat veterans. Joe was just a seventeen-year-old kid when he entered the army during the war and was a veteran of some of the most brutal battles in Europe including Anzio. He ultimately suffered what was then described as "shell shock." Today, he would be diagnosed with post-traumatic stress disorder (PTSD).

Joe was handsome and had a body of stone. He could have been cast as a capo in the *Godfather* movies. Nicknamed "Joe Mama" for his devotion to his mother, he had a gruff and impatient demeanor but possessed a heart of gold. Before the war, he worked in construction to help the family. After the war, he worked as a cement finisher and turned all his earnings over to Angelina. Charlie really loved and respected him. "That guy is a helluva fella," Charlie would say. When you needed work done, you called on Joe.

Aldo, the husband of Connie's sister Jessie, was a man Charlie truly admired. Like Charlie and Joe, Aldo had a harrowing World War II experience. While serving in an army infantry unit, he was captured and confined in a German prison camp until the war ended. Like Charlie and Joe, he never talked about the war. Aldo always seemed happy and jovial. He was a great needler and would do anything to help his family and friends. He always kept himself busy. After working all day as a truck driver, he would toil around the house. "'Hucka' [a nickname used only by Charlie] worked like a dog," marveled Charlie. "He could do anything. And when he was young, he had a helluva curveball."

CHAPTER EIGHT

A SON IS BORN

A S 1946 ENDED AND 1947 BEGAN, STRIKES AND FOOD shortages continued to be front page news. W. T. Grants, Milford's first department store on Main Street, advertised athletic shirts for forty-nine cents and lady's rayon hose for fifty cents. At the grocery stores, beef was selling for fifty-five cents a pound and chicken fifty-seven cents a pound, while a pound of bacon cost sixty-five cents. The price for a ticket to a movie at the State Theater was sixty cents including taxes. Political ads for town office aspirants routinely appeared on the front page of the *Milford Daily News*. March of 1947 became the month the Cold War began, and the Truman Doctrine was proclaimed to help stop the spread of communism.

On March 16, I became the first of Connie and Charlie's four children. They named me Charles J. Brucato, Jr., and my dad immediately nicknamed me "little Bronkie." In an Italian family, a godparent is an esteemed position. My parents selected Michael P. Visconti, a Milford attorney and friend of my dad, as my godfather. He was also the first Italian American to hold an elective position in Milford (school

MOTHERS AND KIDS IN BACK OF BILLBOARD, C. 1949

Front row, left to right: Peter Zacchilli, Mary Ellen Zacchilli, Bronkie.
Second row: Jessie Zacchilli, Mary Zacchilli, Connie.
Back row: Angelina Oliva, Concetta Mastroianni.

committee). My godmother was my father's sister Ninfa, which shows how my father felt about her.

After I was born, we moved from my grandmother's house to the tiny house at 83 East Main Street where Frank and his family had resided. The house had a miniscule kitchen on the first floor with a ten-by-ten foot bathroom adjacent to it that had a cast iron tub, toilet, and sink. The kitchen had a doorway leading to a small dining room. Adjacent to the dining room was a living room which was even smaller. Upstairs was the master bedroom and two closet sized rooms which served as bedrooms. In later years, when the family grew with the addition of three more kids, one closet became my sister Marilyn's bedroom and the other would serve as the bedroom for my brothers and me.

The tradition of Sunday dinner continued in the commune. Angelina rose early each Sunday morning and slaved in the kitchen to prepare homemade bread, macaroni, and meatballs and other Italian delicacies. There would also be an ample supply of homemade red wine. The honored guest was now Uncle Nick. In addition to him and his family, Angelina's sister Mary, her husband, and their three children would come from Fitchburg for the weekly feast. Angelina's two sons, two unmarried daughters, three married daughters, and their kids would also share in the feast. The adults sat in the dining room and the kids were relegated to the kitchen. By the mid- to late 1950s, there would be at least ten kids in the kitchen.

When dinner was over, the kids would leave the kitchen and go outside to play. The women would clear the dining room table and retreat to the kitchen to wash the dishes and pots and pans. The men would get out the cards and play a game called Three Seven. A lot of yelling went on as the game was being played.

Connie especially revered Uncle Nick. He convinced Angelina that she should go to college, and he paid for her education, for which she was forever grateful. None of her siblings had the opportunity to further their education beyond high school. Uncle Nick was also a strong father figure for her as well as a trusted advisor. After she married, Connie's devotion to her family and reliance on Uncle Nick for guidance became a source of friction between her and Charlie.

Charlie resented his wife's devotion to her family and reverence for her uncle. In his family, Charlie was the one who was revered. He had always been the one family and friends looked to for guidance. He would become angry when his wife consulted Uncle Nick for advice.

Charlie also did not like the fact that all Sunday dinners and all holidays were spent with Connie's extended family. The major arguments they had during their marriage centered around this issue.

Life in the Mastroianni-Oliva commune was unique to say the least. While Uncle Nick was the strong patriarch and decision maker for the family and Angelina was the chief cook, others also had roles. Raffaele's wife Elizabeth (Aunt Lizzie) was the family's "witch." She was a character out of central casting. Spry and feisty, she possessed spiritual powers which had been passed down to her by her mother. Since many in the family were superstitious, they often looked to her for help.

Among the many superstitions brought from the "old country" was the *mal'occhio* (evil eye). The belief was that there were people who could inflict this as a curse on someone which would bring harm to them. Aunt Lizzie had the power and tools to diagnose whether someone had been afflicted. She could also be called upon to administer healings for this and certain other illnesses.

When Aldo and Jessie's son Peter was six or seven, his mother thought he might have been a victim of the mal'occhio because he was lethargic. Peter says that he remembers vividly his mother sending him across the yard to Aunt Lizzie's house with instructions that he was to knock on the door and when she let him in, he was to remain silent. Aunt Lizzie guided him to the kitchen table, sat him down, and recited prayers as she placed her hand on his head. When this was done, she placed a bowl of water on the table and proceeded to put two drops of olive oil in the water. After staring at the bowl for a while, she told him to leave.

When he returned home, Peter heard his mother on the phone with Aunt Lizzie. From what he remembers, she told Jessie that he "had it bad." Apparently, she had removed the curse because he was okay after that. His mother made him promise to keep what happened to himself or he would get a slap.

Aldo Zacchilli told a story about Aunt Lizzie that involved Charlie. It was early in the 1950s, and Joe, the cobbler, was living with his wife

Alice and their daughter Concetta on the second floor of the two-family house on Plain Street. The first floor was home to Aunt Lizzie and her five children.

"One night, Charlie and I got a call to go over to Joe's house," Aldo recalled. "Joe had passed out on the kitchen floor of his apartment, and we were called because we were war veterans, and someone believed we would know how to handle the situation. Lizzie was there with Alice when we arrived.

"I looked at Joe, and it appeared that he was dead. I got on the floor anyway and felt for a pulse and there was none. I turned to the two women and told them I thought he was dead. Lizzie ran over to the body and screamed, 'Oh my God, let me hold him before he gets cold.' As sad as the situation was, Lizzie's reaction was not only disturbing but comical. Charlie and I looked at each other and had to leave the room before we both burst out laughing."

My own story with Aunt Lizzie haunts me to the present day. My great grandmother lived with her daughter Angelina at 89 East Main Street and was a character in her own right. (She once explained why she only drank wine and alcohol and not water. In her native tongue she said, "I don't drink water. Look what it does to the pipes.") When I was three or four, she died. The family chose to wake her in the living room of the house, which was not unusual at the time.

During calling hours, I happened to be in the kitchen. Aunt Lizzie saw me, came over, picked me up, and carried me to the living room and the open casket.

She held me over the body and said, "Kiss her good-bye, Bronkie."

I can't remember if I did, but I was very scared.

IN THE SPRING OF 1947, CHARLIE COACHED THE MILFORD High baseball team. The players now knew what was expected of them. The baseball section of the yearbook carried the headline, "Coach Charlie Brucato Was As Proud Of The Team As He Is Of His Newly-Born

Son."[141] The team, which now was playing its games at Fino Field, lost only two games and was crowned Midland League Champions for the first time since 1942. The yearbook in 1948 said the 1947 team "had enjoyed one of the most successful seasons in the history of the school."[142] In addition to the championship, they swept St. Mary's in the annual town series.

The captain of the team was Sisto Petrini, whose first name was given to him because he was the sixth child born in his family, another tradition in some large Italian families. Babe Oliva played first base and hit in the middle of the batting order. On the team was Santo Lasorsa, who had the distinction of being the first high schooler to hit a home run over the left field fence at Fino.

Bob Capuzziello, the catcher for the team, in an interview with the *Milford Daily News*, spoke candidly about his most memorable experience with Coach Brucato. In a game with town rival St. Mary's High, Capuzziello described how his early game jitters led to two passed balls which gave St. Marys a 2-0 lead. "When I returned to the bench at the end of the inning, our coach, Charlie Brucato, really lit into me. I remember he called me afraid and gutless, a trick he used to snap his players out of a fog," Capuzziello explained. As it turned out, after Coach Brucato's tongue lashing, he settled down, getting a couple of key hits and making great plays in the field to lead Milford High to a 5-2 victory.

———

IN 1947, THERE WERE STILL DEEP SCARS FROM THE WAR. A front-page story in the May 6 edition of the *Milford Daily News* reported the apparent suicide of Milford resident Robert Lynch, a twenty-four-year-old student at Amherst College who had been wounded in the war. He had left a note which said that he feared his injuries would be a barrier to his upcoming marriage.

141 1947 *Oak Lily & Ivy*, 79.
142 1948 *Oak Lily & Ivy*, 78.

During the summer, Charlie fulfilled his marine corps reserve duties and was player-manager for the Milford Blackstone Valley League team where he continued to display his talent for smashing the baseball. The local newspaper reported on August 8, "The Bronk's [sic] booming belt, his second round-tripper of the season, was undoubtedly the longest ever parked out of the Fino Field enclosure.... The ball took off like a bat out of Hades, climbed in a skyrocketing trajectory, and landed way, way, way beyond the leftfield barrier."[143]

In September, the National Security Act of 1947, creating the United States Air Force, National Security Council, and the Central Intelligence Agency, became effective. In that same month, Charlie began coaching another successful Milford High Football team.

They won five games, lost two, and tied three. One of the wins was against a powerful St. Mary's team 7-0. Before that game, Charlie knew that St. Mary's posed a difficult challenge. They had a back named Buster Carline, who was unstoppable. Charlie worried all week about how to defend him. His standard defense would not be enough, and losing to Milford High's crosstown rival would be devastating and embarrassing for him. As he lay awake in bed a couple of nights before the game, he came up with a scheme that he thought would work. He called his assistant coach John Calagione, woke him up out of a sound sleep, and told him to come over. Together they worked on the plan until nearly dawn.

The strategy worked. "All eyes soon centered on the annual Thanksgiving Day Classic with St. Mary's. A crowd of 2,two thousand turned out to witness this 'Battle of the Century.' St. Mary's dominated in the first stanza of play but in the second stanza, the [Milford] team shook off their lethargy, collected its forces, and propelled Cocaptain McCausland on a thrilling and dramatic touchdown run. The victory was secured with the extra point added giving Milford a 7-0 victory and

---

143 "Milford Soda Shoppe Whales Rockdale 7-0 in One-Sided Skirmish," *Milford Daily News*, August 8, 1947.

permanent possession of the Alzerini Trophy."[144] More importantly, for Connie, because Charlie's team had won, Thanksgiving dinner was not ruined.

November proved to be a historic time worldwide and a turbulent one in the United States. On November 8, the *Daily News* reported that an eight-year-old Milford boy had been stricken with polio. It was the first case of the year. In the United States, McCarthyism had become a household term. On November 24, Princess Elizabeth (later Elizabeth II), the daughter of George VI of the United Kingdom, married the Duke of Edinburgh at Westminster Abbey in London.

On November 24, the United States House of Representatives voted 346–17 to approve citations of Contempt of Congress against the Hollywood Ten after the screenwriters and directors refused to cooperate with the House Un-American Activities Committee concerning allegations of communist influences in the movie business. The ten men were blacklisted by the Hollywood movie studios on the following day. Later that month, the Milford Police brought seventeen men to court on gaming charges after a raid of the 920 Club on East Main Street, a block away from the Brucato residence.

1948 BEGAN WITH A THREE-DAY SNOWSTORM IN MILFORD followed by record low temperatures the entire month of January. The month ended ominously with the assassination of Indian pacifist and leader Mahatma Gandhi who was shot by Nathuram Godse in New Delhi. On a more positive note, the 1948 Winter Olympics opened in St. Moritz, Switzerland.

In February, nine of the seventeen men arrested in November on gaming charges were found innocent. On February 24, the headline of the lead story on the sports page was "Brucato Resigns As Soda Shoppe Manager; Hangs Up His Spikes." The article said, "Charley [sic] 'The Bronc' Brucato, one of the hardest hitting second basemen in the

144 1948 *Oak Lily & Ivy*, 71.

Blackstone Valley League submitted his resignation as player-manager of the Soda Shoppe team.... Brucato, considered one of the best athletes ever produced here, told a *Daily News* correspondent that he was 'hanging up my spikes for good....'

"'The team needs a player-manager who can get in there and play,' he stated. 'And as far as playing is concerned, my days are limited. I'm slowing up....' In storing his baseball suit in the moth balls, the husky, powerful Valley League slugger has written the climax to a brilliant diamond career."[145]

In the local March election, Michael Visconti was reelected as one of three selectmen, and Charlie's former teammate Bill Bellantuonio was elected to the school committee. Many of those seeking office were Italian Americans. So much was changing in Milford. On March 6, the *Daily News* reported that in nearby Mendon, the last horse drawn milk wagon had been replaced by a truck.

Spring dawned and Charlie welcomed what would become one of Milford's finest baseball teams. Referred to as "the Brucatomen" and led by Captain Ray Elliott and right-handed pitcher Jim Giacomuzzi, the team rattled off seven straight wins to start the season. Joe Stoico, a fourteen-year-old freshman and the team's first baseman, emerged as one of the young stars. Milford easily won the Midland League Championship and went on to play for the Massachusetts Class B (Small School) State Championship at Fenway Park in June. In the championship game, Giacomuzzi, who had become one of the top pitchers in the state, hurled a complete game as Milford High defeated Case High School of Swansea.

"In the final game at the Yawkey orchard, for the state title, Jimmy easily defeated Swansea. Prior to running into Jim's awfully smoky stuff the Cape Cod representatives had piled up something like fourteen victories."[146] At thirty-two years old, Charlie got his first state champion-

---

145 "Brucato Resigns as Soda Shoppe Manager; Hangs Up His Spikes," *Milford Daily News*, February 24, 1948.
146 "Milford High Wins Tourney Crown," *Milford Daily News*, June 17, 1948.

ship as a coach to add to his mythical state championship as a player at Milford High and two official state championships as a Milford Junior Legion player.

The team finished the season at 15-3 by beating St. Mary's in the Town Series two games to one. During the season his friend Sooey DeGaetano and cousin Sammy Tomaso were hired to replace Charlie as player-coaches on the Soda Shoppe team and Charlie took a base coach position with the Hopedale team in the Blackstone Valley League.

In July, as the Cold War persisted, President Truman reinstated the draft. In August, Alger Hiss, a former US government official involved with the forming of the United Nations, was accused of being a Russian spy in the 1930s. He would serve a prison sentence for perjury but continue to deny he was either a communist or a spy.

Charlie completed his annual marine corps reserve training. On July 22, he was promoted to captain. Jeanette and Brother John were still living in Stamford, Connecticut. Their sons Joseph and Rudolf were twenty-three and eighteen now, and their daughters Mary and Barbara were fifteen and eight. Unfortunately, Joseph and Mary were born deaf. Brother John was still working as a police officer in Stamford. Molly and Tope's daughters Jeanne and Barbara were nine and seven. Brother John would visit Milford periodically to see his father, brother, and two sisters.

The front-page banner headline in the *Daily News* on August 17 was "Nation Mourns Babe Ruth's Death." For a town steeped in baseball tradition, this news hit the Milford community hard.

In the fall, Charlie decided that he would not coach football but would stay on as head baseball coach. He also continued to serve as the athletic director. His annual salary was $3,750.00. Unlike today, coaches at the time did not get any extra money. The head coach for the 1948 football team was "Fitter" Cahill assisted by Charlie Espanet.

On September 22, Charlie and the baseball team were feted at a banquet at the Hoboken Citizens Club where the players were awarded jackets and tie pins. Charlie was presented with a trophy signifying the three championships his team had won (Midland League, Massachusetts Small School, and Town Series). When presented with the trophy Charlie said, "In all my years of active playing and coaching, this is the first trophy that I have ever been presented."[147]

In his remarks, Boston Braves scout Doc Gautreau, the main speaker at the banquet, said, "I know Charley [sic] Brucato. I played ball with him. I know that he instills spirit into his clubs and that he is in a game as much as his boys. He always thinks of the welfare of his players and is always trying to help them. He is what I call a great schoolboy coach."[148]

In November, Harry Truman defeated Republican Thomas E. Dewey and "Dixiecrat" Strom Thurmond, the Progressive Party candidate. The entire year had been tumultuous around the globe with Soviet aggression and imperialism, war in the Middle East and Asia, inflation, the beginning of the rebuilding of post war Europe, and the division of Germany into two separate states.

---

147 "Tri-Championship Milford High Baseball Team Honored at Banquet," Milford Daily News, September 23, 1948.

148 "Tri-Championship," *Milford Daily News*, September 23, 1948.

CHAPTER NINE

COACHING SUCCESS AS
THE FAMILY GROWS

I N JANUARY OF 1949, HARRY TRUMAN WAS SWORN IN FOR A
full term as president. In April, the North Atlantic Treaty was signed
in Washington, creating the North Atlantic Treaty Organization
(NATO). On June 8, the Second Red Scare began in the United States
when celebrities—including Helen Keller, Dorothy Parker, Danny Kaye,
Fredric March, John Garfield, Paul Muni, and Edward G. Robinson—
were named in a Federal Bureau of Investigation report as Communist
Party members.

On March 2, the banner headline of the *Milford Daily News* was
"US Bomber Circles the World" with a sub headline, "Non-Stop Ninty-
Four-Hour Flight Shows No Spot Bombproof."[149] In local news, on
March 7, under the headline, "Cock Fight In Milford Raided By State
Police; Eighty-Seven Arrested," it was reported,[150] "The Bonetti Farm
on Birch Street, off Route 109, formerly known as the Bega Farm, was
the scene of the raid, staged by nearly twenty State Troopers."[151] Among
those arrested was one of Charlie's cousins.

---

149 "U.S. Bomber Circles the World," *Milford Daily News,* March 2, 1949.
150 "Cock Fight in Milford Raided by State Police; 87 Arrested," *Milford Daily News*.
151 "Cock Fight," *Milford Daily News*.

Mike Visconti did not run for reelection but was appointed by the new selectmen as Town Counsel on a 2-1 vote with Marco Balzarini and Vince Votolato for him and John J. Casey voting for Attorney Daniel P. Carney. An unusual op-ed piece titled "New Milford Board of Selectmen Face New Bumps on Rough Road of 1949"[152] appeared on the front page of the local newspaper under the by-line of Nicholas J. Tosches. Few, if any, articles in the paper identified the writer and fewer contained opinions and not straight forward recitations of facts.

Tosches wrote, "As has been the case in past years, the selectman's voting will be of the 2-1 variety. Balloting for town counsel already in this now stereotyped vote, with the Progressives (Votolato and Balzarini) electing Attorney Michael P. Visconti while the lone Citizens' man (Casey) voted in vain for Attorney Daniel P, Carney." The implication was not subtle. The Italian Americans voted for their own, and the Irish Americans did likewise.

World or local news did nothing to alter baseball in Milford. As spring began, Charlie greeted fifty-eight candidates at tryouts for the Milford High Baseball team. The team had a tough act to follow with the 1948 team's unprecedented success. At the same time, the news was that it was looking like Milford would not have a team in the Blackstone Valley League.

The high school season began on a high note with Milford trouncing Hudson 16-4, but things went downhill from there. They lost the next game to Clinton 5-2, then reeled off two wins, 10-7 against Framingham and 4-2 against Marlboro, before losing to Maynard 3-2. They faced Maynard again and beat them 10-2, beat Natick 7-4, and lost the next three games. However, they were able to sweep the Town Series against St. Mary's 4-2 and 8-0 in games where Jim "Jacka" Giacomuzzi was dominant striking out nineteen in the first game and twenty-two in the second. The team finished with seven wins and five losses, but there would be no Midland League or State Championships this year.

---

152 Nicholas J. Tosches, "New Milford Board of Selectmen Face New Bumps on Rough Road of 1949," *Milford Daily News*, March 7, 1949.

Joe Stoico, now a sophomore, hit .325 and Giacomuzzi pitched his heart out.

Milford did manage to field a team in the Blackstone Valley League. Fans had conducted a fundraising drive, and townspeople had responded generously. Camel Comolli was named player-manager after retiring as a player in the major leagues. Former Chicago Cub Lennie Merullo joined the team and played shortstop, and Charlie took his baseball suit out of mothballs and his spikes off the hanger. He would be the team's second baseman and cleanup hitter. Former teammate and ex-major leaguer Arthur Kenny would join the team later in the season. It was a blistering hot summer resulting in drought conditions. Farms and gardens were ruined, and without air-conditioners, people suffered. Milford completed a disappointing season finishing second in the Blackstone Valley League and being eliminated from the playoffs in the first series. Charlie had his worst season as a coach followed up with probably his worst baseball season as a player hitting only .238. At thirty-three years old, he regretted his decision to play that summer. Things around the house were tense for Connie to say the least.

When fall began, Charlie Espanet took over the head coaching position for the Milford High football team. The season did not go well. The team won its first game against North Attleboro and its last game against St. Mary's on Thanksgiving Day. They lost every game in between, many by large margins. Stanley Jones chastised the fans for their reaction in an article titled, "Espanet Receiving Knocks, But He Will Have His Day." Jones wrote, "'This is the worst ever. Football is at its lowest ebb.' These doleful, mumbled words were offered by an exasperated J. Francis "Fitter" Cahill.... Milford High is still losing, and the wolves are ready to howl. And Espanet's scalp has become the target of the ever-critical fan."[153]

Jones, whose real last name was Nalewajko, was a unique Milford personality. He started writing for the *Milford Daily News* at an early

---

153 "Espanet Receiving Knocks, But He Will Have His Day," *Milford Daily News*, November 2, 1949.

age, became a well-respected sports and entertainment columnist, and later the paper's sports editor before finally becoming its managing editor. He had a passion for music and was a noted lyricist and publisher, having had several of his songs recorded. He would become one of Charlie's good friends.

On November 18, 1949, Connie gave birth to the second Brucato child, a girl. They named her Marilyn Ann, but soon she would be nicknamed "Moochie" by Aldo Zacchilli and that nickname stuck. I was now almost three years old. We were still living in the small house at 83 East Main Street. We even had a telephone, albeit a party line (telephone number 2627J). At that time, there were no rotary or dial phones.

To make a call, we picked up the phone and waited for an operator. When the operator answered with, "Number please?" we would recite the number we were calling, and she (it was rare for a man to be an operator) would connect us. We had a party line because it was less expensive than a private one. A party line had a drawback—you shared it with some other family. Often when we picked up the phone, we could hear the conversation of the line sharer. The same was true for the sharer's family. In addition, the operators were always listening in. The Italians had a way to keep private conversations private. They spoke in their Italian dialects or used code words. My mother and her sisters used *ink* as code for wine or *oil* as code for liquor for example.

As 1950 dawned, stories related to the Cold War dominated the news. In January, President Truman ordered the development of the hydrogen bomb in response to the Soviet Union detonating its first atomic bomb the previous year. Fear of nuclear war abounded, shaking the nation's psyche.

The local news was just as dire. On January 11, the banner headline in the *Milford Daily News* was, "Mendon Chief and Girl Murdered." The article described a "wild gun battle" at Hensel's Red Rooster in nearby Mendon where Matthew Mantoni, police chief in that town, and a young woman were shot and killed by Harold Ward during an apparent robbery. Photos of the scene accompanied the article and showed two dead bodies.[154] In the ensuing weeks, a fund was set up for the chief's family, and residents in the area were generous with their donations.

On February 15, Milford was buried in twelve inches of snow. This was followed by bitter cold temperatures. Since there was a shortage of coal due in large part to ongoing labor disputes, many Milfordians suffered.

In happier news, Milford High School students put on their annual Minstrel Show, which was a highlight of the school year. The show had been a tradition for thirteen years and would continue well into the 1960s. In the show, several students called "end men" would be black faced and sit in a row of chairs on stage where they would joke with each other to the delight of the audience. Today, such a show, which was degrading to African Americans, would never be permitted, but this was a time when *Amos and Andy* and other similar radio and television shows were popular.

Ethnic humor was not restricted to African Americans in the Minstrel Show of 1950. The yearbook reported, "With the entrance of 'Goldberg's Shamrocks,' a band made up entirely of the Jewish members of the MHS band, the audience all began to roll in the aisles. All dressed in Irish green, the band played and sang to the tune of McNamara's Band."[155]

On March 22, newly reappointed head football coach Charlie Brucato welcomed fifty-five candidates to spring practice. After two unsuccessful football seasons under Cahill and Espanet, Charlie once again took over the reins as head coach. Three days later, Charlie started baseball season by bringing the pitchers and catchers in to throw in the John C. Lynch Auditorium, the tiny gymnasium at the high school. Football practice continued for three weeks under Charlie's assistants when he was involved with the baseball team. For his work as athletic director and head baseball and football coach, his annual salary was now $3,850.00.

"Many say that love accompanies the ushering in of spring, but

---

154 "Mendon Chief and Girl Murdered," *Milford Daily News*, January 11, 1950.
155 1950 *Oak Lily and Ivy*, 71.

sports-minded persons think differently. Spring ushers in the arrival of America's national sport—baseball."[156] This quote from the Milford High School yearbook was certainly true in Milford. On April 5, the baseball team gathered for tryouts. At the same time Milford teachers were seeking maximum annual salaries of $3,800.00 for those with bachelor's degrees, $4,000.00 for those with master's degrees, and $4,200.00 for those with doctorates.

With the loss of fire balling Jacka Giacomuzzi to graduation, Charlie had a huge to fill on his pitching staff. Tall, rangy Bob Gilmore, thin lefty Joe Celozzi, and the multitalented Joe Stoico would have to emerge as pitchers if the team was to be successful. The offense would come from third-baseman Jack Kelley, Stoico, Neil Jionzo, and Sonny Tomaso.

The team began the season by winning five in a row. They beat Wellesley 8-1, Clinton 8-7, North Attleboro 4-0, Maynard 15-1, and Marlboro 3-0 before losing to Franklin 5-4. Gilmore emerged as the ace of the staff as he and Stoico combined for a shutout against North Attleboro, and he went all the way in the Marlboro game, giving up only three hits.

In the second half of the season, they secured their fourth Midland League title in five years with wins over Marlboro 3-1 and Hudson 5-4 before losing to Clinton 4-3. They finished the season with a record of eleven wins and only three losses after beating St. Mary's in the Town Series two games to one. Stoico finished the season with a batting average of .333 followed by Kelley .288 and Jionzo .250. Sonny Tomaso led the team in runs batted in. Gilmore was elected the captain of next year's team.

The season was not without incident. The headline after the loss to Clinton was "Brucato Gets Bounced at Clinton—So Does Milford."[157] The article said, "Coach Charlie Brucato was chased out of the park by a red-faced umpire in the eighth inning." The argument which led to Charlie's ejection was over a slippery baseball. Pitcher Joe Celozzi had

---

156 1950 *Oak Lily and Ivy*, 80.
157 "Brucato Gets Bounced at Clinton—So Does Milford," *Milford Daily News*, May 27, 1950.

asked the umpire for a new ball and the umpire refused, which brought the outraged coach off the bench for a nose-to-nose confrontation with both screaming. "Brucato said later he [Celozzi] was justified in asking for a new ball. 'That ball was slippery and Celozzi was having trouble with it,' he said. 'What if he hit those batters in the head? What then? Who would be responsible?'"[158]

After the season, Charlie was a base coach and pinch hitter for the Milford Blackstone Valley League team. On June 21, Milford High celebrated its Centennial with a large banquet at the Milford Armory. On June 26, the local paper was headlined with "Civil War Breaks Out In Korea."[159] A month later, Charlie left for his annual training with the marine corps reserves. The Korean War would dominate the news for the next year. On July 13, it was reported that Major John F. Smith of Milford was the area's first casualty in the war.

The other major local story of 1950 involved the prosecution of Harold Ward, who had killed the Mendon police chief and a woman. There were periodic reports of the case during the months after the incident. They culminated with front page headline news, "Ward Found Insane, Avoids Murder Trial."[160]

AS SUMMER ENDED AND SEPTEMBER BEGAN, THERE WAS news of another gambling raid in Milford. "Two Dice Raids in Milford, Twenty-Four Are Arrested." The report said that State Police raided Matty's on North Pond and the Bear Hill Schoolhouse on Beaver Street.[161] Not surprisingly, some of the culprits were the same as the previous raids.

Days later, Charlie met his football team and began practice sessions. The local newspaper heralded the upcoming season: "Milford

---

158 "Brucato Gets Bounced at Clinton—So Does Milford," *Milford Daily News*, May 27, 1950.
159 "Civil War Breaks Out in Korea," *Milford Daily News*, June 26, 1950.
160 "Ward Found Insane Avoids Murder, Trial," *Milford Daily News*, August 2, 1950.
161 "Two Dice Raids In Milford 24 Are Arrested," *Milford Daily News*, September 2, 1950.

High May Emerge from Darkness This Fall." In the article, Charlie was quoted saying, "Everyone who shows that desire to play football will receive a uniform and keep it.... I want boys who show a willingness to play, and I seem to have quite a few right now."[162] Though he named Espanet and Calagione his assistants, Espanet was upset about not being head coach, and his relationship with Charlie was never good again.

The decision to coach football would prove to be a great one for Charlie. Led by senior captain Joe Stoico, the team "enjoyed one of the finest seasons in the school's history."[163] They opened the season losing to Clinton 25-6 and tying Marlboro 0-0. The newspaper report of the Marlboro game began, "The Midland League was rocked off its pins and thoroughly startled Saturday afternoon as an improved, positively vicious Milford High football machine wrestled the favored Marlboro High Panthers to a scoreless tie at Fino Field."[164]

The team then rattled off six straight wins to finish the season at 6-1-1. Five of the wins were shutouts. The only team to score on them other than Clinton was Hudson, which managed twelve points. Also impressive were the margins of victory. On October 16, the headline read, "Milford Crushes Maynard 34-0, To Snap League," and the story began, "Cheers. A Toast. And a Hip, Hip, Hooray. The famine is over dear friends. The horrid Midland League jinx that haunted Milford High since October of 1947 was shattered with a thunderous *KUH-RASHH* as the raging Brucatomen ran wild over outclassed Maynard..."[165] The Hudson game was particularly satisfying too.

Entering the game, Milford was the thirteen-point favorite. Hudson forged a 12-0 lead by scoring on a sixty-eight-yard touchdown run on its opening play and then following that up three minutes later with

---

162 "Milford High May Emerge From Darkness This Fall," *Milford Daily News*, September 7, 1950.

163 1951 *Oak Lily & Ivy*, 70.

164 "Milford Underdogs Hold Marlboro to 0-0 Deadlock," *Milford Daily News*, October 6, 1950.

165 "Milford Crushes Maynard 34-0 To Snap League," *Milford Daily News*, October 16, 1950.

Charlie and Joe Stoico

a seventy-three-yard touchdown run. Led by three of Charlie's favorites—senior fullback Stoico, sophomore quarterback Bob Pagnini, and left end Henry Acquafresca—Milford roared back by scoring a touchdown in the first half and three more in the second half while holding Hudson scoreless and won 26-12. However, local news in October was not all good. The paper reported on October 2 that marine Private First Class Lester Lavoie was the first Milford man to be killed in Korea.[166]

Milford High next downed Franklin 18-0, Bartlett 26-0, and North Attleboro 27-0. In the final game against St. Mary's on Thanksgiving Day, they throttled their crosstown rivals 19-0 in a game dedicated to the seniors. In the lead up to that game, Charlie talked about his players.

"We haven't had a serious injury. Scanzaroli [tackle Jim Scanzaroli] played the North Attleboro game with a bad back, but he is all right. Incidentally, he is the most improved lineman on the squad. Taped back and all, he played very well against North Attleboro.... Speaking of

166 "Milford Marine is Killed," *Milford Daily News*, October 2, 1950.

improvement, that goes for Johnny Mignone. His tackling and blocking has been especially good in the last few games.... There is a kid [sophomore Joe Grillo] who hasn't received the credit he deserves. He is the best tackler I have. He is rough and tough and nasty.... They are all good boys. They give everything they have."[167]

After the season ended, Henry Acquafresca and Ed Castiglione were named Midland League All-Stars along with guard Eddie Tighe and halfbacks Lou Guerriere and Joe Stoico. Acquafresca and Stoico also received honorable mention on the Boston Travelers 1950 All-Scholastic team.

Several stories about Charlie and his players highlight his intensity. Acquafresca, who was a bit of a free spirit, tells of the time when he was a freshman and failed to show up for the first day of tryouts for the football team. When freshman team coach Fitter Cahill asked him why, "I told him I went hunting because it was the first day of hunting season. He told me that if I wanted to play, I'd have to see the athletic director. I went to Charlie's office and told him the story. He gritted his teeth and growled at me, 'Jesus Christ, what the hell is wrong with you, Acquafresca?' Then he shook his head and grunted, 'Tell Coach Cahill if he wants you on the team, it's okay with me, but let me tell you, you could never play for me. Get the hell out of here.' Of course, a year later, Charlie picked me for the varsity, and I was the starter at end for him."

Acquafresca also tells a story about the disastrous game against Clinton at Fuller Field in that town. "Clinton was leading in the game and kicked off after one of their touchdowns. Joe Stoico was back with Johnny Mignone to receive the kick. The kicker got into one, and it sailed over Stoico's head into the endzone. When Mignone ran over to down the ball, Joe waved him off and they both trotted to the bench. A Clinton player, knowing as Joe should have that it was a live ball, pounced on the pigskin for another touchdown. The Bronc went nuts. When Joe got to the sideline, he grabbed him by the shirt and screamed,

---

167 "Milford High Stars Preparing for Big Game with St. Mary's Eleven," *Milford Daily News*, November 16, 1950.

'Jesus Christ, Joe, how can you be so goddamn stupid? You know that's a live ball. What the hell were you thinking? Captain! You're the goddamn captain!' The Bronc hated mental mistakes."

Probably the best story involving Charlie and "Acqua" occurred on the bus after the Marlboro game. Acquafresca, who wasn't even the team's placekicker, approached Charlie and said, "Coach, if you had let me kick a field goal, we would have won the game." Charlie, who was a bear after a loss, glared at him and said, "What the hell are you talking about? We had the ball at the thirty-yard line." Henry responded, "I can make a field goal from that distance." Charlie just shook his head and told him to go back to his seat.

The next time the team practiced, Charlie placed the ball about forty yards from the goal post. "Okay, Acquafresca, you said you could make a field goal from this distance. Let's see." With Charlie holding, Henry placekicked the ball through the uprights. Charlie stood up and said, "Get the hell out of here, you son of a bitch!" but from that point on, Henry was the kicker.

Stoico loved to tell of the time Charlie thought he wasn't running hard enough when he got the ball. "We were practicing a dive play for short yardage situations, and Coach wanted me to gain yardage even when there was no hole to go through. He yelled at me after I was unable to gain the needed yard or two, 'Jesus, Stoico, you're the biggest guy on the field and you go down as soon as someone touches you. I need my fullback to bowl people over and make yardage when there is no hole.'

"The Bronc then went over to the defensive huddle and said, 'I am going to tell you where the play is going, and I want you guys to knock Joe on his ass.' He took the offensive line aside and said, 'I don't want any of you to block." We ran the play over and over, with Coach shouting at me, 'Lower your shoulder, keep your feet churning.' I was getting pulverized and was mad as hell, so I started putting my head down and running as hard as I could into whoever was in front of me. The only thing he said was, 'That's the way you have to run. Let's do it again.'"

Stoico's favorite story, however, involves a time when he got hurt during a game. "I got tackled hard and went down," Joe recounted. "I felt a lot of pain in one of my legs and couldn't get up on my feet. The official called time out while I was laying on the field, and the Bronc came out to see me. I told him that my leg was killing me. He looked at the leg, felt it a couple of times, and then said, 'You're all right, Joe. Get up and just run it off.' I limped to the sideline and tried to run like he told me, but it was impossible. Fortunately, Dr. Cichetti, the team doctor, came over, sat me down, and examined my leg. It turned out that I had broken it."

In retrospect, I think my father's response to Joe's injury was one of denial. He hated to see anyone for whom he was responsible suffer. His greatest fear was serious injury to one of his boys. I truly believe telling Joe to run it off was more to assuage his own anxiety than to toughen his player up.

Pagnini related another great tale about Charlie several years later at a banquet to honor his old coach. "Charlie wanted to win as badly as anyone but taught us that games are won on the practice field from hard work, and hard work pays off. In both football and baseball, he covered all the individual skills and team strategies of the game. At practice, he prepared us for every possible situation we might run into in a game.

"I remember one Thanksgiving morning, we were going to play a strong St. Mary's team. Somewhere early that morning, Charlie heard a little birdie tell him that Chick Sayles [St. Mary's coach] might use a spread formation—with the center and QB on one side of the field and the rest of the team on the other. We hadn't covered that in practice that week, so before we went to the field for the game, he took us up to the John C. Lynch Auditorium which was filled with chairs.

"In setting up our defense for that formation he said, 'Acquafresca, you play in the second row on the right. Stoico, you play in the third seat of the second row on the left. Innis, you will play in the seventh seat in the fourth row from the right. Gueriere, you will play in the sixth seat in the tenth row on the right, etc.' until he had us all in position. Then he said, 'Now remember your positions.' Well fortunately, Chick didn't use a spread that day. If he had, we probably wouldn't have remembered where to play because there were no chairs on the field.... "

Stoico went on to Boston University on a full athletic scholarship and would return to Milford after graduation to teach and coach at Milford High. Pagnini would go on to Massachusetts State College (now University of Massachusetts) and return to coach St. Mary's and the Milford Legion baseball team. As coaches, both were successful, and both tried to emulate the Bronc. Pagnini finished his career in education as principal at Milford High. In later years, Acquafresca would become a player in Charlie's weekly poker games.

An emotional Joe Stoico told me on more than one occasion, "Your dad was a second father to me. I love him. He made me the athlete I became, and more than that, he made me a man. I would never have gone to college without him." I heard the same thing from Pagnini and many others.

When the football season ended, I was nearly four years old. Recently diagnosed with astigmatism, I was forced to wear glasses. That fact notwithstanding, my first and most favorite memories were of that 1950 football team. One of the strangest ones involved Stoico. I remember going into the kitchen of our tiny house and hearing a sound in the bathroom. The door was open, so I decided to look in. There, soaking in our tub, was Joe. He had probably pulled a muscle, and since there were no whirlpools, my father had taken it upon himself to treat his star player with moist heat.

I also remember my father bringing me to the high school before or after practice. Those were happy times for me. I would frolic with his players, and they would hand me the football and chase me around. I got to know and idolize his players. I always got to be on the sidelines during the games. This is where my love of sports took root.

Another memory from that time is not so humorous. I was a bit antsy as a kid. One day, I was chasing around and did something my father had drilled in me never to do. I ran into the street. When he saw me do this, he bolted into the street and gave me the first spanking I remember. As he was hitting me, he kept screaming, "I told you never to go into the street. I told you how dangerous that was. Don't you ever do that again."

One of his biggest and most irrational fears involved cars, which he honestly believed were instruments of danger. The crazy thing is that the road I ran into was not the heavily traveled East Main Street. It was Plain Street where it was rare to even see a car and if there were a car traveling down that street, it was so narrow and so short that the car could go no faster than a crawl. To me this was another incident which shows that my dad was dominated by the dread of someone he loved being hurt.

THE WINTER AND SPRING OF 1951 WERE WARMER THAN usual and a little damper. RCA television were selling for $239.00, though many Milfordians (including my family) did not own one. The Cold War had intensified, and the Korean War raged on. The front page of the local newspaper contained daily reports of each battle and any Milford area man who was either killed or wounded. On January 22, Milford was saddened when a report that one of its own, Anthony Ozella, had been badly wounded in Korea.[168] I was too young to remember, but I have to speculate that the war brought unpleasant memories back for my father, and as a thirty-five-year-old marine corps reserve officer and veteran of World War II, he had to be worried about a return to active duty.

There were also stories about war trials involving Nazi atrocities in World War II.

In a court in West Germany, Ilse Koch, the "Witch of Buchenwald," wife of the commandant of the Buchenwald concentration camp, was sentenced to life imprisonment. On a more cheerful note was the story

---

168 "Cpl. David Ozzella, Marine, is Badly Wounded in Korea," *Milford Daily News*, January 22, 1951.

of Joe Stoico being named most valuable player at a banquet to honor the football team.[169]

The Twenty-Second Amendment to the Constitution, limiting future presidents to two terms, was ratified in February. On February 19, in a front-page story titled "Twenty-Four Nabbed in Milford Raid," it was reported, "Police seized dice, playing cards, horse book slips, pool tables...."[170] Many of the same culprits were nabbed. Some people never learn. As a customer of the local bookies and a Sicilian from the wrong side of the tracks, my father never understood law enforcement's focus on what he considered a harmless vice. That said, he became increasingly vigilant and often had others make bets for him.

A new feature on the sports page of the *Daily News* was "My Greatest Sports Thrill," where local athletes from the past would describe their finest moment on the fields of play. On the same day as the report on the raid, Charlie wrote about his, which took place at Fitton Field in 1936 before nineteen thousand fans.

> The clock read about one minute playing time in the final quarter with the score tied 0-0 and our ball on (Carnegie) Tech's forty-three, fourth down and eight. Henry Oulette, the diminutive quarterback...called for a play we had been rehearsing for two weeks, the 'Fake Punt.' The team went into punt formation with Paul Massey, our punter, at tailback. He received the ball from center and went through the perfect motions of punting while handing the ball to me. A pair of blistering blocks from Bill Osmanski and Henry Ouellette shook me into the clear and down the sidelines to the three-yard line. On the next play, Oullette passed to O'Donnell for the score. The extra point was kicked, and Holy Cross won the game 7-0 about forty seconds before the final whistle.[171]

---

169 "Stoico Named Most Valuable Player at Milford High Football Banquet," *Milford Daily News*, January 26, 1951.

170 "24 Nabbed In Milford Raid," *Milford Daily News*, February 19, 1951.

171 Charles Brucato, "My Greatest Sports Thrill," *Milford Daily News*, February 19, 1951.

The local newspaper also started to publish pictures of retiring Draper Corporation employees. A photo of Charlie's father appeared on March 1 with the caption, "Joseph Brucato retires from Drapers after twenty-five years."[172] In that same month, Milford elected John J. Casey, William F. McAvoy, and Marco Balzarini as its selectmen. The Irish had its majority, and Attorney Anna O'Brien was appointed Town Counsel after Attorney Carney resigned to enter the army. Balzarini was pleased with the appointment as well. O'Brien's maiden name was Berardi.

During the winter and early spring, amateur boxing at the Town Hall auditorium drew boxers from all over the state to Milford. Local boxers Dick DeCapua and Ernie Tusino, both of whom who would later serve in the Korean War, distinguished themselves in the matches. In national news, the Senate Crime Committee began its hearings on organized crime with the appearance of mob leader Frank Costello.

At about the same time, Worcester County District Attorney Alfred B. Cenedella, a lifelong Milford resident, began his own assault on crime. In a front-page article titled "Cenedella Maps Out All Out War on Crime in This County," Cenedella boasted, "I'm satisfied that so far as slot machines and 'bookie' joints are concerned that Worcester and Worcester County are cleaner than they have ever been."[173]

Late in March, Charlie started spring football sessions with his high school team. He told the newspaper, "Tremendous all-around improvement...plenty of spirit...trouble for any opposing club."[174]

As April began, the headline in the *Milford Daily News* was "Death for Two Atom Spies—Rosenberg and Wife to Die."[175] Through all the national and local upheavals in the news, one thing remained sacred.

---

172 "Draper Men Retiring," *Milford Daily News*, March 1, 1951.

173 "Cenedella Maps Out All Out War on Crime in This County," *Milford Daily News*, March 29, 1951.

174 "Milford High Squad Steadily Improves in Scrimmages," *Milford Daily News*, March 29, 1951.

175 "Death for Two Atom Spies—Rosenberg and Wife to Die," *Milford Daily News*, April 5, 1951.

Baseball still endured as America's favorite sport, and while coaching spring football, Charlie called his baseball team out for tryouts. He would lead them to another great season. Captained by ace pitcher Bob Gilmore and led by slugging first baseman Joe "Lefty" Stoico, third baseman Jack Kelley, and shortstop Bob Pagnini, the team won ten games while losing only three. Joe Celozzi joined Gimore on the mound to form a potent one-two punch while Kelley batted .358 and Stoico .341 to lead the team in hitting.

They began the season by defeating Wellesley 6-1 with Gilmore hurling a two-hitter. They next suffered a 3-2 defeat at the hands of Clinton in a game that took only an hour and forty minutes to complete. Following that loss, they rattled off three straight wins, defeating Wellesley 9-4 with Celozzi pitching and Bob Whalen belting a three-run homer, Maynard 13-0, and Marlboro 15-5. Gilmore pitched a one-hit shutout in the game against Maynard, and in the Marboro game, Pagnini was five for five. They then lost to Franklin 2-1 before beating Maynard again 9-2, Hudson 8-0, and Marlboro 3-0. Gilmore pitched another one-hit shutout against Hudson and Celozzi pitched a three-hit shutout against Marlboro. Hudson then shut them out 4-0, and they beat Clinton 2-1 on a Bob Whalen hit in the last inning.

In the Town Series, they swept St. Mary's 10-1 and 9-0 with Celozzi pitching another shutout in the season finale. Unfortunately, the Midland League Championship was won by Hudson who also went on to win the State Small School championship. Freshmen pitchers Bob Stoico and Raphael "Lefty" Lumenti began what would become outstanding high school careers. Joe Stoico, Pagnini, and Gilmore were named to the Midland League All-Star team. Gilmore would go on to pitch in the minor leagues.

CONNIE'S SISTER ELEANOR, ONE OF CHARLIE'S FAVORITES, made news of her own that spring. In a front-page article with her picture titled, "Miss Oliva Graduates with Honors," it was reported that

Eleanor had graduated with honors from Modern School of Fashion and Design, and she had been unanimously selected by the faculty as Miss Modern of 1951.[176]

The headline on June 2 was "Arrest Eighteen In Milford Raids— Twelve Troopers, Local Police Take Action, All Men Plead Guilty."[177] Milford's reputation as a gambling town continued. But the major local news of the day came in July. District Attorney Cenedella became embroiled in a controversy which began with him making accusations of graft involving Uxbridge District Court Judge John Derham and an unnamed state official which led to the convening of a grand jury.

This caused such rancor that state officials called for Cenedella to resign. When he refused, Massachusetts Attorney General Francis E. Kelly moved to oust Cenedella from his position. The headline in the local paper on August 6 was "Strip Cenedella of Powers." In the article, it was reported that the attorney general had appointed Special Justice John J. Crehan to take over the Worcester County District Attorney's Office.[178] As these events were unfolding, Charlie was away training with the marine reserves in Virginia and had been promoted to the rank of major. The aftermath of the Cenedella controversy would have a major impact on him.

One of Charlie's favorite pastimes was playing poker with his friends, a passion he acquired many years earlier in the old neighborhood. He particularly enjoyed the weekly game at the Jewish Community House on Pine Street. On August 6, that card game was raided by the State Police. The report of the raid appeared on the first page of the local newspaper under the headline, "State Police Raid Card Game in Milford; Eight Arrested." The report identified Max Karelitz, Attorney Michael P. Visconti, Jack Auerbach, Irving Ferman, Philip Brilliant, Sidney Smith, and Myron Durenbaum as those arrested at the Jewish

---

176 "Miss Oliva Graduates with Honors," *Milford Daily News*, May 19, 1951.

177 "Arrest 18 In Milford Raids—12 Troopers, Local Police Take Action, All Men Plead Guilty," *Milford Daily News*, June 2, 1951.

178 "Strip Cenedella of Powers," *Milford Daily News*, August 6, 1951.

Community Center.[179] These were the same men he regularly played with, and Visconti was one of his best friends. Karelitz, Visconti, and Auerbach pleaded not guilty, and the others pleaded *nolo contendere.* Those with the *nolo* plea received fines, while the three others would go to trial.

In later years, my father explained to me why he and many others believed the State Police raided a "friendly poker game." It had to do with the enmity toward Cenedella. He said, "[Judge] Derham and [Attorney General] Kelly wanted to embarrass Cenedella by having the State Troopers conduct a gambling raid and arrest prominent citizens in his hometown. This was a punishment for Cenedella accusing Derham and Kelly of graft. It is as simple as that. The guys that got caught were good people. They were my friends. They were professional people and businessmen. Hell, I would have been at the game if I was not away at camp. Even your Uncle Nick enjoyed playing in that game. Imagine how your mother's family would feel if he were there that night."

Fortunately, the three who pleaded not guilty were tried and found not guilty by Milford District Court Judge Chester Williams. This did little, however, to remove the tarnish on their otherwise good names.

IN SEPTEMBER, CHARLIE RESUMED HIS DUTIES AS THE HEAD football coach at Milford High School. There were holes to fill with the graduation of star players Joe Stoico, Henry Acquafresca, and Dick Innis, but he had seen promise in spring practice. Bobby Pagnini would be back along with Captain Ed Castiglione, Nick DeRuvo, and Lou Guerriere. Mickey Kowalcyzk and Vinnie Liberto had caught his eye as well.

The Cenedella case was still front-page news. The headline on page one of the September 13 edition of the *Milford Daily News* was "Cenedella Case Tossed Into Lap of Mass. Supreme Court." The article

---

179 "State Police Raid Card Game In Milford; Eight Arrested," *Milford Daily News*, August 7, 1951.

reported, "In dispute is Cenedella's assertion that Judge Derham told him in August 1950 that he had $2,000.00 in his pocket and was on his way to Boston to pay it to Attorney General Kelly for the latter's assistance in settling a land damage case favorably for Derham's client."[180]

A few days later, a heavily favored Milford High football team was upset by Bartlett High 13-7 in the season opener. During the course of the contest, Johnny Mignone took the ball on a sixty-yard run to Bartlett's four-yard line, but Milford failed to score on four attempts. Charlie said, "We were woefully weak in blocking and tackling. We need plenty of work before the Clinton game."[181]

In the next game, Clinton shut out Milford 7-0 for its second straight loss. Stanley Jones detected the unrest among the team's followers and addressed it in an "open letter" to the players on not only the Milford High team but also those who played at St. Mary's. In the emotional letter, he told the boys to "ignore the criticism and have faith in your coaches."[182]

Jones' weekly op-ed column Speaking of Sports would become must reading for fans of local sports for decades. He was a talented writer, well-versed in the history of Milford sports and its impact on this diverse community. Unafraid to express his opinions, Stan's articles were both insightful and provocative. He was witty and warmhearted. Charlie trusted and admired him. Stan was probably the author of the reports of the games in the *Daily News*.

Milford High went on to defeat Shrewsbury 18-7 and then Franklin 26-6 before losing to Marlboro 21-0. In *Game Notes* after the Shrewsbury win, "it was a smiling Coach Charlie Brucato of Milford High speaking Saturday.... 'We got a few breaks towards the end,' he said, 'and the boys made them pay off. We didn't take advantage of the breaks in the other games, and the other teams did. This time it worked out for

180 "Cenedella Case Tossed Into Lap of Mass. Supreme Ct," *Milford Daily News*, September 13, 1951.

181 "Three Milford High Regulars May Miss Clinton Game," *Milford Daily News*, September 19, 1951.

182 Stanley Jones, Speaking of Sports, *Milford Daily News*, September 27, 1951.

1951 MILFORD HIGH SCHOOL FOOTBALL TEAM

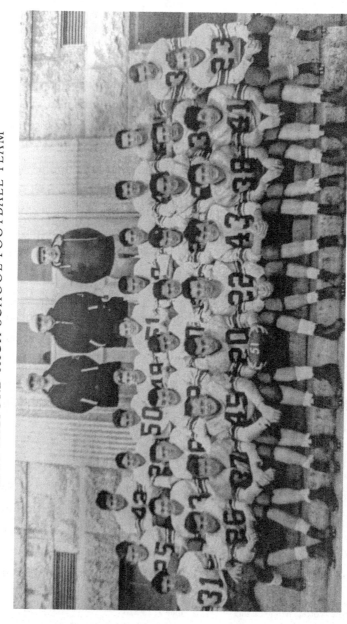

Top row, left to right: Coach Espanet, Head Coach Charlie Brucato, and Coach Calagione.
Front row: No. 41 Henry Aquafresca. Second row, seventh from the left: Bob Pagnini.

us.'"[183] The team beat Maynard 26-0, then lost to Hudson 19-6 and Stoughton 27-19. In the Thanksgiving Day game, they beat St. Mary's 27-7 to finish the season at 5-4.

During the season, Jones used his column to call upon high school administrators to give the sports teams an official name, saying, "Milford High teams have more names than Mexican blue bloods."[184] It was true. Through the years, the writers had referred to the teams using the coaches' names ("Brucatomen," "Cahillmen") or "the red and white" or some combination of both. When Milford High scheduled a banquet for its football team, he called upon St. Mary's fans to do the same for its team. They complied.

Jones also used one of his columns to address the poor officiating in the Hudson game that Charlie had complained about. "Gripes about officiating are common for a loser.... Not from Coach Brucato though.... Seldom have we heard the Bronc criticize the work of an official...."[185] His implication was clear.

Stan did not limit the scope of his reporting to high school sports. When Rocky Marciano knocked out Joe Louis at Boston Garden, he was there and wrote an exciting account of the match while *Daily News.* Editor Nick Tosches provided photos taken at ringside. For the benefit of his Milford audience, he took pains to say that Rocky's real surname was Marchegiano.[186]

———————

AS THE CALENDAR TURNED TO 1952, NEITHER THE COLD WAR nor the Korean War had abated. With the presidential election looming in November, World War II's commander of Allied forces General Dwight D. Eisenhower dipped his feet into the political waters. In England, King George VI died on February 6, and Princess Elizabeth,

———————

183 "Game Notes," *Milford Daily News,* October 1, 1951.
184 Stanley Jones, Speaking of Sports, *Milford Daily News,* October 11, 1951.
185 Stanley Jones, Speaking of Sports, *Milford Daily News,* October 23, 1951.
186 Stanley Jones, "Infighting Hurt Joe Before KO," *Milford Daily News,* October 27, 1951.

Duchess of Edinburgh assumed the throne as Queen Elizabeth II. A massive snowstorm hit Milford on February 18, crippling the town with snow drifts of four feet. In March, the Progressive Citizens (Balzarini, Visconti, and Bellantuonio) were reelected as the town's selectmen, and they appointed Attorney Nathan Rosenfeld, a Jewish attorney, as Town Counsel. Things certainly had changed for the better.

Charlie gathered his football team for spring practice on March 20. Due to the weather, the sessions were initially held at tiny John C. Lynch Auditorium at Milford High School. Fortunately, the team was able to practice outdoors five days later. The big local sports news, however, was the formation of a committee to bring Little League baseball to Milford. Charlie, St. Mary's coach Albert "Chick" Sayles, Legion coach Christopher "Pep" Morcone, and Milford High coach Charlie Espanet became key people in the quest and agreed to manage teams in the league.

Jones eloquently lamented the demise of the Blackstone Valley League while extolling the virtues of the new Little League endeavor. "Blackstone Valley baseball is buried deep in the miseries of the textile industry...and will call it quits in the next two weeks."[187] "The players selection system [in the Little League] helps erase foolish prejudices that do, although we should all feel do not, become rooted in a young boy and are carried into later life.... The Catholic and the Protestant and the Jewish boys, the Italian and the Irish and the Armenian boys are brought together to play side by side on one team and are judged on their baseball ability and not on their faiths and nationalities...."[188]

Following the exciting news of a Milford Little League was the somber news that St. Mary's had dropped football. There would be no intown rivalry with Milford High on Thanksgiving Day for many years. (St. Mary's would resume its football program several years later.)

The high school baseball season started later than usual, and pitching became the major issue in the Midland League according to Jones.

187 Stanley Jones, Speaking of Sports, *Milford Daily News*, April 1, 1952.
188 Stanley Jones, Speaking of Sports, *Milford Daily News*, April 4, 1952.

"Take the case of Charlie Brucato of Milford High for instance.... The league's winningest baseball skipper has constructed his staff around two sophomores, Bob Stoico and Ralph Lumenti, and one senior, Humphry Germagian.... As for the future, Brucato has every reason to grin inwardly.... Stoico and Lumenti, both well advanced for sophomores, are coming back for two more years."[189]

On another front, the Cenedella controversy came to an end with the disbarment of Judge Derham and his resignation from the judgeship in Uxbridge. Cenedella and Kelly survived the inquiry into their conduct in the matter.

The Milford High baseball season began in early May, and it was one of Charlie's finest. After losing the opener to Clinton 11-9 in an error filled game, the team rattled off six straight wins. They beat Maynard 4-2 in eleven innings with Bob Stoico going the distance and Joey Alves driving in the winning run. Stoico then shut out Marlboro in a three-hit complete game performance. Pagnini got three hits in a 4-2 win over Wellesley, and Lumenti pitched a one-hit shutout to beat Franklin 2-0. He lost his no-hitter with two outs in the ninth inning.

In his weekly article, Jones provided an interesting sidelight to Lumenti's performance. "Coach Charlie Brucato of Milford High told us this one coming home from Franklin last week.... Early in the day, he had been asked by Phil Brilliant, local merchant, about his starting pitcher that afternoon.... 'I'm using Lumenti,' said the Bronc.... 'Yes I know the boy,' beamed Brilliant, 'and I hope he pitches a no-hitter.'"[190]

Stoico followed up with a four hitter, and his teammates provided excellent support in a 12-3 romp over Maynard. In the next game, Milford came back three times to beat Hudson 8-7. Pagnini's bases loaded hit sealed the win.

After that game Jones, in his inimitable fashion, wrote the following:

---

189 Stanley Jones, Speaking of Sports, *Milford Daily News*, May 2, 1952.
190 "Milford Little League Managers Submit Player Rosters," *Milford Daily News*, May 13, 1952.

Coach Charlie Brucato of Milford High is at it again.... The man whose schoolboy bat once helped 'Hop' Riopel to sleep nights and whose coaching is reminiscent of the great man has come up with another winning combination.... Strategy, hustle, and alertness, all common house hold words with the Bronc, have catapulted the Scarlets off on a six game winning streak, and a six game winning streak is particularly astonishing for a club that shaped up as only a fair unit last month.... Hustle, a 'must' with Brucato, the players will tell you, has elevated Milford High to the Midland League penthouse, and this same hustle has branded them favorites to win the league title.

Brucato's baseball coaching record over a six-year period is sixty-one wins, sixteen losses, and two ties.... They say material is 75 percent of this schoolboy coaching game while coaching is only 25 percent.... Having watched Brucato crack the whip over a period of years, we would say it is fifty-fifty in this case.... He runs the whole show, and you would have to sit on the bench to see the goings-on.... Few of his players become lax, for laxity is something Brucato holds intolerable.... At the end of a game, he is as weary as anyone on the field...."[191]

Milford's streak was stopped in a 5-2 loss to Hudson, but they finished the season by beating Clinton 7-0 on a Germagian one-hitter, sweeping the Town Series 8-0 and 16-1, trouncing Marlboro 16-4, and winning the Midland League title by beating Clinton 7-2 in a special playoff game. In what many considered a snub, they were not selected for the postseason tournament, and Pagnini was the only player named to the All-Star team.

After beating Clinton, the players were ecstatic on the bus ride home. Jones reported, "A championship victory would naturally touch off a celebration, but we have never seen a Scarlet group so excited about winning a title and that goes back six years.... Usually, the clatter

191 Stanley Jones, Speaking of Sports, *Milford Daily News*, May 20, 1952.

subsides after five or ten minutes, but this excited group tinkered with laryngitis until the bus reached its Spruce Street destination.... 'Did you ever see such spirit?' asked Brucato.... 'This was one of my best-balanced ball clubs.... Look at that line-up—speed, hitting, defense.... These kids had guts, too, always in there plugging.... I think they learned something out of this...You've got to hustle in this game—or in any profession for that matter.... '"[192]

As the high school season progressed, the Milford Little League also flourished. There were four teams each named for its sponsor. The teams were the VFW sponsored by the Veterans of Foreign Wars post, the Eagles sponsored by the local Eagles Lodge, Davorens sponsored by Davoren's Pharmacy, and Sabatinellis sponsored by a local contractor.

Charlie resigned as manager of one of the Little League teams but was appointed as a player agent and was charged with the responsibility of organizing tryouts from which the players would be selected. Not everyone who tried out made the teams. The teams played fifteen games, and after the season an All-Star team was selected to compete in the Little League tournament.

One of the best things about the *Milford Daily News* was its long-standing custom of covering all local teams in all sports. This included not only varsity teams, but JV teams, Junior High teams, and even playground teams. Readers could follow the players from grade school through college. They published accounts of the games, statistics, and even box scores.

The paper treated the Little League games the same way. Every game was reported and every box score published. Boys between the ages of nine and twelve saw their names in headlines when they hit home runs or pitched great games. At the end of the season, all players batting averages were listed. I remember vividly that in my first year in the league, I was 0-4 and the next year I was 4-16, which is why my dad made me a pitcher.

---

192 "Milford Wins Flag With 7-2 Victory Over Clinton," *Milford Daily News*, June 12, 1952.

When the high school season ended, the Junior Legion season began, and the Little League continued its schedule. The Milford Legion team could select players from nearby towns though most either played at Milford High or St. Mary's. Pagnini, Alves, Lumenti and Stoico became key figures in what would be Milford's most successful team in the history of the program to date. During the summer, the Legion team captivated the town by winning the league, state, regional, and Eastern US titles, qualifying the team to play in the tournament for the national title held in Denver, Colorado. Many Milfordians followed the team to every game, and those who did not listened to the games on the radio. When the team lost two games in Denver, they returned home and were cheered by ten thousand as they were paraded through town.

A SHORT TIME BEFORE SCHOOL WAS TO BEGIN IN THE FALL of 1952, Lou Noferi and his father paid a visit to Charlie at the tiny house at 83 East Main Street. Lou, who was from Hopedale, was about to start his sophomore year at St. Mary's and was looking forward to playing football. As a matter of fact, the reason he went to St. Mary's instead of Hopedale High was because Hopedale did not have a football team. When football was discontinued at St. Mary's, he convinced his father to take him to see Charlie and ask if he could go to Milford High to play.

At the time, Lou was about 5'4" tall and weighed 120 pounds.

Charlie looked at him and said to his father, "I think your kid should go back to St. Mary's."

The two left the house, but Lou was determined.

On the first day of school, he took a bus to Milford, walked into the principal's office, and said, "Here I am."

Charlie was there when Lou arrived, and he told the principal, "Let the kid stay."

It was a good decision for Lou and for Milford High.

Now eighty-four, Lou described how that visit affected his life in a letter to me. "I think how fortunate I was to have my life intersect with your dad's in the fall of 1952."

He met his wife at Milford High, was able to play football, which he excelled at, and baseball. Lou went on to play football at Dean Junior College and later at the University of Connecticut. He is in the Dean Hall of Fame. After college, he went to law school and practiced law in Milford for over forty years.

Shortly after the start of school, one of the teachers who taught chemistry and math at Milford High resigned. With virtually no time to find a replacement, the school committee decided to have then principal Joseph Tosches assume the duties of the teacher who left and appointed Charlie as "temporary acting principal." At thirty-six years old, Charlie's plate was full. He was the acting principal, athletic director, and head coach of both football and baseball.

The 1952 football team would prove to be one of his best. The backfield was formidable with Bob Stoico at quarterback, Bob Pagnini and Warren Larson at the halfback positions, and hard-nosed Joe Grillo at fullback. Carlos Curral, Charlie Ramelli, and Frank Gandolfi anchored the line with sophomore Joe Arcudi at one end and Ronnie Brown at the other.

The season got off to a terrible start with the team losing to Clinton 12-0 in the rain. After the game, Charlie told the local paper that poor blocking was a major cause in the defeat. "'It was our weakest point,' said Brucato as he moved out to work with the squad. 'We just didn't have any blocking at all.'"[193] The team worked on it all week and it paid off. They humiliated Marlboro in the next game. The headline of the report of the game was "Sharp Blocking Milford High Astonishes Marlboro 55-6."[194] Grillo, Pagnini, and Larson each had two touchdowns.

---

193 "Milford High Drops Opener to Clinton in Drizzle, 12-0," *Milford Daily News*, September 30, 1952.

194 "Sharp Blocking Milford High Astonishes Marlboro 55-6," *Milford Daily News*, October 14, 1952.

After tying Maynard 6-6 and losing to a powerful Hudson team 19-0, they ran off four straight wins to finish the season at 5-2-1. In those games, they defeated Franklin 15-0, Bartlett 19-12, Stoughton 34-7, and St. Bernard's 34-7 on Thanksgiving Day. In the Bartlett game, Grillo scored all three touchdowns. Pagnini scored three touchdowns in the Stoughton game and two more in the turkey day game. Frank Gandolfi was named to the Midland League All-Star first team and Curral, Ramelli, Stoico, Pagnini, and Grillo were named as second teamers.

Arcudi, who would go on to play football at the University of Richmond, had an interesting story about one of his first experiences with Charlie on the field. "We were scrimmaging, and after watching me, the Bronc took me aside. He said to me, 'Arcudi, you can be a good player if you just don't think. When you think, you don't do very well. So, if you want to play for me, *don't think!*'"

Vinnie Liberto, who was related to Charlie and lived in the same house for a time, was also a sophomore on the team. He said, "The Bronc was hard on me both in school and on the field. He would tuck his tongue under his lip and growl, 'Jesus Christ, Liberto, what the hell is the matter with you? Are you stupid?' One day, me and the other players got even with him. Every season, the Bronc would put the pads on and scrimmage with us. When he did this with our team, each time he carried the ball, we would gang tackle him and hit him as hard as we could." After graduation, Liberto became a Milford police officer and later chief of police.

THE YEAR 1953 WOULD BE A MOMENTOUS ONE. THE COLD War and threat of nuclear extinction weighed heavily on the nation's psyche. Air raid drills were conducted at schools and townwide and many citizens began to construct bomb shelters. In national news, General Fulgencio Batista re-took power in Cuba in a deadly coup, and the world was stunned to learn of the death of Joseph Stalin from a massive stroke. The Korean War raged on, seemingly never ending.

General Dwight D. Eisenhower, who had won an intense presidential campaign against Adlai I. Stevenson, was inaugurated as the first Republican president in many years. The Republicans had majorities in both the Senate and House of Representatives. Good news came when the United States treaty with Japan was ratified. The country was also heartened with the news of the discovery of a polio vaccine by Jonas Salk. Locally during the long cold winter, Milford began mapping out plans for a municipal swimming pool near Fino Field. Televisions were now common in households throughout the country. *I Love Lucy* was the most popular show.

Brother John's family continued to grow as his children began to marry and have families of their own. The visits to Stamford were often for weddings or other family events.

At the football banquet in January, "Coach Brucato declared that football players are not born but are made on the practice field. He said that many of his players were good students despite the time involved in preparation."[195] It would be Charlie's last banquet as head football coach.

As April began, excitement was building about the Milford High baseball team. Lumenti and Stoico, now juniors along with Pagnini and Alves, had proved they could excel under pressure with last year's successes both with the championship high school team and the incredible run to the nationals with the Legion team. Sophomores Jim Marcello, Gardie Rett, Lou Noferi, and Joe Arcudi provided added talent to an already stacked team.

Early on Charlie made the decision to have Rett be the team's catcher and put Arcudi at third base. This did not sit well with Rett, who had always played third. Rett and his father met with Charlie to complain but got nowhere.

"Either he catches, or he doesn't play at all," Charlie told them in no uncertain terms.

Rett seamlessly converted to catcher and would quickly become one of the best backstops in the state.

---

195 "Milford High Football Team Feted By Sons of Italy Lodge," *Milford Daily News,* January 30, 1953.

In the opening game, Milford High beat Clinton 2-1 in eleven innings with Rett catching, Arcudi at third, and Marcello in center. After suffering a loss to Wellesley 4-2, they rattled off ten consecutive wins. Stoico tossed a no-hitter to beat Maynard 8-0 with Rett and Pagnini providing the offense. They trounced Marlboro 16-2 and Lumenti pitched a no-hitter against Maynard in a 12-0 win making him the second Milford pitcher to no-hit Maynard. Lumenti allowed only two runners to reach base in the game.

They next beat Marlboro 8-0 in a game where Stoico allowed only one hit and Framingham 8-0 in a two-hitter by Lumenti. Hudson then fell 4-1 on a Stoico two-hitter, and Clinton got only one hit off Stoico in a 9-0 game which clinched the Midland League title. Franklin then fell 12-0 in another Lumenti shutout.

In world news, during May, Sir Edmund Hillary from New Zealand and Tenzing Norgay from Nepal became the first men to reach the summit of Mount Everest. The most celebrated event, though, occurred on June 2 when Elizabeth II was crowned Queen of England at Westminster Abbey.

The first game of the annual town series was played on Memorial Day, as always, and Milford dispatched St. Mary's 6-1. In the next game, Stoico pitched and batted Milford to a 7-4 win over Braintree. After twelve games, the team was 11-1. Pagnini was leading the team in hitting at .368 with Rett (.326), Alves (.308), and Stoico (.286) following. Arcudi led the team with thirteen runs batted in (RBI). Remarkably, over sixty-one innings, Stoico had allowed only two earned runs, and in forty-one and one-third, Lumenti had allowed only four.

In the state tournament, Milford defeated Malden Catholic 3-1 at Fenway Park. The highlight of the game came when Gardie Rett became the first schoolboy ever to homer over the high leftfield wall (known as "the Green Monster") with a 365-foot blast into the net. Milford next beat Dorchester 8-7 to earn a place in the finals against a strong Concord High team at Fenway.

In the game against Concord, Milford was able to squeak out a 2-1win but not without drama. Concord loaded the bases with two outs in the ninth inning. Lumenti was pitching, and Charlie went to the mound and asked him if he was tired. After he walked away, Lefty struck the next batter out.

Charlie told the local paper later, "'He had spunk, that kid. He looked at me and said 'No, Coach, I'm not tired. Don't worry, I think I can get the next hitter.' I told him I thought he could, too, and he did. He came through as I thought he would.'"[196]

Bobby Pagnini had a different account of that mound meeting many years later when he was making a speech at a banquet to honor his old coach. "Charlie was quite a hummer. Still does it today. Whenever he is doing some thinking he starts humming.... We were leading 2-1 in the last of the ninth inning and Concord had the bases loaded. Lefty Lumenti was pitching, and the count went to 3-2 on the hitter. Charlie called time and went to the mound to settle Lefty down and then went back to the dugout. Lefty struck the batter out on the next pitch to win the game and the tournament.

"After the game, Stanley Jones [sportswriter] asked Charlie what he had said to Lefty to settle him down because it had obviously worked. Charlie said that he told Lefty that it was just another game. 'If we win, we win; if we lose, we lose. Don't worry about it. You're a good pitcher. Just get it over.' So later, Stanley asked Lefty to follow up on what the coach said. Lefty had a completely different version of it, and he said Charlie wasn't humming."

After the Concord game, Milford beat St. Mary's 15-3 to sweep the Town Series. The season came to an end when the team lost to Holyoke, the Western Massachusetts Champ, in the state finals. The 1953 season was one of the best at Milford High. It also was the seventh season in a row with a championship under Charlie. Pagnini led the team in hitting with a .351 average followed by Tony DeLuzio (.308), Rett (.300),

---

196 "Milford Wins Eastern State Title, Defeats Concord 3-1," *Milford Daily News*, June 8, 1953.

and Alves (.277). Rett drove in a team leading seventeen runs followed by Arcudi and Stoico who drove in fourteen each. Stoico posted a 1.10 earned run average (ERA) and struck out ninety-seven while walking only twenty-four. Lumenti posted a 1.13 ERA with seventy-four strike-outs and twenty-five walks.

When the season ended, Charlie was asked to write a story about the team for *the Milford Daily News.*

> I attribute the success of the Milford High school baseball team mainly to the coordinated efforts of its members. They learned initially to play for the good of the team and the school, and soon they learned a supreme effort from each was necessary to ensure a successful season.
>
> I explained that the proper hustle, heads-up play, and love for the game were musts in winning baseball games, and that even though the haul was long and the pull heavy, that with proper character, no haul was too long nor any pull too heavy.
>
> The boys who represented the 1953 team are a fine group.

Charlie then went on to name each player and describe the importance he had to the team's success. Gardie Rett "improved steadily" and "appears destined for baseball greatness." Matt Berardi, who fought through injury, was "an inspiration to the team." Joey Alves "is always under control" and a "natural leader." Bobby Pagnini was the team's "old pro." Joe Arcudi was "the team's most consistent hitter" in the so-called "clutch."

"Raphael Lumenti and Bob Stoico go down in my book as the best pitching staff in the entire baseball history of Milford High." Outfielders Tony DeLuzio, Jimmy Marcello, Henry Covino, and Eddie Costello "each have taken turns for hero roles in many contests."

"I feel a deep respect for the players who haven't experienced too much action in games, but whom I consider just as important." He went on to name Manoog Manoogian, Ronnie Brown, Vin Liberto, Lou Noferi, Ed Russciti, Larry Bonetti, and Dick Manguso and declared

Bob Stoico and Charlie

they "were all necessary in the molding of a championship array." He named the manager Charlie Calcagni, "who asked for no reward but to be with and help the players."

In his concluding remarks, Charlie gave a glimpse of what he believed to be the real importance of sports.

> Anyone who has spent many hours perfecting the fundamentals of baseball has acquired a habit that will make it easier to devote many more hours to mastering the fundamentals of good living. They will make better Americans since they know that they can achieve success if they are willing to work for it.
>
> I have been the recipient of many compliments during the season just past, but the one that stands out above all others came

Raphael "Lefty" Lumenti

following the final game with Concord in the Red Sox dressing room. I approached and asked the two clubhouse boys why they had rooted so hard for Milford since the start of the series. Their reply was: 'They are a nice group of boys, and they play so awfully hard.' I cannot think of a better tribute two strangers could have given to any team.'" [197]

The tales about Charlie and the players during the season are almost as amazing as what they accomplished. As good a coach as Charlie was, he had his idiosyncrasies. As good as the players were, many can only be described as characters.

---

197 Charles J. Brucato, "Brucato Rates Stoico— Lumenti Best in School's History," *Milford Daily News*, June 11, 1953.

Stan Jones told me that he had an interesting relationship with my dad. "I was covering the games for the newspaper, and so I would ride on the bus with the team and sit on the bench with my scorebook. The Bronc was paranoid about the opposing coaches stealing his signs. He approached me one day and said, 'Stan, I want you to give the signs to the boys. I'll tell you what I want, and the boys will look at you for the signs.' I said, 'Jesus, Charlie, I'm a reporter, not a coach. I'm supposed to be neutral.' He said, 'Bullshit, you are going to do it.' And that was that. He simply would not take no for an answer, so I did it."

Sitting on the bench gave Stan a unique insight into Charlie's coaching style. "No one, not even the players, worked as hard as the Bronc during a game. He was exhausted when the last out was made. While he could forgive physical errors, mental mistakes made him crazy, and if a boy did not hustle, he would get an earful. He never showed the kid up. He would take the boy aside and quietly growl at them with his tongue under his lip. And his look was like a death stare. Every player could imitate him.

"As he sat humming away on the bench, you could see the wheels turning in his head. He saw everything, and he was quick with an adjustment or a change of strategy to fit each situation. In the Concord game, Stoico was playing in the outfield and made a great catch of a fly ball to save runs from scoring. Charlie had repositioned him just before the catch and that was why Bobby was able to get the ball.

"He knew the rule book by heart and his arguments with umpires were something else. He never backed down."

The stories about Jimmy Marcello, the sophomore speedster, are also legendary. In one game, Jimmy was on first and Charlie (or Stan) gave him the steal sign, and he apparently missed it because he did not run. This happened two more times. Finally, Charlie got up from the bench and screamed, "Marcello! Steal!" Jimmy was so fast that, even knowing he was going to steal, the catcher was unable to throw him out.

Fellow sophomore Joe Arcudi related a story about Jimmy when the team was playing at Fenway Park. "The Bronc had left the field while

1952 CHAMPION BASEBALL TEAM

First row: Ralph Lumenti, Henry Covino, Eddy Costello, Matteo Berardi, Joe Alves, Bob Pagnini, Ronald Brown, Bob Stoico, Pete Piscia.
Second row: Eddy Ruscitti, Manoog Manoogian, Lou Noferi, Coach Brucato, Anthony DeLuzio, Alfred Tomaso, Gardner Rett.
Third row: Robert Mancuso, Lawrence Bonetti, Vincent Liberto, Joe Arcudi, James Martello.

we were warming up. Jimmy went over, got the bag of balls we used for practice, and from second base, he started hitting the balls into the net over the celebrated thirty-seven-foot high left field wall [now referred to as the Green Monster]. When Charlie came out for infield practice, he noticed that the ball bag was virtually empty. 'Where the hell are the baseballs?' the coach yelled. When he found out what Jimmy had done, he went nuts. 'What the hell is wrong with you, Marcello? How can you be so goddamn stupid? I want you to climb that wall and get the balls out of the net.' Obviously, that was not possible, so the Bronc just shook his head and mumbled to himself."

Vinnie Liberto told the story of the time in the season when he and Charlie's other cousin on the team, Alfie Tomaso, either skipped school or missed practice. "The Bronc suspended us and wouldn't let us practice or play in the next game. When our parents pleaded with him to let us play, he told them, 'These boys need to learn a lesson, especially since the other boys know they are related to me.'"

Henry "Hank" Covino, who played the outfield, said, "I always seemed to do the wrong thing at the wrong time. I pissed Coach off more than any other guy on the team. He was a great coach, but he was tough. If he was upset, you didn't want to mess with him. He would get an inch from your face and had a way of talking through his teeth without opening his mouth.

"I was up at bat in a game against Burlington. The pitcher knocked me down with an inside fastball. I gestured to the ump that the ball hit me, but the ump said it didn't. Coach got off the bench and trotted over to home plate to argue that I was hit and should go to first base. Foolishly, I opened my big mouth and told him it didn't hit me. That ended the argument, and I struck out. I could see him looking at me as I came back to the bench. He followed me. I knew I was in for it. He got right up in my face, muttering through his teeth, 'Covino, if you ever think you got hit, lay on the ground like you're dead ....and don't ever do that to me again!'

"In a close game against Wellesley, Bobby Pagnini was on second base," Covino continued. "Coach Brucato called a timeout. He signaled for me to come off the bench and told me to go coach third base and send Pagnini home on a base hit. The next batter was Joey Alves who lined a single to left. Knowing that Bobby would never beat the throw to home, I put up the stop sign to hold him on third base. Bobby ran right through the sign and was out by about twenty feet.

"We lost the game, and Coach was especially pissed off about Pagnini getting tagged out at home. In the locker room he turned to me and said, 'Covino, what the hell were you thinking sending Bobby home?' I answered, 'Coach, I gave him the stop sign.' He then turned to Bob and asked him if he ran through the stop sign. He admitted that he did, so Coach turned back to me and yelled, 'If that ever happens again, tackle him!'"

CHAPTER TEN

TRANSITIONING

AFTER THE BASEBALL SEASON, CHARLIE LEARNED THAT the school committee was seeking an assistant principal for Milford High School, a position that hadn't been filled in six years. He mulled it over in his mind and decided to apply for the position. He felt he had the inside track because Connie's Uncle Nick and her future brother-in-law Anthony "Cubba" Compagnone were both on the committee. Charlie went to see them, told them his intentions, and asked for their support. He was both shocked and furious by their response.

"We don't think you are ready," they told him.

With his patented tongue under his lip, he growled, "Are you shitting me? I'll tell you what. I am ready, and I am going to get that goddamn job with or without your support. I'll get the four votes I need, mark my words."

Shortly thereafter, he visited his friend Ernie Lombardi, who was also on the committee, and together they "schemed" a way to get the necessary votes without Uncle Nick's or Cubba's.

At the school committee on June 25, 1953, Charlie received the necessary votes and was appointed assistant principal. The committee also reappointed him as athletic director and director of physical education and relieved him of his coaching duties. He had known beforehand that he would have to give up coaching if he was to be assistant principal. He was obviously willing to do this. One can only speculate why.

Perhaps he was looking for more in his career since he never truly valued a lifetime in sports. He had walked away from professional baseball after all. He referred to those who were lifers in sports "jockstraps" who couldn't do anything else. Perhaps there was simply nothing more he wanted to accomplish in athletics. He had never aspired to coach at the college or professional level.

Perhaps the years of coaching had taken a toll on him. Ever the perfectionist, when his teams lost, he was devastated and consumed by planning ways to improve. Winning on the other hand was never enough. There was always the next game to prepare for. At home, he was a bear when his teams lost, and it was not much better when he won. He would sit on the couch every night scheming ways to beat the next opponent.

Connie was always wary of his mood swings. Often, she was the target of his impatience and anger. Sometimes he even took it out on my sister and me. When he returned home from a game, my mother would have me look out the window as he got out of the car and tell her how he looked so she could prepare herself. It was easy for me to read him. If he lost, his head was down and his expression pained. When he won, he was upbeat and sometimes even smiling, which was a rarity for him. It was a roller coaster life at 83 East Main Street, and it was a good thing that his teams rarely lost. Additionally, Connie was pregnant with their third child which would mean more responsibilities at home.

At thirty-seven, Charlie's brilliant coaching career was over. He would leave behind some exceptional athletes with high school eligibility remaining. Rett, Lumenti, Arcudi, Noferi, and Stoico would only get better. Lumenti would receive a $35,000.00 bonus after college and pitch in the major leagues. Rett and Stoico would go on to play in the minor leagues, and Arcudi and Noferi would play major college football. Through the years, these men always credited Charlie with making them good athletes and teaching them to be good men.

––––––––––

THE SUMMER OF 1953 WAS ONE OF THE HOTTEST EVER, AND in June, a deadly tornado struck the City of Worcester. The Milford Legion team led by Stoico, Lumenti, Rett, Pagnini, Arcudi, Marcello, and Alves once again zipped through the state and regional tournaments and advanced to the National Legion Finals in Miami, Florida, much to the delight of the adoring Milford fandom. The Korean War had finally come to an end and, though the Cold War continued, the country was finally free from an armed conflict.

When the school year began in September of 1953, Charlie started what would be an eighteen-year tenure as assistant principal at Milford High. Why he chose this over coaching was puzzling to many townspeople, who believed he was still young, healthy, and at the peak of his game. The athletes he left behind were among the best in the school's history. He had nurtured them along the way in physical education class, Little League, and high school. He had instilled in them a winning attitude. It was now time to reap the benefits. Instead, he had walked away. He exchanged his whistle and coaching clothes for a suit and tie. Maybe he felt that he had nothing left to prove.

It is not as though he was using the assistant principal job as a steppingstone to become principal or superintendent. He wanted no part of those jobs. Joe Tosches was his good friend and was deeply entrenched in the principal position. His friend Dave Davoren was still the superintendent. It is more likely that he viewed a career in sports as something unimportant in the greater scheme of life.

Athletics had its place in education, but success in the classroom was much more important to him. He never understood why athletes or coaches were revered and given elevated status. He never encouraged any of his children to be like him. We heard him ask us repeatedly, "Why would you want to be a jockstrap?" I think he regretted not studying harder and not aspiring to do something more. He often told us that professional baseball was a "horseshit career." It was as if he was embarrassed that his life was defined by his athletic prowess and not his intellect.

The assistant principal job was somewhat prestigious, but it was also unfulfilling. Charlie's major responsibility was discipline, and though he excelled in that area, it simply was not satisfying either emotionally or intellectually. Additionally, since he was no longer coaching, his afternoons and evenings were free, and idle time was not a good thing for him. He was restless and uncomfortable at home and always trying to find something to do. He rarely did anything around the house or with his kids. He played poker at least twice a week and was at the racetrack on many other days. It seemed like he was never home.

When Charlie was at home, he had nothing to occupy himself with. He would sit at the end of the couch deep in thought smoking cigarette after cigarette. He never revealed what he was thinking about, but his expression was usually troubled. He continued to find life in the Mastroianni-Oliva commune on East Main Street stifling.

On the days that he was not at the track or playing poker, he would hang out with Sooey, Sammy, Tate, Mike Visconti, or other buddies. A popular haunt was Rizoli's Drug Store a couple of blocks up East Main Street. Louis "Burkie" Rizoli was a pharmacist and local political maven. The men loved to gather there and gossip about the goings on in town while enjoying a milkshake or an ice-cream cone. (At that time, pharmacies were not like they are today. Most of them had soda counters with stools where people could enjoy a coffee or Coke, order a sandwich, and discuss the events of the day.)

Since he held a respectable position in town, Charlie was cautious about how the townspeople perceived him. He always wore a conservative suit and tie, and he always had a serious demeanor in public. He carried with him the memory of how he and his Italian friends were treated by the Yanks and Irish in the past, and he was apprehensive that they still did not regard him with the respect he felt he earned.

Throughout our lives, he would always tell us not to share our feelings with anyone and never do anything to embarrass the family.

He did not want anyone to know his vices. He would go to great lengths to hide his fondness for poker and the racetrack. When he and his friends went to the track, he would arrange to meet them at secret locations and sneak out of town in one or the others' car for the trip to Rockingham or Suffolk Downs. There were also Charlie's surreptitious encounters with the town's bookies where he would bet on the numbers, or horses.

I remember him driving me over to local bookie "Skeezer's" house to either deliver the plays or pick up winnings. He would always be looking around to make sure that no one was watching. We were never to reveal his habits to anyone. Everything was a family secret. He also tried to keep us in the dark about certain things. I remember a middle-aged man around who was always well dressed in a dark suit and tie. Everyone called him Doc, so my cousin Pete and I thought he was a doctor. When we had the temerity to ask our parents about him, the answer was "mind your own business." We learned much later that Doc ran the numbers racket in town. (In the numbers game, a bettor would pick a three- or four-digit number and bet anywhere from a quarter to ten dollars on it. The daily number was always a specific column of digits in a certain racetrack's report of its gambling receipts which were published in the newspaper. The payoff odds were set at six hundred to one. State lotteries would replace the numbers racket in later years, but the odds of winning were much longer.)

Charlie was truly unique in many ways. Though he was well educated and polished, he never forgot where he came from, never forgot his friends, and never shed his bad habits, street smarts, or the hard life lessons he learned in the Plains. These attributes made him a folk hero in the Italian community. They were proud of all he had accomplished and prouder that he remained one of them.

———————————

CHARLIE ACCLIMATED HIMSELF TO HIS NEW JOB ALMOST immediately and established a reputation for toughness that would continue until he retired. Students were fearful of incurring his wrath. Many trembled and even cried when a teacher sent them to his office to answer for some wrongdoing. He was equally hard on the teachers. The stories about him are almost as legendary as those from his playing and coaching days. He would never hesitate to suspend or expel a student if the offense were significant.

When a relative or a friend's kid was sent to him for wrongdoing, he had unique ways of handling the situation. He would close the door, shove the kid into a chair, and scream at him, sometimes using "color-ful" language to make his point. He knew that the parents would not complain, especially the Italians. Unlike today, this was a time when parents were supportive of educators, and if their children misbehaved, there would be hell to pay and they knew it.

He was particularly hard on the athletes, although if they were needed for a game, suspension was out of the question. The athletes' punishments would be worse than that. Their parents would be called in. On more than one occasion, when a parent did come in and heard what his son had done, the parent would slap the kid in the face right in front of Charlie.

One would think that since he was no longer coaching, he would spend more time with his kids, but this was not the case. When we lived in the Mastroianni-Oliva commune, my father did not spend much time with us and rarely gave me any coaching. He had learned athletics from the older kids in the neighborhood and had honed his skills on his own. It was clear early on that he expected his kids to do the same thing.

I believe that the last thing he wanted was for us to be like him. He envisioned my future as a doctor or dentist or other type of pro-fessional person. He constantly stressed that getting good grades in school was much more important than being a good athlete. I think he was embarrassed that he was not a good student until he got to college. Furthermore, he had had an outstanding career in sports and, unlike others, did not have the need to live his life through me or my brothers.

He probably also feared that we would suffer from the inevitable comparisons to him. Sadly, he was right.

When he did take me outside to help me with sports, things did not go well. He did not have a lot of patience, and even though I was just a boy, he was demanding and expected a lot out of me. Once, when I was six or seven, he picked up a couple of gloves and a ball so that we could play catch. I was ecstatic. He gave me a glove and started to toss me the baseball instructing me how to catch and throw. I was so happy that he had taken the time to play with me that I began jumping around and laughing. I couldn't catch, and my throws were terrible.

After a few minutes of this, he picked up the ball, put it in his glove, and shoved them into my stomach and said, "You'll never be a ballplayer." He then turned and walked into the house.

I was devastated, but I learned that day that if I wanted to be an athlete, I would have to be serious. Ever the coach and perfectionist, my father insisted that if you wanted to play, you "had to act like a ballplayer, look like a ballplayer, and give it your best effort" even during practice. He was no less patient when it came to schoolwork. Charlie was the master of tough love.

When I was a little older and a little more skilled, he brought home a brand-new Wilson baseball glove and gave it to me. It was a beauty—a leather George Kell model. I took it everywhere, even to bed. At nine, I tried out for Little League and made the Sabatanelli's team. That season, I batted just four times, and the results were the same—four strikeouts. My father did not attend one game. During the season, I started to hear the refrains which would haunt me for years. Among them were, "How come you can't run like your father?"; "How come you can't hit like your father?"; "Your father was a great ball player, what happened to you?" It did not help that he had nicknamed me Bronkie.

———————

AS THE NEW YEAR BEGAN, ON JANUARY 5, 1954, IN THE MIDdle of the school year, Connie gave birth to another baby boy. He was named Joseph after Charlie's father Giuseppe. There were now three little Brucatos in the family, and when his first school year as assistant principal ended, Charlie needed a summer job to supplement the family's income. He had finished his commitment with the marine corps reserves so that income was gone. Connie had not had a full-time teaching position in several years, although she did teach English to non-English speaking adults at night school. She could no longer do that.

Fortunately, that summer, Milford opened a municipal swimming pool near Fino Field. Built out of concrete and with a sandy bottom, the pool jutted out into Milford Pond. The job of pool supervisor became available, and Charlie jumped at it. He became the first pool director and spent the summer supervising the lifeguards, swimming lessons, and public swimming. He also began a master's degree in administration program at Boston University.

Later that summer, tragedy struck. Brother John's wife Jeanette became gravely ill, and the family was devastated when she died on July 30. She was only forty-nine. John had known her since her birth, and they had fallen in love when she was just a teenager. They were inseparable. During their marriage, she and he faced some challenges. Two of their children (Joesph and Mary) were born deaf and son Rudy had serious health issues. Through their travails, they remained loving and loyal partners and created a beautiful and close-knit family. They were two of the most wonderful individuals I have ever known.

Connie and Charlie left for Stamford to comfort his brother and nieces and nephews. Ninfa and Molly went with them. They knew that Brother John would be lost without Jeanette.

I was seven when she died, and her passing affected me greatly. I had grown close to Aunt Jeanette and Uncle John and my entire Stamford family, because each summer since I was four years old, my father would take me with him when he traveled to see his brother, aunts, uncles, and cousins who lived there. This continued until my teen years.

We would stay for a week. When we arrived, our first stop was always at the three-decker on Beckley Avenue to see Brother John and Aunt

STAMFORD BRUCATO FAMILY CIRCA 1950

Front row, left to right: Barbara Brucato, Jeannette Brucato, Brother John.
Second row: Rudy Brucato's wife Josephine, Rudy, Joseph Brucato,
Joseph's wife Edith, Mary Brucato.

Jeanette. We would climb the steep wooden stairs of their three decker, and Aunt Jeanette would greet us warmly with a hug and kiss. The greeting between my father and uncle would always be the same. My father would say, "Brother John," and he would reply, "Brother Charles." I was always surprised by their stoicism and the formality of their discussions. Though you could feel the love, warmth, and respect they had for each other, there were no outward displays of emotion. They never hugged. They would sit, drink coffee, smoke, and catch up on the news of their families. Aunt Jeanette always had some pastry on the table.

The roles of the brothers in the relationship had changed. Charlie was now the one giving counsel and guidance to the man he had

BROTHER JOHN'S CHILDREN CIRCA 1960S

Left to right: Barbara, Mary, Rudy, Joseph

idolized and who was his surrogate father. Brother John and Charlie'
s sisters truly believed that because their baby brother was educated,
he had all the answers. If Brother John had confessed some misstep or
another to Charlie, the exchange was the same.

"Jesus Christ, Brother John, what the hell were you thinking?"
Charlie would say shaking his head.

"Brother Charles," John would reply sheepishly, "I'm not as smart
as you. You're a college man." He meant it too.

Being with Uncle John, Aunt Jeanette, and their kids Joe, Mary,
Rudy, and Barbara was a highpoint in my summers. I only had two
Brucato aunts and two Brucato cousins in Milford, and being in
Stamford, I got to establish lifetime relationships with the rest of my
father's family.

Each year, after visiting Brother John and Aunt Jeanette, we would head over to Joe Franchina's house where it was more coffee and pastry. Even if we were there late in the evening, there was always coffee and something sweet to nibble on. Joe's mother was a (Failacci) Brucato, and he and my father looked like brothers. Their facial resemblance and even their mannerisms were similar. Each had brown sympathetic eyes, big Italian noses, and similar olive skin. Like Brother John, Joe married his first cousin, Margaret Franchina. She didn't even have to change her last name. The Franchina's had five kids—Joe Junior, Mary Grace, Rosemary, Patty, and Phil. They were a boisterous bunch, and I had a lot of fun at their house while my father and Joe were deep in discussion.

We would also spend time with Uncle John Faillaci, who retained his birth name. John and his wife Amelia owned and operated a restaurant, and often, we would eat in the kitchen while the chefs and waitresses were busy cooking and tending to the customers. We would also spend time with their sons, Anthony and Blasé Faillaci, and daughters, Molly and Frances. Blasé shared my father's interest in gambling.

Through the years, my father used the trips to and from Stamford to impress upon me his philosophy of life. It was an indoctrination into the Sicilian way. It was on these trips that my father confided in me and told me stories about his past and his expectations for my future. He would also try to explain the vast differences between him and the Mastroianni-Oliva family which produced conflicting emotions in me. His intentions were clear. He was preparing me as his oldest male child to be the next Brucato patriarch. Whether I was emotionally ready for this information is debatable.

AS SUMMER TURNED TO FALL, CHARLIE WENT BACK TO HIS job at the high school and thereafter completed his second year as assistant principal. He had learned a lot from the previous year, and his reputation as a tough guy had grown. As a result, the kids behaved better, and fewer students were sent to the office.

CHARLIE AND CONNIE'S KIDS CIRCA 1955

Left to right: Marilyn, Joseph, Bronkie, John.

As 1955 began, the Brucato family expanded when on January 26, Connie gave birth to Joe's "Irish twin." They named him John after Charlie's favorite, Brother John. We were still living in the tiny house at 83 East Main Street, and it was bursting at the seams. I was sharing a bed in a closet-like room with Joe. My sister had her own small cubby hole, and John was in a crib in my parents' bedroom. The "rooms" were not even separated from my parent's bedroom by a hallway. We had only one bathroom which was downstairs off the kitchen. John's crib was squeezed between my parents' bed and the outside wall.

We now had a black and white television with a small screen encased in a large mahogany cabinet. Prior to us getting a TV, there was one at 89 East Main, which we would occasionally watch. There were few baseball games aired, but I remember my father watching one between the Red Sox and Yankees. He called me over and pointed to the screen as Joe DiMaggio batted. "I want you to look at this and remember because there is the greatest baseball player who ever lived."

In March, the television version of *Peter Pan* starring Mary Martin was aired. That same month, Claudette Colvin, a fifteen-year-old African-American girl, refused to give up her seat on a bus in Montgomery,

Alabama, to a white woman after the driver demanded it. She was carried off the bus backwards while being kicked, handcuffed and harassed on the way to the police station. She became a plaintiff in *Browder v. Gayle* (1956), which ruled bus segregation to be unconstitutional.[198]

One day while he was having his afternoon nap in his crib upstairs, baby John began screaming. Connie went up to determine what was wrong. She was horrified to see that one of his bare legs was extended out of the crib and was resting on the radiator. The outside of his calf was severely burned. Charlie was livid when he learned of the incident. Shortly thereafter, my brother Joe developed a severe case of impetigo. I vividly remember Aunt Jessie Zacchilli coming over the house and administering "treatments" and my brother screaming in pain.

With four children now crowded into the small house at 83 East Main, it became clear that the family needed a larger residence.

Charlie learned that Joe Rosenfeld, one of Milford's wealthiest men and the owner of Rosenfeld Concrete, had created a subdivision off Congress Street on the uptown side of the old railroad tracks. Charlie visited the subdivision, which had been carved out of an apple orchard and decided that this would be a perfect location for a new home.

Since the family had no savings, he convinced Connie to arrange a meeting with Uncle Nick and get a loan from him to purchase a lot. She was reluctant at first but finally agreed. Uncle Nick gave them the loan, and they purchased two adjacent lots on Rosenfeld Avenue with the agreement to later deed one of the lots to Uncle Nick if he wanted it.

After acquiring the lots, Connie and Charlie visited several houses to determine the style of home that would suit them. They decided on a ranch design with the exact floor plan of one of the homes they had seen and liked. Charlie called his high school classmate Henry Consigli and hired Consigli Construction Company to excavate the lot and put in a foundation. He next hired Rico Lombardi to do the carpentry work. Charlie supervised the construction and he drove the workers crazy

198 "1955," *Wikipedia*, https://en.wikipedia.org/wiki/1955.

with his demands. Not a day went by when he was not screaming at Henry or one of the workers. We moved into our brand new home at 16 Rosenfeld Avenue in 1956 when I was nine years old and starting fourth grade.

It was a new experience for me. I spent my kindergarten through third grade years at the old yellow clapboard Plains School which was directly across the street from 89 East Main. I remember the excitement of having police officer Frank Hines stop traffic to permit us to cross the street and enter the school grounds. Miss Sennet taught kindergarten, Miss Mawn first grade, Miss Edwards second, and Miss Seaver third. Though only a stone's throw from my house, Plains School opened a new world to me. For the first time, I got to interact with people who were not related to me. I was surprised to see children with blonde hair and blue eyes and teachers who were not Italian.

Now that we had moved uptown, I would have to walk to Park School which was about a quarter of a mile away. For the first time, we would be apart from Mastroianni-Oliva clan, which made my father very happy. The move did have a drawback. Connie's family would not be around to help her out with the children and babysitters were not an option.

Almost immediately after we got settled in our new house, my father and mother took me into the kitchen, sat me down, and said, "Bronkie, the kids are your responsibility. If anything happens to them, we are going to blame you."

Though it may seem odd that they would place this burden on me as a nine-year-old, it was perfectly normal for my father. Molly and Ninfa had been responsible for him when he was a baby, and they were my age at the time.

Once we had settled in our new house, my father's routine was virtually unchanged. He continued to go to the racetrack and play poker a couple of nights each week. Things were different for not only my mother but also for my sister and me. Without cousins to play with, we had to make friends. We would also be going to new schools. We were nervous but excited by the challenges.

Connie now had a large modern kitchen, and she loved to cook. Since many of the apple trees remained on our land, we would pick the apples and she would make pies.

Often when I was playing wiffle ball with my friends, she would call out, "If you kids pick some apples, I'll make you a pie." She didn't have to ask twice.

On each Saturday afternoon, Connie would make Italian bread. It was a tradition we all cherished, especially my father. My sister Marilyn describes it perfectly.

"'I can smell it!' Dad exclaimed every Saturday as he walked through the front door of 16 Rosenfeld Avenue. It was late afternoon, and he was happy to be home after spending the day at the racetrack with his buddies. His cry was a relief to us four mouth-watering kids who were absolutely forbidden to take a taste of the warm aromatic bread until Dad came home and cut into the loaf.

"She made seven loaves, and always gave two or three away. The process of making the bread was not unlike the ritual at Sunday Mass. Before she fashioned the dough into loaves, she would bless it by making the sign of the cross over the well-kneaded mixture of flour, water, eggs, and yeast, which had risen and swelled into a round mound. After she had formed the loaves, they would be placed in the oven.

"When the loaves were sufficiently baked, she removed them from the oven and placed them onto a large wooden cutting board. The aroma of freshly baked bread wafted throughout the house, but we were not allowed to taste it until Dad took one loaf and 'broke it.' That process involved him pulling a loaf apart, removing the fluffy white interior and spreading the remaining crust with copious amounts of butter.

"After this ritual, he would take a bite and declare, 'That's the long ball! There is nothing like Connie's fresh bread!'

"He would then devour the entire loaf. We would wait, anxiously, for the slices which were meted out to us.

"There was one remaining act to complete the bread ritual. At least two and sometimes three loaves had to be distributed to certain favored individuals. Dave and Inez Davoren, Nick Mastroianni, Jr, Theresa and Mike Visconti, and people who had helped Connie out in some way during the preceding week were among the happy recipients."

The good news about living up town was that I had more freedom and was permitted to walk to school and play at Town Park when not babysitting my two baby brothers. My first lesson on the Sicilian code of omerta occurred one day at the park. I was ten or eleven and had just finished playing ball with my friends and was heading home with a baseball in my hand. A teenage boy who I did not know ran at me, grabbed the ball, knocked me down, and smugly walked away with it. I ran home crying and told my father what happened.

He shouted angrily, "Get in the car and show me who did this to you."

I directed him to the park and pointed out the boy who was still there.

My father barked, "Stay in the car." He then got out, ran up to the boy, took the ball from him, and slapped him in the face. "You like to hit little kids? How do you like it?" he yelled.

I was beaming when he got back in the car.

Once seated, my father turned to me, slapped me with a backhander to the face, and screamed, "Don't you ever come crying to me if something like this happens again!"

I was confused at the time but learned that day I had to fight my own battles and more importantly never be a rat.

He would follow this lesson up many times during our rides to Stamford with other Sicilian rules of conduct that he had learned from his father.

"Keep your feelings to yourself. Listen and don't talk. Don't let anyone know what you are thinking. Be careful when choosing your friends. Don't put your trust in anyone but your family."

I did not realize it at the time, but he was grooming me to replace him as the Brucato family patriarch.

By the time I was eleven, my beloved George Kell glove had seen better days. One Sunday, while I was with all my cousins at the weekly Oliva family feast, my father gave me a box containing a new glove.

When I opened the box and took it out, my face dropped. The glove was not the professional model which I had become accustomed to. It was a glove you could buy at any department store, and it was an Eddie Stanky model. I began crying hysterically.

Through my tears, I kept repeating, "Eddie Stanky, Eddie Stanky, who is Eddie Stanky?"

My cousins just laughed. To this day, when they see me, they remind me by echoing the phrase. But, in my mind, this was another instance of my father's attitude that playing sports was unimportant. Fortunately, he returned the Stanky model and bought me a real glove.

There were other incidents on Sundays at 89 East Main Street when my cousins and I were kids. As a boy, I was a prankster, and it seemed that I was always the one who got into trouble. My cousins all knew this and were constantly egging me on.

One Sunday dinner, all the kids were seated around the table in the kitchen table while the adults were eating in the dining room. My poor cousin Rosemary Bramante, who had been crippled with polio, was sitting next to me. We were having macaroni, and she did not like gravy on hers, so everyone would find those pieces on their plates that were gravy free and give them to her. I wanted to get a laugh. I took some macaroni, put it in my mouth and sucked all the gravy off. As my cousins (except Rosemary) watched, I took the macaroni out of my mouth and put it on Rosemary's plate. She thanked me and proceeded to eat it as my cousins laughed hysterically. We kept this a secret from Rose for about thirty years, and when we finally told her, she was furious.

Another Sunday after dinner, Rose's sister Connie and I decided that we would try smoking cigarettes. Connie went up to Aldo Zacchilli's apartment and pilfered a couple of cigarettes and some matches and we went into the garage with the inverted roof next to the billboard and lit up. Unfortunately, there were bundles of newspapers being stored there for paper drives and they caught fire. Someone ran to tell the adults, and they rushed out to put out the fire. Needless to say, my father gave me a good beating. It was one of many for me.

NEARLY EVERY HOUSEHOLD NOW HAD AT LEAST ONE BLACK and white TV. On Rosenfeld Avenue, we also had a hi-fi record player. If Charlie ever relaxed, it was when he was listening to music. The soundtracks to musicals and operas were his favorites. *South Pacific, My Fair Lady, La Traviata, La Boheme,* and others were staples.

Charlie would often say, "It's not a good song if you can't hum it." When he was humming with a smile, he was happy.

Being away from Connie's family provided Charlie with a modicum of comfort. He felt that he now had his own family independent of and not just a small part of the Mastroianni-Oliva clan. He constantly instilled in us that we were Brucatos. Connie, of course, missed the daily interaction with her mother and siblings. She was insistent that Sundays and holidays be with her family much to the delight of my sister, me, and my brothers.

The holidays, especially, always proved to be tense times for us. On Christmas Eve every year, Charlie's ire would reach its zenith. Uncle Nick annually hosted a party at his house on the evening of December 24, and all Olivas and Mastroiannis would have to attend. As children, we loved the party because we got to play with our cousins and each of us would receive a gift.

Charlie hated this. He was resentful and angry that Christmas Eve had to be spent with Connie's family. He would begin complaining early in the day. His emotions would be raw and driven by his insecurities and repressed anger. Connie revered Uncle Nick and Charlie was jealous. He did not want to "bow down to and pay homage" to Uncle Nick because he was his own man.

He would say, "We are Brucatos not Olivas or Mastroiannis. Why do we always have to be with your family?"

What would ensue was a shouting match between the two of them. By the time we would get to the party, Charlie's ire had diminished, but Connie would remain shaken.

Unlike Connie and her extended family, Charlie was not a partier and rarely drank alcohol. He was self-conscious and guarded. Connie was just

BRUCATOS AND CELOZZIS CIRCA 1960S

Seated, left to right: Jeanne Celozzi, Barbara Celozzi
Standing: Ninfa Brucato, Louis "Tope" Celozzi,
Molly Brucato Celozzi, Giuseppe Brucato

the opposite. Social gatherings with Connie's family made Charlie edgy and nervous, perhaps because he was unaccustomed to huge gregarious throngs of relatives having been brought up in a small, insular family. One Christmas Eve, he decided that we would stay home and host his sisters. Connie reluctantly agreed, and we were not happy about it.

I have often wished that I could have met my father when he was young. Was he as guarded and fearful? Was he ever outgoing and cheerful? Was he ever able to express love and affection? He never hugged or kissed us and was always uncomfortable with any kind of intimacy. Ironically, within his tough veneer was a kind and gentle man who always championed the underdog.

It is not as though we never saw our father's family. We would visit 98 Hayward Street frequently. Ninfa and Giuseppe lived there in a small apartment with Molly, her husband Tope, and their two children Jeanne and Barbara.

BRUCATO FAMILY AT RUDY'S WEDDING

Front row, left to right: Barbara Celozzi, Jeanne Marie Celozzi, Barbara Brucato.
Second row: Molly Celozzi, Jeannette Brucato, Rudy Brucato,
Josephine Brucato, unknown bridesmaid.
Third row: Ninfa Brucato, Mary Brucato, Brother John, unknown,
Back row: Connie Brucato, Charlie Brucato, Joseph Brucato,
Edith Brucato, Giuseppe Brucato, unknown.

We were treated like royalty when we arrived. Our aunts doted on us, showered us with attention, and were always complimenting us. My grandfather would look on quietly with a look of pride. We always left feeling better about ourselves.

THE YEAR 1958 STARTED OMINOUSLY. ON JANUARY 17, NINFA telephoned Charlie to report that Giuseppe had died. It was a shock to me. He did not appear to be ill. On the other hand, the fact that he had lived to the ripe old age of seventy-eight was remarkable considering that he was frail, had worked hard, and smoked cigarettes.

My memories of him are vivid. He looked world-weary and could not have weighed much more than a hundred pounds. He had a full head of white hair. His face was wrinkled, gaunt, and always coated with a three-day scruffy growth of white whiskers. Any time we visited, he would grin, call me over, and look me up and down almost as if he was admiring what he saw.

He then would say in Italian, "*Guarda. Guarda questo bellissimo raga-zzo.*" ("Look. Look at this beautiful boy.") Molly and Ninfa would nod in agreement. I truly felt loved. I would like to think that he achieved peace and contentment in his final years.

After Giuseppe's funeral, friends and relatives gathered at our house for the "mercy meal." Connie and her sisters along with family friends prepared the food for an elaborate buffet. One incident which I witnessed in the kitchen stands out from that day. A former neighbor from the Plains was sitting at the kitchen table and he rose to approach my father, who had just walked in.

"Hey, Charlie," the neighbor said. "How come you had Edwards [Funeral Home] handle the funeral and not DePasquale? All the Italians use DePasquale."

My father became enraged. "It's none of your goddamn business. Get the hell out of here, you goddamn fool!" he bellowed, almost pulling the man off the chair.

I was shocked at this outburst at the time. There were a lot of people in the room and I had never seen my father act this way in public. I realized later that my father was insulted and infuriated by the man's implication that he was violating some sacred code by choosing an Irishman and not an Italian to handle the funeral. The reason he chose Edwards was he trusted and respected him. He did not feel the same way about DePasquale. As a matter of fact, he disliked him.

The news during that year centered on the space race between the United States and the Soviet Union. In nearby Cuba, Fidel Castro and his revolutionaries were beginning an armed campaign to seize control of the country. Nikita Khrushchev became premier of the Soviet Union and Herb Elliott; an Australian runner ran a 3 minutes, 54 seconds mile in Dublin, knocking three seconds off the world record.

The school year ended in June, and it was customary for my family and Uncle Aldo and Aunt Jesse Zacchilli's family to vacation together at Uncle Nick's "cottage" on New Silver Beach in Falmouth on Cape Cod. We were always there for the last week of June, and though we did spend some time vacationing, the trade-off for our stay was that we had to get the place ready for Uncle Nick and his family.

The "cottage" was more like an inn than a residence. It was a large, shingled building with two floors and a porch that wrapped around the exterior of the first floor. It had a small kitchen, large dining room, and an even larger living room on the first level. There was a bathroom and six small rooms for sleeping and storage on the second floor and a make-shift shower in the basement. It was neither insulated nor heated and was occupied only during the summer.

When we arrived, the lawn would be overgrown and the interior of the house musty and covered with cobwebs. Connie was notorious for being an obsessive cleaner, and she and Jessie would spend the week washing the dishes, vacuuming, scrubbing and polishing the floors, and generally making the place spotless. Aldo would spend all his time cutting the lawn, tidying up the grounds, pruning trees, painting, and repairing what needed to be fixed. He never stopped working. My cousin Pete and my sister and I would also have chores. My brothers were too young, and in addition to helping with chores, I was charged with babysitting them.

My father did very little and, in fact, resented the fact that we were in servitude and not on vacation. He was so restless and aggravated that his wife was working so hard that he was rarely around. He would travel to the track or go back and forth to Milford during the week, sometimes taking me with him so I would not miss any Little League games.

When my father was at the Cape, he would often take Pete and me on rides around the area. On one occasion while both of us were in his car, he was plodding along, humming with his arm out the window, as was his usual manner. We could not have been going twenty miles an hour. A man in the car traveling behind us on the winding road kept beeping his horn for us to go faster. My father ignored him. When we finally got to a straight part of the road, the man passed us and angrily gave my father the finger.

My father was enraged and yelled back, "Up your ass," and chased after the guy muttering, "that son of a bitch."

Pete and I were five or six, and we were scared. It looked to us like he was going to either crash into the guy or stop and fight him. I think the guy was as afraid as we were. He kept speeding up and looking back. My father cooled off and decided to turn around. We were relieved.

When I was a little older and we were at the Cape for a week, he would take me to a field and pitch to me. I was not a good hitter, and it frustrated him so much that it seemed that he was always yelling at me. I got to experience first-hand how his players must have felt, and like them, I didn't want to let him down. I tried as hard as I could but never was able to swing the way he wanted me to.

There was also the day he took me to a batting cage once at an amusement park at the Cape. I went into the cage and kept swinging and missing the balls thrown by the pitching machine. After each swing, he would have a comment.

Finally, the cage operator came over and said to him, "You think you could do better?"

My father replied, "I not only think. I know I can."

The operator put the machine on the fastest setting and said, "If you can hit this, I will give your son as many free rounds as he wants."

My father picked up a bat, swung it a couple of times, and then went into the cage. The machine delivered six of the fastest pitches I had ever seen, and my father smashed every pitch with stinging line drives. He then tossed the bat down and walked away as the operator's jaw dropped.

CHAPTER ELEVEN

THE TUMULTUOUS SIXTIES

T HE YEAR 1959 PROVED TO BE A PRECURSOR OF THE TUR-
bulence of the next decade and beyond. In Cuba, Fidel Castro's rebels
had forced President Fulgencio Batista to flee Havana, setting the stage
for a coup. The Soviet Union immediately recognized the new Castro
government. Alaska was admitted as the forty-ninth state, and Eisenhower was finishing his second term as president of the United States.

As 1960 began, there were developments which would alter the
course of history in the United States. In March, it was announced that
3,500 troops were being sent to Vietnam and President Eisenhower
approved a covert Central Intelligence Agency plan to train a paramilitary force against Cuba. In May, he signed the Civil Rights Act of 1960.
That same month, the Soviets shot down Gary Powers's U-2 plane,
captured him, and sentenced him to ten years in prison for espionage.

The Republican Party nominated Vice President Richard M. Nixon as
its presidential candidate and the Democrats nominated Senator John F.
Kennedy of Massachusetts to oppose him. In November, after a historic
television debate between the two, Kennedy was elected the thirty-fifth
president of the United States in one of the closest elections in history.

I completed my Little League in 1959 and was set for Babe Ruth League in 1960. My baseball career had not gone the way I had expected, but I was sure that with the pitcher's mound going from fifty feet to sixty feet, six inches, I would be a much better hitter. I did hit a lot better in Babe Ruth and I thought I was a decent shortstop, but my father did not agree.

He took me aside one day and said, "I know you love baseball Bronkie, but you can't hit, and you can't run. You do have a good throwing arm so if you want to play, we will have to make you a pitcher."

I was crushed that he felt this way about me, and I was embarrassed that I could never live up to his standards, but in the end, I realized he was right.

From that point on, my father spent hours with me teaching me how to pitch. We set up a mound in the empty lot adjacent to our house, and at least two or three times a week, he would have me throw to him. It was not easy. He was a stickler on pitching mechanics, from how I gripped the baseball to my wind-up and how I threw. He insisted upon a full wind-up and overhand delivery.

We started throwing at half speed so I could master control. We then moved to full speed and then he taught me what he called a "big league curveball." Sometimes he was so harsh with his criticisms or instructions that I would become so angry that I wanted to throw the ball through him. When I missed the target he gave me, he would intentionally not catch the ball. He would then make me run to retrieve the ball. He also had running drills, bend and pick up drills, and many other drills to condition my body. He even brought in a professional baseball scout to talk to me about pitching. He forbid me from pitching in a game until I had mastered my delivery and had good control.

One day late in the process, I became a little too cocky for his liking. I told him I thought I was throwing really hard and would be tough to hit. He told me to throw my best fastball. As I wound up and reached back to throw, he flung the catcher's mitt aside and caught the ball bare-handed. He did not like cockiness. His coaching techniques would probably not be acceptable today, but they helped me get the best out of whatever talent I had, and more than that, they helped me become a better person.

AS KENNEDY ASSUMED THE PRESIDENCY IN JANUARY OF 1961, tensions with Cuba and the Soviets were at a boiling point. Prior to leaving office, Eisenhower had severed relations with Cuba. The CIA convinced the new president to proceed with its plan to invade the nearby island with a paramilitary force, and on April 17, the plan was carried out in the Bay of Pigs. The force was soundly defeated in three days. As a result, Castro became a hero and Cuba's relationship with the Soviets was solidified.

In addition to the troubles with Cuba and the USSR, the country was being divided by the civil rights movement. In Alabama, riots caused the governor to declare martial law, and in Jackson, Mississippi, the Freedom Riders were arrested and charged with disturbing the peace.

A few years earlier, Brother John, against my father's advice, married a Tomaso cousin from Milford. He had been lonely since Jeanette died, but my father did not feel the woman was right for him. He felt that it would be difficult for her to leave Milford and live in Stamford and Brother John was not going to leave his job and children to live in Milford. After the marriage, they did live in Stamford but made many trips to Milford, which was a good thing because my father got to see his brother more often.

Unfortunately, on August 11, 1961, Brother John dropped dead at Grand Central Station in New York City. He was sixty-one years old. When my father got the news, I saw him cry for the first time. He was truly devastated. He had lost the man he loved and respected most. He would not soon get over it. He, Connie, Ninfa, and Molly travelled to Stamford to mourn his passing with John's family and friends. They all would miss him and his kind and gentle ways. His death at such a young age just didn't seem fair.

WITH FOUR GROWING CHILDREN IN THE FAMILY, LIFE WAS hectic in the Brucato household to say the least. Each child had a different personality, and Charlie and Connie treated each differently. One thing, however, was constant. There was no outward display of affection from parent to child. There was no hugging or kissing. Connie and Charlie were task masters, tolerating nothing but the best efforts from their children and accepting no excuses.

We were brought up with old world values and tough love. Respect for others was ingrained in us at an early age. We also learned that there were consequences for our actions. Wrongdoing was punished with what we called a beating, which really was a slap or spanking. Times were different in the 1950s and '60s and this was an accepted form of discipline then. Unlike today when psychologists have convinced society that physical punishment is harmful, "Spare the rod and spoil the child" was a belief our parents endorsed.

We were also taught the importance of family unity. We always ate supper together and did not begin the meal until my father was seated at the head of the table. John always sat on my father's backhand side because he was prone to acting up. My father had little patience. On one occasion, John spilled his glass of soda on my father's lap and my father took his drink and threw it in John's face.

"How do you like it?" he yelled.

We all roared, including John. At dinner, there was always a discussion of the day, and everyone participated. The TV was never on. It was family time.

As educators, both parents expressed the importance of doing well in school. Bad grades were not acceptable, and we would pay a price if we ever brought one home. As we got older, punishments for any wrongdoing were meted out. Joe was once prevented from playing in a Little League championship game when he showed up late for dinner.

Each child had a different relationship with our father. My relationship with him was the most complicated. As his firstborn son, he spent an inordinate amount of time with me and shared with me his unique perspectives on life. He charted out the path that I would follow as I got older. At a very early age, he confided in me and told me all the mistakes he had made over the years. He did not want me to be like him. Long before I hit puberty, Charlie instilled in me a sense of duty to my sister and brothers.

He told me that he and my mother had decided that I had to work hard in school, go to a top-notch college, and become a doctor. More importantly, he told me that I had an obligation to take care of the kids (my brothers). Perhaps that is why he did not want me to be an athlete. Perhaps that is why he was so hard on me. I was a dutiful son and never questioned him, even though I wanted to be just like him—an athlete and teacher-coach.

As a child, I was happy-go-lucky and into all kinds of mischief. When I did something wrong, he would take out the razor strop and hit me in the ass. As I got older, I changed due in large part to the fact that I was afraid to let him down in any way and because I hated to incur his wrath. I became more serious, less careless, and much more responsible. My cousins liked me much better when I was acting up.

Charlie was motivated by fear, and he motivated us with fear. Connie motivated us with guilt. A common refrain to me was, "The kids are your responsibility Bronkie. If anything happens to them, it will be your fault." From age fourteen, when my parents went out, I was the babysitter. By the time I was sixteen, if they went away for a couple of days, I was left in charge. I took my brothers to their games and stayed to watch them. I even coached some of their teams. It was an awesome responsibility. To this day, I feel responsible for them.

While the boys in the family regularly got the rod, Marilyn did not. She was reared by Connie, and Charlie rarely disciplined her.

She recalls, "From the time we moved into the new house on 16 Rosenfeld Avenue when I was five years old to the time when I left for nursing school when I was seventeen, whenever my dad came home from work (or if it was a Saturday evening, from the track), I would run

up to him yelling 'Daddy!' and give him a hug. He would bend down
to offer his cheek. It was difficult for him to show his emotions, but I
felt them. His face was smooth and warm and smelled like Old Spice.
It is not a popular aftershave now, but over the years, whenever I would
catch a whiff of Old Spice, I would remember the feeling of warmth and
safety and love, and the strong and gentle man who carried it."

Possibly because she was his only daughter, she saw the very best
qualities of Charlie.

"Dad was very kind," she said. "He was always bringing people home
with him to share a meal. Mom would freak as he never gave her notice
that someone was coming, but she always had something scrumptious.
On Friday nights, it would inevitably be pasta fagioli, pizza, or fried
smelts. Often, the surprise guest would be Phil "Pinky" O'Donnell who
weighed well over 280 pounds. There was always enough food. Interestingly, this custom was passed on to all of us. There was not a holiday
dinner at any of our homes when we didn't have extra people join us.
We called them 'strays' because they had nowhere else to go.

"Although I was the second of four children and the only girl,"
Marilyn continued, "my status in the family was that of a middle child,
personified by my being an FBI [full-blooded Italian]. Though both of
my parents were highly educated, we were first, last, and always Italian.
When I think of what defined me, it was this: I was Marilyn Brucato,
Italian ....pretty much in that order. My job was to be a nice girl, and
anything less than that would be a poor reflection of my parents. Period.

"My friends loved my father. While we were in school, sometimes
during lunch, he would excuse us and send us on errands. He would give
me the keys to his Olds, and Paula, Donna, and I would take off. Some
of our favorite times were when the superintendent was out, and Dad
was the one to decide whether to call off school during a snowstorm.

"He would look at us and ask, 'Whaddaya think?'

"We would say, 'Call it off!'

"Then he would say, 'No school for all schools!'

"It was like we had helped make the decision.

"I remember walking home from football games on a late Saturday fall afternoon in my majorette uniform, turning the corner onto Rosenfeld Avenue, that wonderful aroma of homemade bread pulling me up the driveway into the house to the tune of my mother's 'Young lady, don't take off your uniform. I want you to deliver these loaves while they're still warm!' Dad would just shrug his shoulders and smile.

"We all attended Mass on Sunday as a family except for my father who said, 'I went to Mass every day at Holy Cross, so I don't have to now.' He also refused to adhere to the Catholic rule of no meat on Friday. When we said, 'Dad, it's Friday, you can't eat meat,' he would playfully say, 'It's your sin for telling me.'"

———————

IN MARCH OF 1961, I TURNED FOURTEEN AND WOULD ENTER high school in the fall. My brothers were in grade school, and my mother had returned to teaching a few years earlier, starting out as a third-grade teacher. Earlier that year, my father had talked to me about prep school. I really wanted to go to Milford High and play sports in my hometown, but he insisted that I take the prep school aptitude test.

Late in August, he took me for an interview at Deerfield Academy about two and a half hours west of Milford. It was a boarding school, and the campus was magnificent. The school had an indoor pool, indoor hockey rink, a huge gym, and a movie theatre on campus. I was in awe.

At the end of my interview, admissions director John Boyden, who called me Bronc after he learned my nickname, said, "I cannot take you in this year's class because we have already filled it, but I can take you next year if you want to come here."

I did not realize at the time that Deerfield Academy was one of the most selective prep schools in the country.

On the ride home, my father asked me if I wanted to go to Deerfield next year. I didn't really want to leave Milford and my friends, but I knew that my family couldn't afford to pay the huge expense anyway, so I said yes.

He said, "Okay, you can go there starting sophomore year."

"But" I said, "you can't afford it."

He just nodded. I later learned that Boyden had asked him how much he could afford. My father said $500.00 per year. Boyden agreed that I could have room, board, and tuition for $500.00 per year.

It turns out that Paul Raftery, the principal of Stacy Junior High School where I was a student, received a flyer about Deerfield and had given it to my father saying it might be a good school for me. I believe that my father did not want me at Milford High. He did not want to expose me to the endless comparisons to him. He feared that the teachers and coaches who didn't like him would take it out on me. He wanted me to succeed or fail on my own, and most of all, he did not want me to be a jockstrap like him. I don't know whether he shared these feelings with Mr. Raftery and that prompted Mr. Raftery to give him the flyer, but it does seem reasonable.

I completed my freshman year at Milford High in June of 1962 as a lame duck, since everyone knew that I would be going to Deerfield. I played quarterback on the freshman football team, forward on the freshman basketball team, and pitched and played shortstop on the freshman baseball team. My coach for football and basketball was none other than Joe Stoico, one of my father's best players. He treated me the same way my father treated him, constantly pushing me to be better and never letting up.

There were some issues at Milford High that confirmed my father's fears. I was thrown out of class one day and told to go down to the office to see him. He immediately realized that the teacher, who did not like him, did this to embarrass both of us when I told him why I was sent to his office. He calmly told me to sit down for the period and he'd take care of the situation, but I could see that he was angry, and his anger was not directed at me.

At the end of the school year, the Class of 1962 dedicated the yearbook to my father which was a surprise to everyone considering his reputation as a disciplinarian. In a two-page tribute with photos showing him as a marine corps officer and a football player at Holy Cross, the class wrote,

> As our four happy and profitable years at Milford High School draw to an end, it is most fitting that we try to express our deep appreciation for his patient instruction, his contagious enthusiasm as a coach in days gone by, and his sincere friendship. This dedication can only be thought of as a small token in return for his many efforts on our behalf.
>
> It is with pride and affection that we, the Class of 1962, the one-hundredth graduating class of Milford High School dedicate this edition of the *Oak, Lily and Ivy* to Charles J. Brucato.

———

IN SEPTEMBER OF 1962, AT FIFTEEN YEARS OLD, MY PARENTS left me off at Deerfield, and for the first time in my life, I was living away from home. My sister was twelve, Joe was eight, and John was seven. As surrogate father to my two brothers, they hated to see me go. My mother took a position as a language teacher at Hopedale High School where Bob Pagnini was principal.

At Deerfield, which was an all-male school at the time, we were required to dress in jacket and tie during the school day and a dark jacket and tie at dinner. I had never owned a jacket and tie and had only one pair of dress pants. Outfitting me for school would put a serious dent in the family's budget. As always, my father had a scheme to deal with this.

A couple of weeks before we were to leave, my father took me down to our old yard on East Main Street. A few minutes after we got there, a man named George pulled into the driveway and nodded for us to come over to his car. When we got there, he opened the trunk and there were suits, pants, ties, and jackets piled up in it. I was "fitted" in a few jackets and trousers; cash was exchanged, and I had some of the clothes I needed. There were no labels on any of them.

To complete my wardrobe, we drove to a residence somewhere in Rhode Island where another man took us into his basement which had rows and rows of clothing hanging from racks. We followed the same procedure and left with the remaining things I needed. My father swore me to secrecy about these two episodes. While my father was educated, cultured, and image conscious, he was still Sicilian at heart. It was perfectly acceptable to bend the law if it was for the good of your family. In some ways, he had two different and conflicting sets of values.

In October, tensions between the Soviets and the United States reached its zenith with the Cuban Missile Crisis, which brought both countries to the brink of nuclear war. Thinking that Kennedy was weak, the Soviets under Nikita Khrushchev installed offensive ballistic missiles in Cuba, ninety miles away from the coast of Florida. The Executive Committee of National Security Council recommended that Kennedy authorize an air strike on the installations and an invasion of Cuba. After much deliberation, on October 22, he ordered a naval quarantine to prevent further missiles from coming to Cuba.

Kennedy then went on television from the Oval Office and told the nation what had transpired. I remember his speech vividly. The nation was shaken, fearing that this would lead to nuclear war. After tense negotiations, Khrushchev backed down and agreed to disassemble the missiles and ship them back to Russia. This was quite possibly Kennedy's finest hour.

By year end, the Vietnam War had intensified, the arms race continued unabated, the civil rights movement continued to divide the country, and Kennedy vowed to have a man on the moon at the end of the decade.

ON NOVEMBER 22, 1963, I WAS IN STUDY HALL AT DEERFIELD when the news of John F. Kennedy's assassination reached us. The United States would never be the same. Soon thereafter, the war in Vietnam intensified, and as American young men began coming home in body bags, an antiwar movement took roots.

When I came home for the summer of my junior year, it was obvious to me that my father was in turmoil. He would sit for hours on the couch smoking cigarettes deep in what appeared to be troubled thought. It was 1964, and I was playing for the Milford Legion baseball team and dating Mandy Eddy. One night, we were out on a double date with another couple, and I lost track of time. I arrived back home after one a.m. and my father was on the couch sobbing.

"You let me down, Bronkie. I didn't know where you were. I was worried sick," he said.

It would have been much better if he had screamed at me. To see him like this really upset me. Here was a man known for his toughness, but now he looked defeated and despondent. I felt pity for him and guilt and shame for myself. Looking back on that day, I think this was when he had begun to unravel.

To add to Charlie's discontent, Marilyn, who was now at Milford High, felt the sting of a teacher's animus toward her father.

"I was thrown out of home room by Miss Dorothy Callahan, a notoriously crabby teacher. She embarrassed me in front of my classmates, by telling me I wasn't the student my older brother was and wasn't a true daughter to my parents because I was only taking one language course. I told her, 'I am my own person, and you should not compare me to my brother.'

"I went to the office, and when I told Dad the story, he was angry at the teacher and not me. He was actually sympathetic. He said I should sit in the office, and he would handle it. Years later, the tables were turned when I was a nurse, and she was a patient at Milford Hospital. My orders were to give her the "3 H Enema:" high, hot, and a helluva lot!"

I graduated from Deerfield Academy in May of 1965. Though I had been exposed to things there that I would never have been exposed to in Milford and I had received an enviable education, I have many regrets. I had a successful baseball career there, but I never played varsity basketball and I was a second-string quarterback and the place kicker on the varsity football team. Added to that, I was just an average student and my father's dream that I go to an ivy league college was not to be. Instead, I was accepted at Holy Cross and the University of Vermont. I chose UVM.

My father was happy with my choice, and looking back, I think this was because he did not want to me to go to Holy Cross where there would be inevitable comparisons to him. I had visited Holy Cross with him earlier, and he and I met with his old coach, Hop Riopel, who was now head baseball coach there.

While we were meeting, Hop turned to me and asked, "Son, this is very important. Do you know the width of first base?"

Before I could say I did not, my father interrupted, "Are you shitting me, Hop? Who the hell cares about something like that?"

We left shortly thereafter. In the car, my father said, "That was horseshit." He then told me the story of when Hop called him a foul ball after he made an error.

That summer, I was eighteen and playing my final year of Legion baseball. Unlike when I was younger, my father would come to the games. He would position himself far away from the playing field and stand alone, not wanting to hear what was being said by the fans. He was still serious when it came to baseball. One day, I got a lesson on how not to act when you are on a team, a lesson I will never forget.

We were at Lake Park in Worcester playing one of our Legion rivals and I was the starting pitcher. In the first inning, with one out, I walked a guy. The next batter hit a tailor-made double play ball to our short-stop, but he bobbled it, and we didn't even get one out. There were now runners on first and second, but I remained composed. The next batter hit a high foul pop up to the right side of the infield. Our first baseman got under it but dropped the ball. With a new life, the batter hit a sharp single to center scoring one run as the man on first went to third.

With one run in and runners at first and third, and one out, I still was not flustered, but Pep Morcone, the head coach, called time out, came to the mound and said, "I'm taking you out."

I was shocked. I said, "Why are you taking me out?"

He replied, "Things aren't going well with you in there."

He took the ball from me and signaled for a relief pitcher. I stormed off the mound, said something I should not have said, and threw my glove about fifty feet.

There were at least three hundred fans watching the game, one of whom was my father. When I got to the bench, I picked up my gear and retreated to a place under a tree about one hundred feet away. I was so upset, I put my hands over my face and started bawling. I spent the remainder of the game there and refused to get on the bus for the ride home.

I trudged dejectedly to the parking lot and got into my father's car which was in a line of vehicles exiting the ballpark. My brother Joe was in the back seat.

Thinking that my father would be sympathetic, I turned to him and said, "Do you believe he took me out?"

The words were not out of my mouth when Dad hit me across the face with a backhander.

"You made a pig's ass out of yourself and me too!" he shouted.

My brother Joe cowered in the back seat as my father blasted me during the entire forty-five-minute ride home.

During the ride, he kept repeating, "You acted like a real horseshit. I can't believe it. Who the hell do you think you are? You aren't a ballplayer. I think you should turn in your uniform."

I am sure that he meant it. I had seen him angry before but never like this. I hung my head in embarrassment.

Pep Morcone was probably the nicest guy in the world. He did not deserve that conduct from me. The next day, I went to him and apologized. I told him that I would turn in my uniform if he wanted me to. Fortunately, he did not. I apologized to the team and was back in uniform the next day. Another life lesson learned. I never again acted that way on the baseball field regardless of the circumstances. When you are playing sports, the team comes first.

While I was away at Deerfield, my father was becoming more and more disenchanted with his position at Milford High. He was not accustomed to the brazen attitudes of many students. Paul Raftery had replaced Joe Tosches as principal and my father's role as assistant principal had not changed. He was still involved with discipline. One night at about three a.m., he got a call from the police telling him that someone had chopped down the fifty-foot-high pine tree that adorned the entrance to the high school auditorium. He was disgusted.

"Anyone who could do that," he said, "could probably commit murder."

On another occasion, he incurred a mother's wrath when he told a scantily attired young lady to "go home and put some clothes on."

IN SEPTEMBER OF 1965, I SET OFF TO UVM WITH MY FATHER. Neither of us had been there before, and there were few major highways heading to Burlington, Vermont. We had to spend much of the drive on two lane, winding country roads. It took over six hours to get there, and my father vowed that he would never take that trip again. When classes began, I reluctantly enrolled in the pre-med course as mandated by my father. To say that I struggled with chemistry is an understatement, and before long, I was on academic probation.

In early fall, my grandmother Angelina died, and I decided that I would hitch back to Milford for the funeral. I told only my sister what I was doing and swore her to secrecy. I was not a good hitchhiker, and it was nighttime before I even got to Massachusetts. When my sister broke down and told Dad what I was doing, he went ballistic. Finally, tired and frustrated, I called home, and my father picked me up somewhere near Springfield. I was fully prepared for the rant he would go on until we reached home. My father was consumed by fear when he learned what I had done. He could not control the outcome which added to his angst.

When I came home after the first semester, Dad had bought me an old Chevy, and I drove myself to school even though freshmen were not permitted to have cars. I flunked chemistry at the end of the first year and flunked physics the next. My father's dream that I become a doctor was shattered.

During my years at UVM, the civil rights movement and the war in Vietnam continued to divide the country. In remote Burlington, we were unaffected. On April 4, 1968, Reverend Martin Luther King, Jr., a black activist, and leader in the civil rights movement, was assassinated. Drugs had made their way to Milford, and social unrest exploded across the nation. On June 6, 1968, Robert F. Kennedy, who was seeking the nomination to be the next president, was assassinated. It had not been five years since his brother was killed. The tension in the country was at an all-time high.

At UVM, though I did not do well in school, I had a pretty good three-year career as a pitcher on the varsity baseball team and even received a small baseball scholarship. At UVM, male students had to take two years of ROTC, and at the end of the second year, we could elect to continue for the next two years and get a commission in the army or simply opt out. If you stayed in, you would receive a second lieutenant commission upon graduation and had to serve on active duty for two years. The incentive for staying in was that you were in the army and received a check for $50.00 each month until graduation. I needed the money and elected to stay in the program, even though the Vietnam War was raging, and I would likely be sent there after I got my commission.

I graduated from UVM in May of 1969, and that summer I was commissioned as a second lieutenant in the army with a position in field artillery. I thought my father would be proud. He was not. Though he did not say it, I suspect he did not want me to experience in Vietnam the horror he had in World War II. Fortunately, I had been accepted to Boston College Law School, and while there were no deferments for civilians, the army had a policy of deferring service for soldiers who were furthering their education. I got to attend law school. Joe and John were now teenagers, and Marilyn was finishing up nursing school. I had been virtually absent from home since I left for Deerfield.

JOE AND JOHN HAD DIFFERENT AND MORE DISTANT RELA-tionships with Charlie than Marilyn and me. He rarely spent significant time with them. As a result, they had trouble understanding him or dealing with his idiosyncrasies. Joe was generally quiet, serious, and obedient. He looked like Giuseppe. As a child, he was afraid of monsters. To conquer his fear, he decided to get as many toy goblins and ogres as possible. He would array them on the bureau facing the bed and stare at them. Joe and I shared a bed, and it was not until I went away to school that I had a room or bed of my own.

When Joe was an eighth grader, a female classmate who had a crush on him told her father that Joe had thrown a ball at her and hit her in the back. Her father called Charlie and reported the incident saying that his daughter had welts on her back. Joe was in the bathtub when Charlie finished the call and he busted into the bathroom and gave Joe a beating while he was still in the tub. The only way Joe knew why he was taking a beating was Charlie kept shouting, "What kind of a guy throws balls at a girl? Are you stupid?" Charlie never even tried to get Joe's version of what happened. Many years later, the girl told Joe that she had exaggerated the story to make him angry.

Joe regularly violated the Sicilian code of never letting anyone know what you are thinking, which enraged Charlie. An example of this occurred one day when Dave Davoren's wife Inez was having dinner with Charlie and Connie. At the time Jack Davoren was secretary of state and was the subject of a scathing report by the *Boston Globe* Spotlight Team. Joe was at the table and started to talk about the report. Charlie pinched him in the thigh under the table to shut him up.

Instead of shutting up Joe shouted, "Stop pinching me. I'll say whatever I want."

Charlie just glared at him, but Joe didn't back down.

John was the rebel of the family. He could not sit still and did some of the craziest things imaginable. He had what we now know as ADHD. One day when he was three years old, Sooey came over to visit my father and John grabbed the garden hose and started squirting him. On another occasion about a year later when the bread man was at the house making a delivery, John hopped in his van and started driving it down the street. The breadman was able to jump in and stop the truck thereby averting disaster. On still another, he took a knife and carved a gash into one of the wooden kitchen chairs during dinner. Each time he pulled off one of these stunts, my father would chase him around and give him a "good licking." John would not cry. Instead, he would taunt him and say, "Didn't hurt a bit." Looking back on this, I think he was trying to get my father's attention.

Another incident took place when John was a boy and was playing with some neighborhood kids.

During the day, for some reason, John said to the boy, "Your father is a 'hay shaker.'"

This was a term Charlie used in private to describe someone he thought was uncouth and John had obviously picked it up. In any event, the father called Charlie and John took a beating.

Joe and John also had views of Charlie that were vastly different from his older children. Joe recalls, "Dad was jacked. He had huge biceps and triceps. His pecs were broad and firm. He was short and stocky, built like a light heavyweight fighter. There was not a pound of fat on him. He strolled around in his boxer shorts like a king in his palace. His neck was thick, upon which rested a boxed-like head, a flat face, and a large-hooked nose. He had thin lips that seemed painted to a square jaw. His facial characteristics resembled those of the actor Danny Thomas. His outward appearance was that of a bear who paced the living room humming random show tunes. His favorite was *Sound of Music*. He'd go on endlessly with "the hills are alive with the sound of music...."

"He hated what he termed 'followers' [people who would follow what others dictated]. He wanted his kids to be leaders. One of the reasons why Dad got out of school administration had to do with a cafeteria boycott arranged by Johnny Calagione's oldest son from the class of 1968. Dad was quite upset. In the spring of 1971 of my senior year, Dad caught wind of another cafeteria strike. He was very nervous. Anticipating this event, he ordered me to get together with my friends

CHARLIE AND LIFELONG FRIENDS CIRCA 1970S

Left to right: Michael "Weasel" Visconti, Henry "Camel" Comolli, Charlie,
Louis "Sooey" DeGaetano, Henry "Tate" Bodio.

to buy lunch the day of the so-called food protest. As it turned out, the boycott never took place, but Dad, who hated followers, made sure that I was to be the leader of the pack of strike breakers."

John had a more insightful view of Charlie. "He was a bit peculiar. His peer group would fit that bill as well. They all had nicknames. There was the 'Weasel' [Michael P. Visconti], 'White Mouse' [Henry 'Tate' Bodio], 'Rag Bags' [Angelo Ragonese], and 'Pea Head' [Anthony Iacovelli] to name a few. Their interests were limited to card playing, the racetrack, and going out for ice cream. They loved baseball but one would rarely see them at the ballpark. Dad, also known as the "the Bronc" and "Chaloo," partook in these almost religious, ritualistic pastimes for other reasons.

"For Dad, they were escapes more than recreational activities. He was a horse player more than a gambler. Coming home a winner was not as important to him as 'killing the day.' He didn't like confrontation, but if pissed off, he would be 'broken record' confrontational. If you were the victim of his haranguing, you could count on hearing the same insult repetitively. Additionally, you needed to explain why you did what you did even though there was never a suitable explanation.

"Dad was fond of the descriptor '*stupit*' [stupid], which became his insult of choice. He was an introspective, intense, pensive individual. He did not mull things over. His issues would cause him to obsess, fixate, and scheme. It was obvious when he was in conflict or gearing up to explode. He had many tells which included pacing, humming, chain smoking, and drinking lots of coffee. His technique with coffee was bizarre. When it was hot, he would pour it into a glass then transfer it to another and repeat the procedure before pouring it back in his drinking mug.

"His resolve was a matter of finding the means to an end. Perhaps he was always paranoid rather than cautious or suspicious as we suspected. I say this because he used words like 'chicanery' and 'collusion.' That said, he did not trust many people and very much saw things from his own perspective.

"Growing up motherless, experiencing prejudice, the Great Depression, and the horrors of war, he was guarded and perception conscious. This caused him to be reactive and explosive. In social situations involving people other than family where control had to be maintained, it was easy knowing if you screwed up. Dad would stick his tongue deep into his lower lip and glare.

"He was not maligning or over the top with us because he was mean and hateful. On the contrary, he was a very loving, caring person dominated by fear and mistrust. He truly feared for our lives. When crossing the street, he would hold your hand with a death grip. When he was teaching you how to drive, he warned that automobiles were 'killers.' He wanted his kids to always drive the cars and not others. We would never allow him to learn we were in a car with certain people.

"Actually, a name would not matter much, because Dad did not remember names and would refer to people as 'huddya call' or 'so and so' or 'whatchamacallit.' One could perceive him as aloof, but there were no airs about him. Most of the time he was distracted. Other times, he was uneasy having to interact to those he considered 'fakers' or 'horseshits.'

"Family social gatherings with Connie's family made him edgy and nervous, perhaps because he was insecure. He especially did not like the fact that his wife, her mother, and her siblings patronized and worshiped 'Uncle Nick' Mastroianni who was a surgeon and the patriarch of the Mastroianni-Oliva family. No one dared to make any decision without consulting him. These things resulted in many arguments with Connie.

"He didn't drink alcohol and was always spiked up on caffeine and nicotine. He was so tightly wound that he probably got intoxicated only twice in his adult life. On one occasion, he got drunk with his neighbor 'Spike' Moran, a survivor of the Bataan Death March, and a second time with his favorite brother-in-law, Aldo Zacchilli, who had survived World War II in a German prison camp. He had a special closeness to them because they had endured as much as he had during the war. During his binge with Aldo, he insisted that they play the record *The Johnson Rag* at least twenty times, and he sang the chorus each time.

"In terms of parenting, it was only Brother Bronkie who fathered Joe and me. He was the oldest, so Dad, who was a real Sicilian with old country values, prepared him to be the acting father of his other three children, even though Connie had that under control. Bronkie also became a confidant to Dad, and unfortunately, he had to assume the role of *consigliere* at an age that would rob him of the innocence of youth.

"Marilyn was three years younger than Bronkie and may have had a semblance of a relationship with Dad, but for Joe, who was seven years younger than Bronkie, and me, who was eight years younger, the father-son relationship was virtually nonexistent. We had little contact with Dad, whom we nicknamed 'Orb,' and stayed out of his way. He scared the hell out of Joe. As the youngest and the most headstrong, I was defiant and would not conform. He punished me throughout my youth, and thereafter, I would take as many risks as possible so not to be ruled by fear as Dad was. As we got older, Dad became even more of an enigma to Joe and me."

CHAPTER TWELVE

THE REVOLUTIONARY
SEVENTIES

DURING 1969 AND 1970, WHICH WAS MY FIRST YEAR AT BC Law, tensions in the country were at a pinnacle. On May 4, 1970, the Ohio National Guard was called to Kent State University to quell a student protest against the war. For no apparent reason, twenty-eight of the guardsmen fired on the crowd of protesters. Four students were killed and nine others were wounded, one of whom suffered permanent paralysis. The incident galvanized student protest throughout the country and led to a student strike and organized walk outs at schools and universities throughout the nation.

In Boston, there were massive marches with students shouting, "One, two, three, four, we don't want your fucking war." It was a sight I will never forget. I was conflicted. Law school closed, exams were canceled, and we were sent home with passing grades. I left my apartment and went back to Milford. A few days after I arrived, my mother and Tate Bodio's wife set me up on a blind date with Angela Parente, who was from Milford, but I had never met her.

When I arrived for the date, Angela's parents greeted me and told me I would have to wait because she was off doing a nursing job. Marie and

Babe Parente were staunch supporters of the war and when they learned I was "on strike from school" (actually, the school had closed been closed by the administration), Babe lit into me. I did not back down. We were shouting when Angela came home, and she said that she could hear us from a block away. I looked at her and told the Parentes I would be back. The fact of the matter is that I was ambivalent about the war. I was, after all, a second lieutenant in the United States Army. Though I was against the war, I was fully prepared to do my duty for my country.

Taking a page out of my parents' book, Angela and I were engaged in three months and would be married in November. I will never forget my father's reaction when I told him I was going to be married. He just nodded, so I asked him what he thought.

In classic Bronc stoic fashion, he replied, "I learned a long time ago that when a man decides to get married, there is nothing anyone can say about it."

I still have no idea whether he was happy about my decision. On November 22, 1970, Angela and I were married and had 550 "friends and relatives" at the reception. It seemed that the entire Italian community had been invited.

In 1971, while the war protests and social unrest continued, Charlie saw an even more dramatic change in the attitudes of some of the high schoolers. There was little respect for authority. Where, in the past, he could count on the parents to support or at least understand why their children were suspended, now they protected and supported their kids and somehow tried to justify their wrongdoing. They made appeals and complaints about the administration to the superintendent, school committee members, and local politicians.

In the spring of 1971, Charlie's anxiety and apprehension had become more apparent.

On a typical Sunday afternoon, he was stretched out on the couch in the breezeway, apparently relaxing.

Joe was home and explained, "My mother asked my father to complete some chores in the yard which he had neglected. After a second urging from her, he became completely undone and snapped. Agitated and angry he exclaimed, 'Connie, you're killing me! You're killing me!'"

As fall began, my sister Marilyn had begun her career in nursing. My brother Joe had graduated from Milford High and had begun his freshman year at Holy Cross College, and my brother John left Milford High School to attend boarding school at Vermont Academy. I was living in an apartment in Milford and had started my final year at Boston College Law School with my cousin Pete. He graduated from Dartmouth College in 1969 while I completed my undergraduate studies at the University of Vermont that same year. We were happy to have escaped Vietnam but not exactly sure we wanted to become lawyers. For Pete, law school was a way of avoiding the war. I was simply following the wishes of my parents. That's just what I always did.

Initially, John's decision to go to prep school was puzzling, but he explained his reasoning. "Though I was only one year younger than Joe, I was two grades behind him in school. Knowing my inclination for recklessness and trouble, Dad made sure that on weekends I went out with Joe and his buddies. Joe apparently had inherited Bronkie's role as caretaker. As a result, I spent most of my time socializing with his classmates rather than my own, and they became my friends. When it came time for Joe to graduate, I decided to go to prep school because those friends would no longer be around."

Charlie was supportive of John's decision. He knew that Dean Academy proved to be a key steppingstone to his success at Holy Cross and believed that I received an exceptional education at Deerfield Academy. He was also happy that with Joe in Worcester and John in Vermont, he would have even more reasons to escape his job at Milford High School, which had become unbearable. By that time, he was spending more time out of the building during school hours.

Though he was no longer athletic director, Charlie still had a keen interest in Milford High sports. The baseball team's tradition of excellence remained a constant, but the football program had fallen on hard times. In need of a new head coach, Charlie was instrumental in the hiring of Richard Corbin, who began his tenure in the fall of 1971. Corbin put together an incredible staff of excellent young coaches and began a football tradition which would become among the finest in the state.

During his first season, Corbin would often seek Charlie out for advice about the team. He learned immediately that the Bronc didn't mince his words. After a game that Corbin's team lost early in the season when one of his backs fumbled at the goal line, he was distraught. He went to Charlie's house for some consolation.

When Corbin told Charlie that he had called a reverse on the fumble that cost the team the game, Charlie glared at him and said, "You called a reverse on the goal line? You deserve to lose, you stupid son of a bitch. You can't toss the ball around down there. You just power it in. Jesus Christ, Dick, what were you thinking?"

———————

IN SEPTEMBER, CHARLIE DROVE JOHN TO VERMONT ACADEMY in his Pontiac Grandville, a boat of a car that could seat seven passengers comfortably like a modern-day SUV. After leaving John off and returning to Milford, the night was still young when John called home. Homesick and overwhelmed, he asked Charlie to come get him. Without as much as a small dialogue to dissuade him, Charlie got back in the car, drove to Vermont, and gathered up John and his belongings. He was perhaps reminded of his first days at Dean when he decided to quit only to be told by Giuseppe that if he left school, he would have to find another place to live. Charlie's reaction to his son's unhappiness was totally different.

John explains, "I was embarrassed and humiliated. When Dad picked me up, I thought he would be upset or angry. He was neither. He was instead empathetic. We drove back to Milford in silence. My mother had dinner ready when we arrived home.

"Dad said he would make a call to see if I would still be eligible to play football at Milford High. When he got off the phone, he told me I was not eligible. He said I could go back to Vermont and play football or stay home and watch from the sidelines. I was amazed at how calm and matter of fact he was about the entire situation.

"Not playing football was simply not an option for me. I told him I wanted to go back. We never unpacked the car. I stayed the night and the next morning we drove back to Vermont. On the way there, he told me about going to Dean, coming home, and then going back. For the first time, I saw my father as the kind, gentle, and understanding man he was beneath his tough exterior.

"I was no less homesick when I got back to Vermont Academy, but I adjusted, feeling most at home on the football field. The team was loaded with great players, mostly postgraduates. I quickly earned their respect as one of the toughest players on the team.

"Dad came to all my games, be they home or away. When I played in Milford, he rarely attended a game and we hardly ever discussed football. I could tell he was happy I decided to stay in Vermont. I know now that getting away from Milford High School and the town in general was good for me at that time."

One of the family's funniest and favorite stories took place on a ride from Vermont Academy after one of John's football games.

"It was a cool clear autumn day," John recalls. "My father, brothers, and our cousin Pete traveled to Vermont to see a game. I was especially excited because after the game I was going back home with them for a long weekend.

"I had a great game, and we beat Winchendon. I quickly showered and jumped in the back seat of the Grandville with my brother Bronkie and cousin Pete. My brother Joe was in the front seat with my father who was driving. We were clowning around, laughing and being quite loud.

"We were on the Mass Pike heading east when Joe spotted a hitchhiker holding a sign that said, 'Holy Cross.' He alerted my father who immediately pulled over to pick the young man up. He was obviously a student and possibly one of Joe's classmates. The young man was happy to be picked up, and Joe slid over to the right of Charlie so the hitchhiker could join him in the front seat. We were all making small talk and the stranger was seemingly comfortable.

"It was not too long before we again started clowning around in the back seat. That is when the calamity started. At the time, Bronkie was smoking, and he lit one up. When he finished the cigarette, he looked to extinguish it. Noticing that the driver's side window was slightly open, he attempted to flick the lit butt out the window. The attempt failed, as the butt bounced off the window and landed between my father's back and the front seat. Pete and I became hysterical and Bronkie was in a panic.

"Tapping Dad on the shoulder, he said, 'Dad, there's a lit cigarette down your back!'

"'What...? What...?' Dad shouted as he thrust his ass forward with one hand on the wheel and the other brushing behind his back.

"He managed to maintain control of the car, slow down, and pull over to the side of the road. The cigarette had gone out without any resulting damage, but Bronkie was bracing for the aftermath while Pete and I continued laughing hysterically. Joe was somber and tense while the stranger we picked up looked scared.

"As we got back on the highway, Charlie was both bewildered and irate. 'How can you be so goddamn stupid?' he screamed. 'What the hell were you thinking of? Just tell me why you did it. Only a damn fool could be that stupid.'

"Pete and I were laughing so hard we were crying. Bronkie tried to get serious, but he also started laughing. This got Dad even more angry, and he began talking to the passenger we picked up.

"'Do you believe this? Those two horseshits back there are in law school. The two of them. They are a couple of fools.'

"This was a common theme for him when one of us did something to make him mad. As Dad continued his haranguing for another five minutes or so, the passenger, eager to get out of the car, finally asked to be dropped off. Dad pulled over and let him out, but the rest of the way home he did not relent. At times, he was talking to himself."

After the season, John was elected captain of the Vermont Academy football team for the next season. Though he had made a mark for him-self there, he continued to be unhappy. He would call home regularly, and Charlie was always calm, understanding, and supportive. Any time John wanted to come home, Charlie would drive to Vermont to pick him up and take him home then back after the visit. He never com-plained and never criticized his youngest son.

John said, "Though Dad could never express his emotions, his actions demonstrated to me that he was a compassionate and kind man."

At the end of the school year, it was apparent that Charlie was in resolve regarding the end of his career in education. He no longer had the unconditional respect and trust of parents and the students had become products of a war-torn society. They were rebellious, opposi-tional, defiant, and mistrustful of authority. The last of the US troops would return from Vietnam, and the Nixon Watergate scandal was on the horizon. After officiating the graduation ceremony, he retired. He was only fifty-six years old and in good health.

The straw that broke the proverbial camel's back came when a stu-dent complained about how the assistant principal treated him and Charlie had to appear in court.

When asked on the witness stand what he said to the boy, Charlie replied, "I told him that he was a very nice boy."

Believe it or not, he was telling the truth, but when he uttered those words to the boy, he was being cutting and sarcastic.

Ever the disciplinarian as a former marine officer and high school coach, Charlie realized that he could not adapt to the behavior of the students and their parents and was convinced that it was no longer worth the toll it was taking on him. This was another sign that he was beginning to unhinge. Perhaps he was anxious about how things were changing in the world, his life, and family. Perhaps he was begin-ning to lose control of those things which kept him insulated from the repressed demons of his unresolved past. His coping mechanisms were faltering and the feelings that were surfacing must have frightened him. More than ever, he was seeking distractions.

JOHN DECIDED TO RETURN TO MILFORD FOR HIS SENIOR year in the fall of 1972. Charlie supported his decision. His class would be in the last to graduate from the old high school. A new high school had been built and would open in the fall of 1973. John had an excellent season for Corbin in football. It culminated with him stripping the football from St. Mary's leading running back twice and leading the team to victory in the annual Thanksgiving Day game. There would be only one more Thanksgiving Day game with St. Mary's. That school closed the next year.

In the years after St. Mary's closure, Milford High, under Corbin's leadership, would become a central Massachusetts football powerhouse. This resurgence was due in part to the fact that the boys who would have gone to St. Mary's were now at Milford High.

At this point, John and Joe's attitude about Charlie had begun to change. Both had gotten closer to him and saw him as much kinder and more understanding. They had become more sympathetic seeing him struggle with his emotions and they were beginning to realize that his outward coldness obscured an inner kindness.

Joe recalls, "Since I was my dad's only son to go to Holy Cross College, his alma mater, I think he was proud of me. On Sunday nights, he'd drive me back to school after I had spent a weekend at home. Sometimes he would have a friend come along. I recall George Pyne, one of his insurance associates, as being in the passenger seat more than once. They would chat about business while I listened in the back seat.

"As we headed toward the college, one could see the spires of the campus church, the administration building, and the dorms on the hill from a distance.

"At that point, Dad would invariably say, 'Mount St. James, the College of the Holy Cross.'

"When we pulled up to my dorm, Wheeler Hall, I would grab my bag and any food that Mom packed for me and head for the door.

"Dad would always stop me and say, 'Do you need any money?'

"Generally, I would say no because he probably had given me forty dollars the week before. He would then shove another twenty dollars in my hand.

"'Dad, I don't need any more money, I have plenty,' I would say.

"His typical response was, 'Big deal. Take a friend out and buy some dinner.'

"Dad was so generous like that. He was always giving.

"During my junior year at Holy Cross, while at home, I happened to mention my buying a class ring. I was totally prepared to foot the bill on my own since I had worked during the previous summer with the Milford Highway Department and saved a generous amount. Dad casually asked how much. When I told him it would cost $250.00, he went to his bill box, took out his checkbook and proceeded to write out a check to me in that amount. Though I tried my best to tell him that I had the money he would have none of it.

"'What's the big deal?' he said.

"My schooling was expensive. The College of the Holy Cross was a private Jesuit institution not easily afforded by one on a high school administrator's pay. I graduated with only a tiny loan to pay off. Dad had financed most of my education and left me with minuscule debt. Never once did I ever hear him or Mom complain about a tuition payment.

"After having graduated from college in 1975, I lived at home until I married in 1981. During that time Dad never pressured me to get a place of my own. I came and went as I pleased. My brother John and I paid $100 for room and board only because Mom insisted on it. Had it been up to Dad, neither of us would have paid a dime."

Both Joe and John followed in their parents' footsteps. Joe became a teacher when he graduated. John went on to Trinity College in Hartford, Connecticut. Upon graduation, he became a teacher and coach. Marilyn graduated from Framingham Union Hospital School of Nursing and became a registered nurse. I graduated from law school in May of 1972 and in February of 1973, I began active duty at Fort Sill Oklahoma Field Artillery School.

In May, I passed the bar and finished my stint at Fort Sill. My commander told me that since the war was over and there were too many artillery officers, I had been ordered to enter the army reserves for five years in lieu of my two-year active duty commitment. My wife was pregnant, and we returned home. In the summer, I started my legal career at McGuire and Collias, a law firm in Fall River, Massachusetts.

On October 1, 1973, my wife delivered a son, and we named him Charles J. Brucato III after his grandfather. He was Connie and Charlie's first grandson.

CHAPTER THIRTEEN

RETIREMENT

B Y THE END OF THE 1971-72 SCHOOL YEAR, CHARLIE HAD had enough. In June of 1972, he retired. He was only fifty-six years old and still in good health. Connie continued to teach at Hopedale High where there was far less disruption. He had thought long and hard about retirement for the past few years. He had done research and schemed a plan for maximizing his post-retirement income. With the combination of his military service and time in the school system, he was in a unique class. He would be able to receive not only his Massachusetts teachers' retirement and health benefits, but also get Social Security. Additionally, he would continue to receive a monthly military disability check for the injuries he sustained in the war.

With Charlie's background and experiences, retirement at such a young age would prove to be a bad idea. It gave him too much free time to ruminate and obsess about his past and worry about the future. His nightly routine had always been the same. He would be bare chested and stripped to his boxer shorts and sitting alone at the end of the couch. The living room at our 1950s style ranch house on 16 Rosenfeld Avenue in Milford, Massachusetts, was his refuge. His right thumb clasped under his right armpit, his eyes wide open and his face taut with a troubled expression, he appeared deep in thought, oblivious to all things around him.

What is he thinking about? I thought to myself as I had many times before. Once, I even had the temerity to ask him.

His response was terse. "I'm not thinking about anything."

In past years, we thought that he was scheming about how to handle one situation or another. Now there was nothing to scheme about except how to spend the next day.

His brother-in-law Aldo Zacchilli provided a simple yet profound reason for Charlie's behavior: "He is always thinking about things he shouldn't be thinking about."

Looking at Charlie's pedigree and the traumatic hits he withstood along his life journey, Aldo nailed it.

He had never been idle, and his interests were limited to playing cards and going to the racetrack. He never played golf or exercised. He was uncomfortable at social functions, did not drink, and generally liked to be alone. Without anything to do, the days were long and he was on the couch not only after supper but also for hours during the day. After several weeks of boredom, he decided that he had to get some type of work to occupy himself.

After a lot of deliberation, he came up with the idea of setting up a travel agency. He convinced John Rizoli, an old friend, to be his partner in this venture. They secured a location and opened the business. Their personalities were very different, and they clashed almost immediately about how to run the agency. The partnership lasted only a few months and almost cost him a friendship.

He had also been umpiring baseball games in the spring, but that only occupied him for three hours or so and it did not stimulate him. He took a job as a scout for the California Angels and that reunited him with his old cronies in the sport he loved. He enjoyed that for a time, but the pay was not good, and once the major league teams started to use a central scouting bureau, that job disappeared.

Finally, looking for a way to "kill the day," he convinced me to give him a job at my law office, so "he could increase his Social Security earnings." (I had spent four years at McGuire and Collias but returned home and formed a partnership with old friend Aldo Consigli.) Consigli and Brucato hired him to transcribe billable hours spent on a file from the lawyers' diaries onto the appropriate clients' accounts. It was menial work to say the least, but it did keep him busy for two or three hours a day. It was clear that he was more restless and bored.

When they were not away at school and after they graduated, Joe and John lived at home at 16 Rosenfeld Avenue. Though their relationship with Charlie had improved, neither understood Charlie's idiosyncrasies, and they still resented the fact that he had given them little attention during their formative years. Charlie also didn't understand them. My sister and I had always been obedient and respectful even when Charlie was irrational. Joe and John were children of the '60s and challenged him constantly.

The drinking age had been changed to eighteen when Joe and John were in high school. This created more tension as they were always out drinking and carousing with their friends. Charlie didn't understand this. He was not a drinker and was afraid that they would be driving while under the influence. As a compromise, he had a room built for them in the basement with a TV and record player so that they could have friends over and did not have to drive themselves. That worked only for a short period of time.

Joe recalls, "Johnny and I would occasionally throw parties at our home on Rosenfeld Avenue when Mom and Dad took time to go to see a play in New York or visit friends in other parts of the country. Dad had a fear of us driving. He knew that we would be drinking. He did not condone it, but his view was that as long as we were at home and not driving around under the influence, we were safe and he'd have peace of mind. My brother and I would then go ahead, order a keg of beer, and invite a dozen or so friends to party at our house."

Joe also relates a story about how he and his brother haunted Charlie, who they had now nicknamed "the Orb" for some foolish reason.

"One night Johnny and I came home late from a night at a bar. We were feeling good. Both of us were joking around rather loudly in the bathroom next to Mom and Dad's bedroom. At first, we heard a pounding on the wall and then Dad started shouting, 'Quiet down in there, your mother is trying to sleep!'

"Knowing fully well that it was he that had been awakened, we began to get silly. We started to laugh and joke around, creating more of a disturbance. The pounding on the wall continued but we would not stop. Finally, he'd had enough. In a flash, he jumped out of bed and appeared at the bathroom door. There he was like a specter in the night. Adorned in only his boxer shorts and squinting in the bright light, he looked like an animal ready to pounce.

"'You kids,' he said, 'are a couple of real fools.'

"With that, we grew even more silly. Dad flew into a rage and started swinging. Johnny landed in the bathtub, still laughing, and I dashed into the shower stall, fully protected.

"We were in our twenties then, and it was obvious that we were out of his control. Dad was totally frustrated by now. He returned to his bedroom, muttering obscenities under his breath.

"'You kids are a bunch of real losers,' he ended. Meanwhile, Mom had been fast asleep and never heard a thing."

One of the best things that happened during Charlie's retirement was that J. Fred "Spike" Moran and his wife Louisa moved into the house next door. Though Charlie had known him for years, they were not friends. After a few "hellos" across the yards, they decided that it would be nice to sit out in the yard together and enjoy a cold soda or iced tea. Soon they developed a close relationship which each cherished. The fact that Spike was an uptown Irishman, and Charlie was a Sicilian from the Plains made the relationship as unlikely as it was delightful and meaningful.

Spike had a wealth of knowledge and experience, especially about Milford politics and Milford people. They would chat for hours, and Charlie would always be smiling when he went back into the house.

"That Spike is a helluva fella," he would often say.

THE BRUCATO FAMILY CIRCA 1976

Kneeling in front, from left to right: Bronkie, holding daughter Lisa;
Angela Brucato, holding son C.J.
Back row: Marilyn Brucato Tobin, John Brucato, Connie Brucato,
Charlie, Joseph Brucato holding dog Afro.

Both were veterans of World War II so that was one thing they had in common. Another was that Charlie was one of the few marine officers to survive Iwo, and Spike was one of the few survivors of the Bataan Death March.

In 1978, my sister and I were both married with two children. Joe and John were single and teaching and coaching at Milford High. Charlie still had an interest in education and specifically who would be the next principal at the high school, so he ran for a position on the Milford school committee and was elected. With Charlie's support, the committee appointed Bob Pagnini, one of his favorite players.

Charlie's term on the committee ended in 1981 and he decided to run for reelection. Unfortunately, the state had enacted a law limiting the amount towns could spend. Called Proposition 2 1/2, it forced the committee to lay off teachers. (His own son John was a victim of the layoffs.) This became the main issue in the campaign and because of it, Charlie was defeated in the local election.

It was a severe blow to his ego in that he was a lifelong resident, well-respected educator, and an excellent member of the board. What hurt Charlie the most was that he lost the precincts in the Plains neighborhoods, and the victors were not even Italians. The loss in the election left Charlie with much less to do and more time to ruminate.

He did find the time to contribute one more time to Milford baseball. Powers American Legion Post 59, which sponsored the Junior Legion Baseball time, was having trouble raising money. Charlie and old friend Tate decided that they had to step in and help. They formed a committee consisting of Charlie's former players, established a nonprofit corporation, and began raising money.

Charlie became the first president and Pagnini, Joe and Bob Stoico, Lefty Lumenti, and others were committee members. Under Charlie's leadership, the team not only got new uniforms and equipment, but it would also be transported to games in a bus rather than private cars. The team was the envy of all its opponents. It was a truly professional operation. A few years later, Tate and Charlie were instrumental in bringing the state tournament to Fino Field, attracting literally thousands to Milford. The money raised from this endeavor ensured that the program would be a first-class operation for many years to come.

The rebuilding of the Milford's Legion program was Charlie's final contribution to the town's illustrious baseball tradition. His baseball career had come full circle. He had helped bring two state championships to the Legion team as a player. He had been a key member of Milford High School's mythical state championship teams. He had brought two state championships to Milford High as a coach. He had coached two players (Joe Stoico and Bob Pagnini) who went on to coach great teams at Milford High, St. Mary's, and the Milford Legion. He cofounded Milford's Little League program. Through all of this, he had impacted the lives of hundreds of young men. In many ways he was instrumental in breaking the ethnic barrier which had existed in town for so long. Not bad for a poor Sicilian kid from the Plains.

AS 1980 DAWNED, JOE WAS THE ONLY CHILD STILL LIVING AT home. Marilyn and I were married with kids of our own. John was in Miami, Florida, working at a private school as head football coach and school administrator. Soon, Joe would be leaving the nest to start his own family, and Connie and Charlie would be alone.

At sixty-four, Charlie should have been ready to enjoy his golden years. This was not to be. Connie was still teaching, so most of his days were spent alone. Without any real interests, his days were becoming longer and longer. During the summer, he would half-watch Red Sox games on television. He spent an inordinate amount of time sitting on the couch smoking and ruminating. If you dared to ask him what he was thinking about, he would curtly respond, "I am not thinking about anything."

During the day, he puttered in the yard doing gardening and trimming the plants.

Joe also recalls, "I remember him mowing the lawn in the pitch dark of night. He had a rider, and I can still see the headlights as he drove around the front lawn. He often watered the lawn in the dark too." His best times were in the afternoons when he and Spike Moran would spend a couple of hours sitting in Spike's yard drinking iced tea and talking about 'the good old days.' Some nights, he would play poker or 'go out for ice cream' with Tate or Pee Wee Iacovelli. His favorite expression about his life routine was 'I am just trying to kill the day.'"

Sometimes he would sit and make notes. Found among his belonging's years later, these notes revealed a softer side of the man. They also revealed some of his fears and insecurities as well as his views on mortality. Written in his hand on cards from a Rolodex, many are quotations of other people.

A father is a man who expects his son to be as good a man as he meant to be.
FRANK CLARK

Those who expect to reap the blessings of freedom must, like men,
undergo the fatigue of supporting it.
THOMAS PAINE

The universe is change; our life is what our thoughts make it.
MARCUS AURELIUS

Now my weary lips I close, leave me, leave me to repose.
GRAY

There are two kinds of people on this earth,
the people who lift and the people who lean.
ELLA WHEELER WILCOX

Luck is the residue of design.
JOHN MILTON, BRANCH RICKEY

It's not how many times you fall, it's the number of times you get up.
ABRAHAM LINCOLN

These are the times that try men's souls.
THOMAS PAINE

Still like muffled drums, our hearts beat a funeral march to the grave.
PARAPHRASING HENRY WADSWORTH LONGFELLOW

In his belongings was an article, *Man in Sport* by Robert Riger. Charlie highlighted a passage which appears to describe how he looked at sports.

> *It seems most of us are suspended on the tedious lock of indifference. Nothing happens. There is little time, little chance, little energy, little reason, little feeling. There is a numbness, and against the soft edges of inaction, we make no crucial decisions because there are none exciting enough to make. For many of us, most things in a day just happen.*
>
> *The athlete is blessed. His line is clear cut. The time of decision for him is absolute. He faces it again and again and his feelings are real. There is a total awareness to the full scale of emotions all the time. No one tells him what he should feel. He experiences it. This experience, this feeling is worth all of his brutal effort and dedication.*

One of the most revealing quotes is Frank Clark's, "A father is a man who expects his son to be as good a man as he meant to be." If Charlie believed this about himself then it validates the theory that, in spite of all his accomplishments, he still did not feel a sense of self-worth. It explains why he did not want his sons to be like he was. It also explains why he pushed so hard for me, especially, to be a student and not an athlete, a professional not a teacher or coach, a man to be respected for his intelligence and class rather than for his physical strength and abilities.

I remember a time when we were shooting pool at my Uncle Bill and Aunt Eleanor's house. We were not very good because we had never been allowed in pool halls. In any event, my father came into the den and asked if he could take a few shots. We handed him the pool cue thinking he would not know what to do. He proceeded to shoot each of the balls on the table into the pockets he called out. I was amazed and asked him how he learned to play so well. His reply was terse.

"Evidence of a misspent youth," he replied, and he was not joking.

ON JUNE 3, 1981, CHARLIE'S LIFE TOOK A DRAMATIC TURN. The day was sunny and warm, and he was on his riding lawn mower cutting the grass at 16 Rosenfeld Avenue. Suddenly, he felt something in his left eye. His vision became blurred, and he felt like there was sand or dust in it. He had reached his sixty-fifth birthday a couple of months earlier and was in excellent health. Earlier in the year, he had begun to experience light flashing in the eye which blurred his vision for fifteen to twenty seconds at a time.

After a few such episodes, he visited his good friend Pee Wee Iacovelli, who was an optometrist with an office in Milford. Dr. Iacovelli examined him and determined he had 20/20 vision, and his eyes were clear. He returned to Dr. Iacovelli immediately after the lawn mowing incident and asked him to remove the particles he felt in his left eye. His friend conducted another examination after which he told Charlie that there was nothing in the eye, but he suspected that Charlie had a cataract. He referred him to an ophthalmologist specializing in cataract surgery in nearby Framingham, Massachusetts.

On June 4, 1981, Charlie visited the ophthalmologist. I was with him. After examining the eye with an instrument for about thirty or forty seconds the specialist told him that he had a "ripe cataract," and a lens implant operation would restore his vision. Charlie asked him if the surgery was urgent since his son, Joe, was to be married in July and he was concerned that he may not recover by then. The doctor told him there was no urgency and the surgery could be done after the wedding. This set off a chain of events which, in retrospect, should never have occurred.

Charlie attended the wedding, and on August 25, the ophthalmologist performed the cataract operation at Framingham Union Hospital. It involved the removal of the existing lens on the left eye and replacing it with a lens implant. At that time, surgery for cataract removal and lens implant was not routine. It was a relatively major surgery. After this procedure, the patient's vision is supposed to come back almost immediately. This did not happen. In fact, not only was Charlie's vision not restored, but he also began to experience severe pain in the eye.

On August 29, he visited the doctor again. He told Charlie that he could not understand why his vision did not improve because the surgery had "gone well."

He then said he wanted to examine the retina admitting, "I assumed the retina was okay." When the doctor tried to examine the retina, he told Charlie he could not see it with the equipment he had and referred him to a retina specialist in Boston.

Charlie saw the specialist on August 31, and after examining the retina with sophisticated equipment, the specialist told him, "You have a serious problem and will require major surgery."

The diagnosis was that he had a detached retina. The specialist also found a small retinal tear in his right eye. The doctor went on to say that "he couldn't guarantee anything because of the bleeding and build-up of scar tissue." The news was devastating, and Charlie sought a second opinion, which confirmed the diagnosis.

September 6 was Connie's birthday. Usually, Charlie was not emotional, but this time, he gave her roses and a card, which read,

> *These roses are bringing a wish to you,*
> *For joys both large and small.*
> *May you have a happy birthday,*
> *And the finest year of all.*

Below it he wrote,

> To my wife: The 62nd [sic] is your best birthday—it shall mark the beginning of full happiness for you—my job shall be to make sure that it does.
>
> Love, Dad

Unfortunately, the next two years were anything but happy for Connie, Charlie, and their four adult children.

On September 13, Charlie was admitted to Massachusetts Eye and Ear Infirmary where the retina specialist performed surgery to reattach the retina in the left eye and repair the tear in the right eye. After the operation, Charlie remained in the hospital where he had to lie face down on his hospital bed. He was in severe pain and was weakened by the effects of two major surgeries within a month. He was discharged on September 21, still in severe pain and still without vision in his left eye. Had the retinal detachment been discovered by the cataract doctor and surgery been performed immediately to reattach, it is likely that it would have been successful and restored his vision.

When he left Mass Eye and Ear, Charlie was still in severe pain, and he had also become despondent. He feared that he had permanently lost the vision in his left eye. He was angry that the cataract doctor had failed to even examine his retina. He started having dull headaches and the pain in his eye was unrelenting. As the days went by, he became withdrawn and refused to see friends. He lost his appetite and began losing weight. He was inconsolable and experienced bouts of crying. This behavior persisted for days, then weeks, and then months.

It was heartbreaking to see this once magnificent athlete, a former marine who withstood four major campaigns in the Pacific during World War II, and coach with a reputation for toughness shrink not only in size but also in confidence and self-esteem. Connie and his children tried everything to snap him out of it, but his emotional condition continued to deteriorate. He became a shell of his former self. His once muscular body had melted into emaciation. He quit smoking. When I asked him why, he replied, "Lost interest." It should not have surprised me. He had lost interest in everything.

Finally in March of 1982, Connie insisted that he begin treating with a psychiatrist. He did this, but antidepressant medication and counseling did nothing to improve his condition. By June, as his emotional state worsened, he changed psychiatrists. The new psychiatrist treated him with different medication and did psychotherapy. This lasted for six weeks without any improvement.

It was a difficult time for everyone in the family. Charlie's mornings were the worst. Each day, he would call one of us over to the house to be with him. Sometimes, we would all be there trying to cheer him up or snap him out of it. None of us had ever seen him complain. He never showed weakness. He was "the Bronc" after all. Seeing him cry uncontrollably and act defeated was devastating. None of us knew what else to do. His friends and former players were equally shocked and distressed. They called regularly, but he refused to speak to them. They tried to visit but he would not see them.

On September 14, Charlie lost his grip on reality. He drove himself to the Milford Police Station, parked his car, and sat there for several minutes. Vinnie Liberto, who had played for him, was now the police chief. He called me at my office because he suspected there was something wrong. I immediately came to find out what was going on.

When I got into my father's car and asked him what he was doing he responded, "I am here to turn myself in. I am a demon."

Hearing this, it was clear to me that he had crossed the line, and when I brought him home Connie and I convinced him that he needed hospitalization. After she packed his bags and toiletries, we drove him to St. Vincent's Hospital in Worcester. Along the way, he kept insisting that we were being followed by "the Russians" and that they were "inside the car radio." I was so exasperated that I shouted into the radio, "Fuck you, Russians!"

When we arrived at the hospital and checked him into his room, he was almost child-like in the way he acted. He looked lost. He had trouble answering simple questions. He had lost so much weight that he had become very frail. I could not bear to see him like that, and when I left the hospital and got back into the car, I began to cry. My mother was more composed and tried her hardest to console me. She had always told us that she was like the "Rock of Gibraltar," and she truly was that day and in the ones that followed.

Charlie remained in the hospital until October 3, when he was discharged. His condition improved to the extent that he was no longer psychotic, but he was still experiencing a debilitating depression. He returned home and tried hard to get better. Connie was not only patient, but she was also resolved to help him get well. My brothers, sister, and I all worked diligently to raise his spirits. Unfortunately, his condition worsened again.

In the early summer of 1983, he sank to his lowest ebb.

He called me at my law office and said, "Bronkie, please come over. I tried to hurt myself."

Connie was at school at the time. When I arrived, I found my father with Luke, one of his young grandsons. There were cuts on my father' throat. He had tried to kill himself. Fortunately, the knife he used was too dull to do much damage.

When Connie got home, she screamed at him, "You promised me you would not try to hurt yourself. You let me down. How can I ever trust you?"

On June 8, we took him to Whitinsville Hospital about ten miles from Milford, and he was admitted to the psych unit. He had once again lost touch with reality. The hospital records on his admission stated that he manifested "profound psycho motor retardation and retardation of speech. He was suspicious, believing he was being followed by the local police." During his stay at the hospital, he refused medication and would not eat or drink. If this continued, he would die.

Under Massachusetts law, a psychiatric patient has a right to be noncompliant and the hospital staff cannot force food or medication on him without his consent. We had to take decision making away from him, which is a drastic step and must be court ordered. I immediately filed a petition with the Worcester Probate Court to have Connie appointed as his guardian so that she could make medical decisions for him. The court allowed the petition.

We learned a day or so later that he was involved in an incident where he slapped a woman patient at the hospital. It was completely out of character for him to act that way. The hospital officials determined that he could no longer remain there because he was a danger to other patients. Our family was at wit's end. Connie, after consulting with all of us, made the decision as guardian to have him transferred to Bournewood Hospital in Norwood, and he was admitted there on June 20, 1983.

Dr. Leo Alexander, an elderly psychiatrist at the hospital, met with us and recommended electroconvulsive therapy (ECT) for Charlie. ECT is a treatment that involves sending an electric current through one's head, causing a brief surge of electrical activity within the brain (a seizure). Its use is controversial as many regard the treatment as barbaric. We felt that we had no other option. Since this was a drastic step, it, too, required a court order. I filed a petition with the Worcester Probate Court for permission for the ECT treatments, and the judge allowed the petition.

Charlie had four treatments. The first was administered on July 1, 1983, and the final was administered on July 8. Dr. Alexander wrote in the Bournewood Hospital's discharge summary, "The results were astonishingly superb." The day following the first treatment, "the patient appeared definitely improved: was more relaxed and he himself stated: 'I feel better—I don't feel as down as I was.' He was even smiling with animation." Dr. Alexander further stated that after the final treatment, "he [Charlie] considered himself restored to his own best self and he was to accept encouraging psychotherapy."

Dr. Alexander concluded the summary with, "By July 11, 1983, he was remarkably cheerful and at ease. Psychological testing including testing of his memory revealed entirely normal findings....One week later, he was animated, lively, considered himself and was considered by his wife to be his own best self. It is my opinion that the patient had achieved a full state of recovery." We were elated. When he came home, Charlie was not "his own best self"; he was better than that. We had never seen him so happy.

One of Charlie's earliest psychiatrists, Dr. J. Edward Prunier, addressed the cause of the depression in a letter which set forth his observations during treatment. "It is my medical opinion that, although

Mr. Brucato has had in his life a number of experiences which could have made him vulnerable to suffering a depression, this current depression was indeed precipitated and aggravated by the complications related to his eye problems. His depression is severe and protracted."

While losing his vision in one eye may have been the final catalyst for Charlie's depression, his other traumatic "life experiences" had made him susceptible to that brutal disease. Like a balloon which can only take in so much air before it bursts, so, too, the human psyche can withstand only so much trauma before it breaks down.

The emotional neglect lingering from Charlie's childhood following the loss of his mother in his infancy coupled with the lack of emotional nurturing and confirmation from his father tells an important story. So, too, does his learning at an early age to keep his thoughts and feelings to himself and never express his emotions. This led to the suppression of emotions which made coping with difficult situations less traumatic but prevented him from discovering his true self. There are consequences for suppressing emotions and using ego defense mechanisms to keep unpleasant memories from surfacing. Whatever is left unresolved will eventually surface. The health of the human psyche depends on it.

The next traumatic blows occurred in his youth when he felt the sting of discrimination from even his grade schoolteachers and the horror of one of his friends drowning. These experiences inspired emotion which was repressed and unresolved. Then came World War II. There was so much to deal with from the guilt of being a survivor to the horror of bearing witness to the death of thousands—some friends, some just young boys, most with families, all with loved ones.

When factoring in how an already emotionally fragile Charlie was impacted by the war, we can better describe his adult years, including the idiosyncrasies and peculiarities which defined his behavior and personality. In looking at the major events in his life that shaped him, we can also get closer to answering the question about his happiness, which was circumstantial and situational but never long lasting. There were certain things which brought him joy and satisfaction, but those periods of distance, isolation, worry, and outbursts of anger were far more prevalent throughout his adult years.

Psychologist Jonice Webb, recognized as the pioneer of childhood emotional neglect, sheds light on how emotional neglect lingers from childhood. In describing emotional neglect, Webb also explains how neglected children feel and behave in adulthood. According to Webb, emotional neglect from childhood teaches people to ignore or be ashamed of their feelings and live in a gray world, always feeling like a cloud is hanging over their head.

Growing up in an environment where emotional life is not recognized, one learns to deny their emotions, which, according to Webb, teaches them to disregard, ignore, or become ashamed at how they feel. Understandably, the emotionally neglected become emotionally numb and feel different from others. Emotional neglect is not a result of something a parent does to a child but what they fail to do. "Childhood emotional neglect does not happen to the child like abuse or trauma. Instead, it is something that fails to happen to the child, like emotional awareness, emotional validation, and emotional discussion."[199]

Charlie was just over a year old when his mother died. Giuseppe, his cold, aloof, stoic Sicilian father, was incapable of providing any semblance of emotional support for him or his siblings. To make matters worse, Giuseppe remarried a first cousin who treated the children poorly. Charlie was robbed of the love of his birth mother and now had a stepmother who could not meet his emotional needs. His sisters Molly and Ninfa and his brother John loved him dearly but were no substitutes for a nurturing mother. Charlie became a quiet, withdrawn, sullen child.

We know from research and science that the absence of both parents can be traumatic for a child, but children growing up without mothers are especially disadvantaged. Traditionally, 85 percent of children in the US and Europe grew up in two parent homes. This did not

199 Jonice Webb, "Childhood Emotional Neglect," *Psychology Today*, December 4, 2021.

change until the 1970s. According to Dr. Preet Pal's research, children without mothers tend to be emotionally immature and detached. As adults, these children may have difficulty developing relationships and friendships. They become rigid and inflexible. Additionally, low stress tolerance can make them vulnerable to various psychological disorders.

"They are less likely to form a long and loving bond with others, as they have a fear of losing someone, fear of love and attachment. They develop a defense mechanism that prevents them from being emotionally close to anyone, trust them. Thus, they are less likely to feel happy in life."[200]

Without question, Charlie loved his wife and children but more so in a cognitive sense. He was protective of his own but clearly struggled with expressing the love he was incapable of feeling. He did not hug and kiss his wife or children and we never heard him say, "I love you." Perhaps he did, in fact, equate love and affection with fear and loss. He was rigid and inflexible. He was also opinionated and a self-proclaimed judge of character. Insincere people who "talked a big game but never laid it on the line" when it counted most were his least favorite. Charlie would refer to them as "fakers."

When he developed a mindset about something, it could not be discussed or negotiated.

Charlie did not handle stress well. When placed in stressful situations, he would become angry and explode. We can remember most of the times he flew off the handle because they were dramatic. He became quite animated and unhinged like the time when he was lying on the couch in the breezeway and started screaming, "Connie, you're killing me. Killing me." Something was obviously bothering him, but this was just another instance of not knowing what.

Charlie also expended a great deal of energy ensuring that his reputation and the way people perceived him was never compromised, especially by his children. We learned when we were old enough to

---

200 Dr. Preet Pal, SB, "Psychological Effects of Growing Up Without A Mother," *Woman Junction*, August 13, 2020.

understand how we behaved outside of the home was a direct reflection on him. Repeating something he may have said was an *infamnia*. Further, we had to be cautious of expressing our own opinions. He expected us to suppress our emotions by following the same code of omerta which was imposed upon him. Hanan Parvez, in writing about the causes and consequences of emotional suppression, provides an interesting perspective in the following assessment.

"If you break it down, there are a host of psychological reasons why people suppress their emotions, some directly or indirectly related to maintaining one's social image: negative emotions are painful to experience and acknowledge, so suppressing them is a means to escape them. People want to appear perfect to others and to themselves. So, acknowledging their mistakes and failures and the feelings associated with them can be hard. Many people believe that expressing negative emotions makes a person appear weak and lacking control."[201]

While the unfortunate experiences of his youth help explain the psycho-emotional difficulties of his adult years, it is important to consider the positive influences and circumstances which made him strong, resilient, and capable of overcoming the hatred and prejudice against the children of southern Italian immigrants. To begin with, he had many cousins in Stamford, Connecticut, and Milford who looked after him and kept him out of trouble. His father and sisters would go to work to pay the bills and provide for him. They made sure he had what was needed to play sports and stay in school.

He was a naturally gifted athlete who earned respect for his outstanding feats on the baseball and football fields. His brother John was a father to him and most importantly, Charlie developed friendships that would last a lifetime. He had just started high school when the Great Depression caused hardship for everyone. When many of his peers had to drop out of school, Charlie continued to earn notice as one of the best baseball and football athletes Milford had ever seen.

---

201 Hanan Parvez, "Emotional Supression: Causes and Consequences," *PsychMechanics*, May 18, 2021.

Without the support of his friends and family, the legend Charlie Brucato may have never been. His confidence and self-esteem had to be directly related to the fame he earned as an athlete. To maintain that level of excellence throughout high school, junior college and college had to exert the kind of pressure that broke and destroyed just as many talented athletes—but Charlie was never broken. He never had any bad years. He just got better.

Perhaps it was the emotional neglect of his youth which insulated him from the pressure to always be the best player on the field. We can speculate the pressure never got to him because he just couldn't feel it. Humble in his accomplishments, Charlie was never flashy or outspoken. In fact, the sportswriters would frequently comment about how he did his talking on the playing field. He was withdrawn, like most introverts, but had a fire burning within. We can speculate that all that time on the field provided him with an outlet, an escape from the mundane existence which kept him and his kind in their place. Pride had to be his greatest motivator. He was one of the Italian kids who made it.

When returning from the war, he was no less humble or reserved, but now he was carrying a new set of baggage. From then on, he would live with those horrific memories, trying to sort them out and keep them from becoming debilitating. Understandably, fear would now serve as his greatest motivator.

His baseball prowess would no longer be what defined him. His greatest honor, although he did not mention it for some forty years later, was his service to his country as a United States Marine in the Pacific. Charlie was no different than any of the other combat soldiers who survived WWII. The deep but invisible psychological wounds would never heal. All combat veterans would adopt various coping mechanisms, but the sadness would persist for the remainder of their lives. The memories were much too vivid to completely repress, and one could argue that none would ever again experience lasting peace or happiness.

Larry Decuers, a curator for the National WWII Museum explained that for many veterans, the symptoms of combat stress temporarily faded when they returned home, but for others the effects were long lasting and debilitating. Many never made it out of the VA treatment centers. Psychiatric medicine then was archaic, and numerous soldiers were given lobotomies. Others were permanently damaged by shock treatments, as ECTs was in the experimental stage.

"Some veterans quickly grew bored of civilian life as it paled in comparison to the overstimulation that only combat provides. As a result, many came home adrenaline junkies."[202] This seems to explain why Charlie would drink coffee and smoke cigarettes nonstop while spending the majority of his free time playing cards or at the racetrack. He would often say that he had to "kill the day." He could not sit still for long periods of time and would pace constantly.

Decuers goes on to explain how the stress of combat for most veterans would eventually resurface. This, of course, was post-traumatic stress (PTSD) which was not defined or properly treated until the 1980s, years after the war in Vietnam had ended. For those who suffer from PTSD, the fight-or-flight response vital to their surviving combat can be triggered by stressful experiences that are not life threatening. An episode of PTSD can bring on intrusive thoughts which can make it difficult to concentrate or perform simple tasks.

Some individuals become paranoid or hypervigilant, locking doors or looking out windows while others may have nightmares or flashbacks. Outbursts of rage, insomnia, and bouts of depression are also common, causing problems in one's job or relationships. The results of these behaviors will obviously diminish the quality of life for both the victims of PTSD and their loved ones. Additionally, the most prevalent symptom of PTSD is avoidance.[203] That's why so many WWII combat veterans did not tell war stories. Charlie was no different and regularly displayed many of the behaviors described. Without question, he suffered from PTSD.

Tim Madigan, a freelance writer from Texas and author of the book

---

202 Decuers, Larry, The National WWII Museum, June 27, 2020.
203 Deucurs, National WWII Museum.

Every Common Sight containing the stories of WWII veterans who fought at Omaha Beach, the Ardennes Forest, and Pacific Islands where Charlie fought, was published in 2015. In an editorial published that same year in the *Washington Post*, titled, "Their War Ended Seventy Years Ago. Their Trauma Didn't," Madigan declares that while each soldier was a survivor, the psychic residue of combat shattered their golden years.

"They talked of night terrors, heavy drinking, survivors' guilt, depression, startle response, profound lingering sadness. The symptoms were familiar to the world by then, but post-traumatic stress disorder, the diagnosis that came into being in 1980, was widely assumed to be unique to veterans of Vietnam."[204]

Madigan opines that by the 1990s, amid the mythology of the Greatest Generation, the psychological costs of the last "good war" were forgotten. Further, the painful stories he heard in his interviews were proof that even though the nation tried to ignore them, or how Tom Brokaw's bestselling book *The Greatest Generation* may have glossed over it, the hidden anguish of the Greatest Generation has always been there.

As some WWII combat veterans aged beyond retirement and were no longer distracted by their careers or raising families, there became an unwelcome void in their minds. The death of a spouse or idle time were often the doorways which opened for unpleasant memories to return. As a result, VA treatment centers were flooded with WWII vets seeking treatment for PTSD in the 1990s.[205] It was after retirement and provoked by the loss of sight in one eye that Charlie suffered his first major breakdown, resulting in an endogenous depression that landed him at Bournewood Psychiatric Hospital. Aldo Zacchilli was right when he commented on Charlie's rapid decline by saying that he was thinking about things he should not be thinking about.

In her book *The Hidden Legacy of WWII*, published in 2011, Carol

---

204 Tim Madigan, "Their War Ended 70 Years Ago. Their Trauma Didn't," *Washington Post*, September 11, 2015.
205 Decuers, National WWII Museum.

Shultz Vento describes the struggles of her suicidal father Dutch Shultz, a hero of the Battle of the Bulge and poster boy for the Greatest Generation. She told Tim Madigan about the time she persuaded her suicidal father to put down the gun.

"For all his bravado and success, Dad had returned home after the war a shattered and broken man. Dutch Schultz managed to conquer the demons of war before his death in 2005, but it took him half a century and, his daughter believes, required as much courage than anything he faced on the battlefield."[206]

The executive director of the National Center for PTSD, Paula Schnurr, has worked with numerous WWII vets since the 1990s and noted that many of them may have looked okay because they went to work, got married, and had families—but it doesn't mean they did not have PTSD. For so many veterans, when they finally learned they were not crazy or weak because of all the information available about PTSD, thousands found their way to treatment. By this time, they were all in their seventies and eighties. Today, there are only 240,000 of the 16 million who served in WWII remaining. It is tragic that identifying what was called "shell shock" or "combat fatigue" took so many years, cost so many lives, and destroyed so many families. So many more could have been helped.

Coincidentally, for Charlie, the outcome was much different. Although his breakdown caused him to have delusions and auditory hallucinations, there were no talking therapies or medications that helped him. He did call himself a demon but never said why. Did he consider himself a demon because of what he did in the war or were there other actions during his life which made him shameful? We will never know. He was numb and completely incapable of articulating how he felt emotionally. After a regimen of ECT, something remarkable occurred. It was as if he had been awakened from a nightmare that he had been in at least since the end of the war. After he was discharged from the hospital, he seemed to have morphed into an entirely different person.

206 Madigan, "Their War Ended."

Carrying the emotional baggage of his youth, Charlie entered World War II, and his experiences in the horrific battles in the Pacific added fuel to the fire burning in his psyche. There is little question that he suffered from PTSD, though that diagnosis did not exist until 1980. His outbursts of rage, mood swings, and ultimate depression are evidence of this. Additionally, the most prevalent symptom of PTSD is avoidance.[207] That's why Charlie, like so many other combat veterans, did not tell war stories.

It is remarkable that he was able to function at such a high level with a past so filled with stressors. It is no wonder that when he finally broke down, the depression he suffered was brutal and seemingly unending.

───────────

WHILE CHARLIE WAS SUFFERING AND WAS AT HIS WORST, HE was not aware that his pal Spike Moran was having medical issues. He was also unaware that Spike had died on June 20. When he returned from Bournewood, Charlie was given the news. Soon thereafter, he composed a poem and gave it to Spikes' sister.

Spike Lives On

Now I understand the meaning of "the spirit will live on."
For Spike has never left us his voice is heard around.
"Don't mourn for me, I'm happy," he states with cane in hand,
"I'm able to watch over many and guide them through this land."
It's difficult to understand the mystery of life beyond,
Spike has made it simple to turn the unknown around.
"My life on earth was pleasant, crowned with love and care,
"Now my work brings joy for all who care to share,"
Spike is missed by many, family and friends alike,
His presence on earth so rejoicing his wit and humor a delight.
C. J. B.

───────────

207 Decuers, National WWII Museum.

In his own hand he wrote at the bottom,

> Hi Grace, Your brother was an outstanding man who loved his
> family members and friends. Chas

For a man unaccustomed to expressing his feelings to anyone, this was evidence that he had finally taken the lid off his bottled-up emotions.

CHAPTER FOURTEEN

THE BEST YEARS

For twenty-one months, the Bronc had endured his second term in hell, and now he was back better than ever. None of us had ever seen the man who left Bournewood Hospital. He was happy and worry free. After the ECT treatments he was not, as Dr. Alexander put it, "his own best self." He had morphed into an entirely different person. Perhaps, this was the way he was before the war. Connie thought that, but even she did not know him then.

Now sixty-six years old, Charlie was finally ready to let himself be happy. It was an exciting time. There was, however, one piece of unfinished business. He hired me and my law firm to pursue a medical malpractice case against the ophthalmologist who failed to diagnose his detached retina and put him through two painful and unsuccessful surgeries. After months of litigation, the case settled on the day it was to be tried. He gave each of his four children a nice check from the settlement proceeds, and for the first time in his life, Charlie had money in the bank.

Connie retired from teaching, and for the next twelve years they traveled, socialized, with family and friends, and enjoyed themselves,

MARINE CORPS REUNION

Charlie in right front pointing.

Charlie (right) and Benny Giallonardo at racetrack

maybe for the first time. Charlie began reuniting with old friends, teammates from his past, boys he had coached, and his marine buddies, many of whom he had not seen since the war. His travels included a trip to Sicily where he visited the towns where his parents had lived and Fourth Marine Division reunions where he socialized and exchanged experiences with his comrades-in-arms.

Connie was always at his side. He even put together a scrapbook of his experiences. They had annual extended vacations in Florida where Connie spent time on the beach and Charlie made daily trips to the horse races.

While in Florida, they also spent time with their son, John, who was an administrator and head football coach at Miami Country Day School in Miami. John tells a couple of stories about how much Charlie had changed.

"During the three years I spent as football coach and dean of students at Miami Country Day, Mom and Dad would spend four to six weeks with me in Miami, usually in February and March. These were arguably the happiest years of Dad's life. He loved coming to visit. During these visits he was in rare form and a totally different person. Sociable, gregarious, and animated, the new Charlie loved hanging out with my new friends and colleagues, especially Sandy Lewis.

"Sandy's son, Steven, was one of my football captains, and Sandy handled car rentals and other personal business for most of the members of the Baltimore Orioles who had their spring training in Miami. Sandy would love to take us out to dinner and to Orioles games, where we would get VIP treatment. Dad was a professional baseball scout, so he knew many of the players and coaches. After the games, he would go down on the field, 'shaking his ass' like he was a member of the organization. I looked on in amazement as he laughed and exchanged stories with manager Joe Altobelli, pitchers Jim Palmer and Mike Flanagan, and infielders Cal Ripken, Jr., and Eddie Murray with whom Sandy was particularly friendly.

"I knew these were special moments and had plenty of time to take pictures. Dad would have kept the players and coaches there the entire night if they did not have to hit the showers. The old Charlie would have kept his distance and never gone on the field to interact with the players. For me, what was especially cool was the fact that in 1983, these were some of the most elite players in professional baseball.

"One night, when we got back to my place after a game, Dad pulled me aside and half whispered, 'Johnny, I think that Lewis woman is friggin' Eddie Murray.'

"I almost hit the floor. It was great to see him so relaxed and so comfortable in his own skin. I had never seen him that way.

"The only way to substantiate Dad's transformation from PTSD and severe debilitating depression to whatever we might call normal, is to provide more anecdotal evidence. One thing I can say for certain is that in the past, Dad would regularly avoid situations and circumstances involving conflict or controversy. Now he wanted to get involved in the thick of it. The man who made sure that his opinions and private agenda were suppressed had changed.

"An example of this occurred in the fall of 1984 when he and Mom came to Miami for an October visit. Dad wanted to see my football team in action. We were on a roll and had a big game scheduled with Plantation American Heritage in Fort Lauderdale. It was their Homecoming, and we were ranked among the elite of Dade County in our division. I need to mention that other than a few of my football games at Vermont Academy, the closest Dad got to the field was from a parked car where he could not see all that was going on. It was even more important that he couldn't hear what was going on. He stayed away from fans or anyone who may be vocal about the athletic contest. Remember, he was a coach. He was not tolerant of the jibber jabber of the loudmouths in the stands. It always made him uncomfortable.

"On that warm October evening in Fort Lauderdale, we had come to play, but the Heritage Patriots were the home team. We were getting the typical 'visitors' welcome.' It was a tie game at halftime. Both teams struggled to move the ball. The slower pace of the game gave me the opportunity to see Dad pacing the sidelines behind my bench. Another first. We scored in the third quarter to take a 7-0 lead, but they answered, and we were deadlocked with a quarter left to play.

"My assistant coach, Dave Franks, called the defense. He was not much younger than my father and had coached football all over Florida for years. Franks was aloof, ornery, loud, and often obnoxious, but he was great with the kids. I gave him a lot of rope, partially out of respect, but mostly because he was one of the best football coaches in South Florida. After a couple of questionable calls going against us with eight or so minutes left to play, Franks went crazy on the sidelines. After he hollered obscenities at the officials, we took two consecutive fifteen-yard penalties for unsportsmanlike conduct. I tried to calm him down, but I knew Dave. This was why he had so many different coaching jobs and never stayed in one place too long.

"The pace of the game became frantic. After telling Dave to shut the fuck up and calm down, I walked to the opposite end of our bench and tried to gather my thoughts for play calling. We just got the ball back in great field position after a muffed punt. I knew we had to score on this possession to win the game. I needed to concentrate, but Dad was right behind me.

"'Johnny,' he pleaded, 'you have to get that fella under control, or he's gonna cost you the game!' He then started gesturing at Dave, giving him the two handed 'calm down.'

"Dave was pissed and waved Dad off. It was bad enough having to deal with Franks. Now I was concerned that things with Dad and Franks were going to escalate. I had to burn a timeout to regroup and make sure my offense understood they had to execute and not give the officials any opportunity to penalize us. I could see that the referee on our sideline was itching to hit us with another penalty. Before the time out ended, I called over my captain and tailback Jonathan Wald.

"'Waldo,' I said, 'we're going to run power, and you're getting the ball. Tell Mick (Mickey DiGeronimo, our fullback) to put the D-end on his ass every play. Can you take it to the house?'

"'Yes sir,' he responded.

"We ran power right and power left. Mick did his job, and Jonathan made five to ten yards on each carry and eventually put it in the endzone. We kicked the point after and, with one minute left to play, stopped them cold. The boys were elated with our 14-7 win, knowing they had played their best game of the season. I was especially satisfied because Dad was there to see it. I huddled the team at the edge of the field to congratulate them. I looked up and saw Dave Franks get into his car and drive off. That was typical of Dave. He was a big baby. As I addressed my players, Dad was right by my side. He was beaming and I was proud.

"It was a very special moment. I was finally confirmed by my father. But there was one more thing that happened that night. As I walked to the bus for the victory ride home, I watched Mom and Dad head for their car. They were holding hands. Dad in a public display of affection? It was yet another first. It wasn't until years later after Dad's passing that brother Bronkie showed me a letter Dad had written about the game and how impressed he was with my team and especially Jonathan Wald, who went on to play four years of college football at Amherst."

CONNIE AND CHARLIE ALSO WENT TO OHIO WHERE THEY visited old fellow marine officer John Halibran, himself a college football star, who had served with him on Iwo. It was a reunion that the two marines relished, and an old friendship was rekindled.

As time went on, Charlie began to receive honors which were long overdue. He was named Plains Man of the Year at the Plains Association annual banquet held at the Milford Italian American Veterans grounds. On January 26, 1985, he was selected as Milford's Heart Man of the Year. The keynote speaker at the event was one of his favorite players, Bob Pagnini, who went on to follow in Charlie's footsteps as a coach and school administrator. His address that night tells the story of his mentor and coach from the perspective of those who played for the Bronc.

> Charlie Brucato dedicated his life to public service in many ways. He was a teacher-coach, a school administrator, a member of the school committee—and he served in the marines in World War II. Charlie enjoyed all of these experiences, but I think he treasures his experiences with his boys the most, and I remember him best as 'the coach.' He influenced the lives of all of us who had the pleasure to play football and baseball for him. Oh—he had many outstanding teams winning many championships. But more important was what we learned from Coach Brucato, which helped prepare us for life.

If I had to characterize Charlie as a coach, I would say that he was a strong father image. We had so much respect for him that we felt like we couldn't let him down. He was thorough. He covered every aspect of the game. The day after each game, we would sit as a team, as a family, and Coach would go over the game. He could forgive physical errors but not mental mistakes. He would continually stress this at our meetings. If you fumbled a ground ball in a game, all you had to do at the next practice was field about two hundred ground balls. That was much easier to take than his famous gritted teeth, verbal assault for a mental error.

Charlie wanted to win as badly as anyone but taught us that games are won on the practice field from hard work and hard work pays off. In both football and baseball, he covered all the individual skills and team strategies of the game. At practice, he prepared us for every possible situation we might run into in a game....

Pagnini then recounted some funny stories which have appeared earlier in this book and then concluded his remarks.

According to Luke, "For where your treasure is, there will be your heart also." Charlie's heart has been in his family and in public service. The community of Milford and its members are lucky to have had someone like Charlie Brucato....

In conclusion, there was no way I could say what all of us feel for you, Charlie. I hope you have a little idea of how we feel. We are so happy and fortunate that you chose teaching and coaching for your career. It was a great choice, one from which we all benefited a great deal. Henry Brooks Adams said, "A teacher affects eternity; he can never tell where his influence stops."

Coach, we thank you and we love you!

At that same event, Milford District Court judge Francis J. Larkin said, "All of his diverse talents have given proof of the grace and gallantry of the human spirit....None wore the Purple [Holy Cross's uniform color] more fittingly or courageously than Charlie Brucato." State senator Louis P. Bertonazzi declared, "He is a standard by which I measure a man....To any kid coming out of the Plains, Charlie Brucato was a living legend. Meeting him was like meeting Ted Williams. And he would always make you feel so good because he would stop and talk to you."

Charlie's remarks at the event were vintage Charlie Brucato: humble, understated and heart felt.

> ...It's always a joyous occasion to be among my family members, colleagues, friends, and a special group whom I have always referred to as "my boys." I refer to the student athletes whom I coached during my tenure at Milford High School.
>
> I would be remiss if I didn't include those whom I was privileged to administrate in a secondary school environment. I've closely followed your respective professional and occupational careers and, more importantly, your community involvement—your successes along the way have made me proud to have been associated with you.
>
> The happiest occasions are when I'm with my reverent family members. My sisters, Molly and Nee, are two special persons [sic] to us. My four children were fortunate indeed to have had two extra mothers to help care for them during their childhood.
>
> What can I say about my devoted Concetta? I can admit perhaps that the executive committee of the Milford Chapter may have selected the wrong Brucato as the nominee. Connie has been the refining influence in our family for the past thirty-eight years of our marriage...."

On May 18, 1985, he was inducted into the Holy Cross Sports Hall of Fame for his exploits on the football field and baseball diamond. (He had previously been inducted into the Dean Junior College Sports Hall of Fame, and after his death, he became the first athlete to be inducted into the Milford High School Hall of Fame.) In August of 1989, he was selected as one of the Milford Highlander's Outstanding Citizens at their annual ball. On each occasion, he was accompanied by Connie, who listened with pride as speaker after speaker sang his praises.

After he was inducted into the Holy Cross Hall of Fame, Charlie said, "Being named to the Holy Cross Hall of Fame is a great honor for me. But I never compare anything to the feeling of pride I have about fighting beside...courageous marines."

Charlie's life had come full circle. He had risen from poverty as the son of immigrants to the pinnacle of success as an athlete only to find himself suffering the perils of war, then to reach the top once again as a coach before descending through the depths of depression—reemerging finally to reap the rewards for his diligence, hard work, and service to his country and community.

CHAPTER FIFTEEN

THE FINAL YEARS

WHILE THE RECOGNITION AND THE HONORS HE received were great, I think that if you asked Charlie, he would say his greatest joys were his grandchildren, whom he loved uncondi-tionally. He and Connie lived to see the birth of all seven. While he was a strict disciplinarian with his own children, that was not the case with them. They saw the very best of him. He was always happy and at ease whenever any of them visited. He never preached to them. He never criticized them. He never demanded anything of them.

My son Charles J. Brucato III (C. J.) and my daughter Lisa were his oldest followed by my sister's two boys, John and Luke, and my brother Joe's kids, Christopher and Scott. My brother John's kids, Jonathan, Jake, and Gianna, were younger. Charlie took a keen interest in each and was very kind and generous to them. He also showed more outward affection to them than any of his four children. Connie would still cook meals and those of us who were in town would descend on 16 Rosen-feld Avenue for a Sunday dinner and often stay for long visits. Grandpa Charlie was always happy on these occasions.

During those years when the grandchildren were young, we would

CHARLIE'S GRANDCHILDREN CIRCA 1999

Front row, left to right: Jonathan, Charles, III, Gianna, Lisa, Jacob Brucato.
Second row: Scott Brucato, John Tobin, Christopher Brucato, Luke Tobin.

still have holidays together and would celebrate birthdays. These were memorable times. At birthday parties, after singing "Happy Birthday" and watching the candles being blown out, we would always sing, "Hooray for ——, hooray for ——, hooray for ——, he/she is a horse's ass." Everyone would then roar.

Each of the grandchildren was different and Charlie enjoyed hearing about what they were doing. C. J. was the most like him in that he was quiet and was a great athlete. Like his grandfather, he was an outstanding baseball player, played on a Milford High State Championship team, led his teams in hitting, and was both a league and county all-star. He was also elected captain of the team in his senior year. But unlike his grandfather, his true love was football. He played fullback and middle linebacker in high school where he earned league and county all-star status. He went on to play football at Princeton University.

Speaking of his grandfather, he said:

> My grandfather was a man of few words, but when he spoke, he either said something profound or profoundly hilarious—most of the time intentionally. His words were born of thoughts, deep thoughts, and ruminations on all sorts of subjects. Mostly sports, primarily baseball, sometimes politics, possibly gambling, often what it meant to be an honorable man—all substantive. Or at least substantive to him. My memories of him are nearly all a commentary on these subjects, and our conversations almost always dealt with sports, especially baseball.
>
> He was a great man who'd seen much in his life and lived the most formidable part before I was even born. He lived a difficult life albeit a very large and extraordinary one. He literally came from nowhere and nothing but possessed incredible talents and street smarts that led him to world class athleticism on the biggest stages and war heroism on a global stage.
>
> His memories were torment in the awful things he experienced, but I think his torment was equally about the burden of relating to those around him who were not remotely as talented, nor would we ever achieve or be recognized anywhere near to him. After all of his achievement, rubbing elbows with literal legends and heroes and I'm sure what he considered missed opportunity, he returned to a small town and our small minds. I'm sure he thought about how the war cut his elite athletic career short every day. How could we be anything less than disappointing? Or "horseshits" as he would say. He was a god walking among mortals.
>
> Understanding his background and perspective has helped me make sense of my grandfather being a man of few words. As his namesake, I seemingly inherited his brevity, and our words with one another were limited and mostly from him to me and not vice

versa. We mostly "talked" about hitting a baseball. But in reflection many years later, I realized that baseball was a metaphor for life. He cared about me deeply, and he wanted me to succeed even though he knew I could never be as great as him, which I am sure pained him.

He talked about "pulling the ball" which was about getting ahead of the ball (life) and "hitting" it when you are in the most powerful position. This would give you the best chance of hitting a (metaphorical) home run. He talked about "working the pitch count," turning the situational odds (of life) in your favor and patiently waiting for your pitch (opportunity). He talked about "hitting for power," again attacking the ball (life). There was a lesson in this one about what he deemed "being a man." He talked about how much hard work and thousands of hours of batting practice the great ones like Ted Williams would take to become great hitters.

For me, these were profound, fundamental, and invaluable lessons that I have carried with me in everything I've done from baseball to football to school to business to being a father, husband, and family man. These lessons allowed me to get the best out of my talent. I may not be the elite Charles J. Brucato, but I am the not-so-bad Charles J. Brucato III. I hope someone someday will say I did the name proud. I think I did, but I'm just happy that I am not a "horseshit" after all.

Lisa was two years younger than her brother and played softball and various other sports in high school, but she was interested more in the social aspects of school life. She graduated from the University of Vermont with a degree in education followed by a master's degree from Leslie College. Like her grandfather, she is in administration as principal of an elementary school.

About Charlie, Lisa said, "I have so many memories from time spent at Rosenfeld Avenue at my paternal grandparents' home. Grandpa Charlie was an intimidating figure, perhaps even a little bit scary. But not to me, not even as a little girl. Even though he was stoic and strong, he was warm and caring, and I always felt loved. There was always an open door and an invitation to sit down and share a home cooked meal. He was the quintessential patriarch of our family, sitting at the head of the table and instilling in us that family is everything. I wish that Chris [husband], Maddie, and Ryan [children] got the opportunity to meet him."

Marilyn was divorced when her two children were young, and the house on Rosenfeld Avenue became a haven for the two boys. "Johntobin" (as we always refer to him) was approaching high school at the time and was angry and rebellious. A good baseball player, he chose not to play in high school. After graduation, he enrolled at the University of Massachusetts in Amherst. A deep thinker, his relationship with his grandfather was complicated. His admiration for the man was not. He said,

No living person ever *really* knows who a true legend was. That's what makes them legendary. Everything is heard second-, third-, or fourth-hand. The stories are passed down through the generations, and each generation adds their own layer to the story. These are our folk heroes, their feats seen by seemingly everyone but us who are cursed to live in the times after him. John Henry. Babe Ruth. George Washington. Charles Joseph Brucato, Sr.

There are two parts of my grandfather in my mind that I have a difficult time merging. First, there's the legend. That man was the standout athlete who somehow lived through the Great Depression by stealing milk for his family only to fight in a brutal war and live because he overruled the orders of a foolish navy coxswain. That's who I always thought of as the man who everyone in town respected and looked up to.

The other part is the very real and flawed man that I knew. He was patriarch of the family and a man that I don't think I ever really knew, and that was because I was too afraid to approach him as his reputation preceded him. He had an air of power and force. Looking back, he seemed broken at the end. I remember a tired soul who was very likely the product of a lifetime of a constant, if quiet, internal struggle. I now wonder if he was impatiently awaiting his end and was irritated that it was taking so long to find the peace he may never have known in life.

But even in death, he sits at the head of the family table. You can't be in the presence of any of his children and not hear some reference to him. There may be no better example of legacy than that, to hold court in a room almost thirty years after exiting the stage of life. Each story and impression a curtain call, the hopes of an encore that sadly will never be.

Legends always leave you wanting more.

His brother Luke was just a boy at the time of the divorce, and he was neither angry nor rebellious. He had a much different and closer relationship with Charlie. Though he was not a great baseball player, he loved the game and spent a lot of time with Grandpa Charlie watching the Red Sox on television. He graduated from St. Anselms College and is an aspiring writer. He writes a weekly column under the heading "Bleacher Brawls" which he posts on the internet. He devoted one column under the heading "The Orb—My Baseball Mentor" to Charlie, and it poignantly describes the special relationship he had with his grandfather.

He couldn't hammer a nail, happily left all the housework to his wife, coddled his only daughter, and was stern with his three boys. He was the strong, silent type who had little use for movies or novels, but he loved to play cards, visit the racetrack, and watch his Red Sox....

After a botched eye surgery and some struggles sapped much of his enthusiasm, I found myself spending more time with him in his final years than virtually anyone else....I learned about baseball at the feet of true masters...Jerry Remy [Red Sox TV commentator and former Red Sox] and Charlie Brucato.... The Orb taught me so many baseball nuances that usually never make the airways of an MLB broadcast....

For instance, one day when he was telling me about his days as a player/coach of a minor league team in Nova Scotia, I asked him where he batted in the lineup.

"Well, remember, I was the coach. I made the lineup. So where do you think I batted?"

"First?"

"Come on!"

"Fourth?"

"I was the coach, Lukey! I batted third!"

That marked the day that I learned that the best hitters always batted third....

How big of an influence can people around you shape your passions?

I've been a baseball guy my entire life, and it all started with watching too much TV in a house where the Boston Red Sox were appointment viewing. What would my thing have been if I hadn't spent so much of my formative years with the Orb?...

If not for him, I may have never had the opportunity to tell you all how much I know about the greatest game in the world.

And for that, we all owe the Orb a debt of gratitude.

Thanks, Grampa.

Joe's children, Christopher and Scott, were the most different of all the grandchildren. Each was an artist rather than an athlete. Chris loved music and acting, starred in all the high school plays, and was voted president of his class. He graduated from Wheelock College and spent time on Broadway in some administrative positions until getting a master's in social work from Hunter College. He said,

My fondest memories of childhood have always involved the gathering of family. I can describe these early remembrances as moving images of cousins playing ball or the entire clan clustered on a hot Cape Cod beach strewn with blankets, chairs, and swim tubes that claimed our space.

These images, along with the smells of garlic-laced marinara and boisterous laughter heard at family gatherings, are engrained in my mind as fine experiences of shared belonging. The ache in my stomach of having to leave a family function for bedtime is still felt. I enjoyed every word, from every story, particularly the ones involving Grandpa Charlie.

I remember him speaking little, although the gaze from under his dark tinted glasses communicated a command of the room I marveled at. To this day, I am mindful of my manners at the dinner table, as it only took one look at my six-year-old self that suggested playing battleship with utensils was not appropriate. Through his silent observation, I sensed he was the wheel keeping our family traditions in motion.

As someone who enjoys thoughtful, quiet reflection, I can appreciate this kind of presence. I remember feeling peaceful watching him enjoy a morning cigarette as he'd turn the pages of his newspaper while sitting on the porch of my Uncle Charlie's summer home. Observing that simple activity gave me an appreciation of the uninterrupted, uncomplicated moments of life.

Above all was the attention shown to his grandchildren, a cohort I am proud to be a part of. There was no greater feeling than to approach the steps of the Rosenfeld Avenue ranch house with a report card or extracurricular accomplishment to share. Grandpa Charlie's approval held a special kind of value and wisdom, one that encouraged a self-motivating drive that I still hold on to. As family instills the sense of belonging that is foundational for many of us, I hope to carry and to share these memories of him long into my adult life.

Scott liked to draw and briefly tried his hand in baseball and football up to high school. He graduated from Keene State College and is a graphic designer and part-time stand-up comedian.

He said, "My grandpa was an intriguing figure, radiating an air of mystery that captivated those around him. His intelligence was unparalleled, and he possessed a depth of knowledge that seemed boundless. Whether it was through his cryptic conversations or his enigmatic actions, he left people wondering about the depths of his mind."

John's sons, Jonathan and Jacob, were good high school football players, and Jacob played some college football at Norwich. Jonathan graduated from Wentworth College and played some club rugby.

Jake says, "I was very young when Grampa Charlie was sick and struggling. I realized that he was a shell of his former self after seeing pictures of him as an athlete and marine. I remember him as quiet and always in his bathrobe. When we visited, he was always in the breezeway watching a ball game. Unless we engaged him, there would not be much conversation.

"When the TV was not on, he seemed to have a blank stare. When he saw us, he would smile and give us candy. He loved to hear we were playing Pop Warner football and that my brother was wearing number eleven."

Gianna was also young when Charlie died. Her memory of him is, "Grandpa Charlie always had candy. I couldn't have been any older than six when he died, but I remember he used to hand me Life Savers and Hershey's Kisses whenever I'd see him. If my memory has any accuracy, I recall the candy stash being located in his sock drawer."

IT IS SAD THAT AS TIME WENT ON, CHARLIE WAS LOSING HIS hearing and eyesight, but there were some very funny things that transpired because of it. I recall a gathering for either Jonathan or Jake at my brother John's house. We were all seated in the family room. There was a golf match on television. This is when Tiger Woods was in his prime. The sunlight coming through the window caused a reflection making it appear that the golfers were on John's front lawn. Charlie, who had not said much of anything, suddenly got everyone's attention.

Pointing out to the front lawn, he stood up and said, "What's that

Tiger Woods fella doing on Johnnie's front lawn?" It was a classic moment which we all remember fondly.

On another occasion, we were all out to dinner at a Chinese restaurant in Milford. Charlie was seated next to Connie and seated on either side of them were other family members. My wife, kids, and I were on the opposite side of the table and behind us was a floor to ceiling mirror. I could see my father staring across the table.

He said, "Look over behind you, Bronkie. There is a woman who looks just like Connie."

I turned around and saw the mirror reflecting our table.

I said, "Yeah, Dad, and the guy next to her looks just like you."

We all roared. Dad laughed the hardest of all.

Charlie's newly found happiness would not last. By the summer of 1992, there were signs that he was regressing. He was less and less active and was beginning to become despondent again. The ECT treatments apparently had shelf life. He was not as depressed as he was at his worst, but he was far from being "his own best self." He began once again to lose weight and became withdrawn. He began complaining about being in pain. He was no longer comfortable driving so he decided that Connie should take over that responsibility.

Though Connie had a driver's license, she had not driven a car in several years, and when she had driven in the past, she was not very good at it. She had little confidence in her abilities behind the wheel, had trouble backing up, and really couldn't control the car even going forward. One of her favorite expressions was, "necessity is the mother of invention." With Charlie unable to drive, the necessity part was in place. To prepare her, Charlie decided to take her out for a lesson. It did not go well.

They went to the large parking lot at Fino Field and Charlie turned over the wheel to her. Not more than a few minutes into the lesson, Connie lost control of the car and ran into a chain link fence. After the impact, the fence enveloped the car, and they were unable to get out. Fortunately, a police officer came to the scene, extricated them, and called me to drive them home. That was the end of Connie's driving career. From that point on, all the members of our family took turns driving the two of them around.

Late in the fall of 1994, Charlie mustered up enough energy to go to Princeton with Connie to see one of C. J.'s last college football games. I drove them, and I was happy to see my father show some enthusiasm. We arrived the day before the game, and Charlie got to see C. J. practice with the team. He was genuinely excited as he watched the practice. The next day, however, he could not summon up enough courage or energy to see the game. It was unfortunate because Princeton won, and C. J. had a touchdown.

When he returned to Milford, Charlie's downward spiral continued. He agreed to more ECT treatments, but they had no positive effect. Connie stood by him and catered to his every want and need, but it was clear that he would not recover. For the next four years, he was virtually housebound.

In January of 1996, Charlie's sister Ninfa became gravely ill. She had been diagnosed with stomach cancer and did not have much time to live. Ninfa had never married. She had always lived with Giuseppe, Molly, and Molly's family. She was the cook and housekeeper and had devoted her entire life to caring for them. She was a surrogate mother to Molly's two daughters and Charlie's four children. She was loved by everyone, had a great sense of humor, and told the best stories about the family's past. Now it was just Molly and her living at 98 Hayward Street.

Aunt Nee, as everyone called her, was my godmother, an exalted position in the Sicilian family. The fact that I was Charlie's first child, and he and Connie chose her, shows what they thought of her. We were all incredibly sad when she became ill. She had been the heart and soul of the Brucato family. When it became clear that she was dying, we thought that Charlie should visit her to say goodbye.

I approached him at the house on Rosenfeld Avenue and said, "Dad, I think you should let me take you to see Aunt Nee."

His response was bizarre. He said, "Is she in the bier?"

When I explained that she was not dead but was dying, he agreed to visit her. He put on his winter coat and a felt hat and off we went. He had become so gaunt and his face so sunken it seemed that all that was visible under the hat was his large Roman nose.

Aunt Molly greeted us and showed us to Ninfa's room. She was in bed and my sister Marilyn was caring for her. When my father entered the room, Ninfa's eyes lit up.

She said, "Charlie, it's so good to see you. Can I get you something to eat or drink?"

Here she was on her deathbed, and she wanted to wait on her brother as she always had. My father, still clad in his coat and hat, inched his way to her bedside. It was obvious that he was uncomfortable and did not know how to act or what to do. When he got to her bed, he bent down and tapped her on the head. He then turned and left the room. She died on January 15, 1996.

A couple of years later, Charlie was nearly as depressed as he was in the early 1980s, and his physical condition was now deteriorating. Caring for him was a 24/7 job for Connie. He was eighty-two and she was seventy-nine. He insisted that Connie be always with him. He constantly complained of pain and became obsessed with his inability to have bowel movements. There was one doctor visit after another. He was miserable.

Connie was unbelievably patient. She concocted a potion to help him with his constipation. She called it "black majic." She was at his beck and call and never complained. Her love and devotion to him was total. One day when Charlie was at his lowest ebb, I called her to ask how he was doing.

She responded in her inimitable way of speaking. "Your father is neither fish nor fowl."

Finally, he was diagnosed with stomach cancer, and after much deliberation, the family decided that Connie could no longer care for him. We placed him in a local nursing home and a short time later, on August 7, 1999, he died peacefully. He was eighty-three years old.

At his funeral, there was an outpouring of love and praise for one of Milford's best athletes and coaches. *Milford Daily News* sports editor David Maril wrote,

> Athletes and coaches don't come any better than the late Charlie Brucato....
>
> Brucato was an impact baseball and football player who went on to influence many students and athletes as a coach and educator... was a key building block in the progression of Milford coaching.... His legacy will live on in Milford through all the coaches who were influenced directly by him or by people he coached....[208]

Ken Hamwey, whom I interviewed and who wrote the foreword of this book said,

> "Charlie Brucato can only be referred to with superlatives attached to his name. Whether it was in athletics as a player or coach, as an educator, or during his military service, the Bronc strived for excellence. Discipline was his calling card. Winning was important, but he never lost sight during his incredible tenure that education was the meat and potatoes that led to success."

THERE IS AN OLD CHINESE SAYING THAT, TRANSLATED INTO English, means, "May you live in interesting times." Charlie's lifespan had to be one of the most interesting times of all. During that time, he had seen transportation go from horse and buggy to automobiles to jet planes. He had endured the Great Depression, seen four wars, and was a soldier in the worst one. He had seen a man land on the moon and communication go from telegraphs to telephones to computers.

More importantly, he had reached the highest heights and lowest lows. The child of immigrant parents and motherless when he was

---

208 David Maril, "Nobody Asked But...," *Milford Daily News*, August 13, 1999.

just sixteen months old, his journey had a rocky start. Learning at an early age from his father the Sicilian philosophies of omerta, fear, and distrust of others made him guarded and insecure. Feeling the sting of ethnic discrimination as a boy validated what his father had taught him and placed another layer of emotional baggage on his shoulders. His experiences in World War II were a blow to his already fragile psyche. The loss of vision was the knockout punch.

Charlie overcame all these obstacles, and in the end, his was a life well lived. He had made himself into an exceptional athlete. He earned a college degree at a time when few with his background achieved this. He had gained fame and the respect of all who knew him. He led men into battle. He molded the minds of many as a coach and educator. He and Connie raised four children, educated all of them, and instilled in them a sense of purpose and an obligation to help others.

For a brief time, after receiving ECT, he got to enjoy life and reap the benefits of his hard work. Perhaps that is all he needed. I certainly hope so. He always said, "Treat me well while I'm alive because when I am dead it will not matter." I know he believed my mother had. I hope he felt the same way about his children.

THE END

ACKNOWLEDGMENTS

I BEGAN WRITING THIS BOOK IN THE WINTER OF 2021 WITH the intention of distributing it to my children and grandchildren and the children and grandchildren of my sister and two brothers. I wanted them to know about my father and all the successes, trials, and tribulation he had experienced in his eighty-three years on earth. I have always thought it important that they know about and understand their heritage. My brother John, having recently retired, loved the idea and offered to assist me. Since I was the oldest child of Charles J. Brucato and he was the youngest, it proved to be an excellent collaboration.

As we were deep into our research, John and I began to realize that our father's life story was one which symbolized the travails and triumphs of a generation during years of dramatic change in the United States. For that reason, we thought that the story would be of interest to the people in our hometown and possibly other Americans. This book is not an attempt to glorify my father as an athlete, coach, and war hero. Rather, I have attempted to show that despite his many accomplishments, he, like many of his contemporaries, was ultimately broken by the tragedies of the twentieth century and the horrors of war.

I have endeavored to include historical events in this narrative to give context to the story. My brother John wrote the chapter about

World War II and contributed heavily to the other chapters. As a psychology major, he was able to delve into the emotional analysis of our father's life. We have intentionally chosen to include the names and nicknames of the people who were my father's friends, relatives, teammates, coaches, fellow soldiers, players, and others (even though they may be hard to pronounce). While most will be unknown to the reader, each was important in my father's life and deserve to be credited.

I have relied heavily on *Wikipedia* for historical facts and articles in the *Milford Daily News, Worcester Telegram and Gazette,* and several editions of the *Oak Lily and Ivy* (Milford High School yearbook) and *Purple Patcher* (Holy Cross Yearbook) for the information about Charlie's athletic and coaching careers. John relied on several books and marine corps articles as well as books and articles on psychology. We also scoured old scrapbooks and family photographs for inclusion. The remainder of the information in the book comes from memories and interviews with those few individuals who were still alive to help us out.

I am deeply indebted to Constance Burns and Ken Hamwey who took the time to edit the book. Their input was critical. Ken also wrote the foreword. I thank my brother John for his contributions. I am indebted to my brother Joe and sister Marilyn and my children, niece, and nephews who added their unique stories. I thank Shannon Rideout McDonald who used her skills to make the photographs presentable. Many were old, yellow, and tattered. I thank my cousins Pete Zacchilli, Barbara Piccinotti, Barbara and Bill Livolsi, and Debbie Furano for providing valuable family stories and photographs.

I thank the staff at the Milford Public Library and Milford Historical Commission for pointing me to the places where I could get information and photographs. I especially thank the librarians for setting up the microfilm machine for me and showing patience when I mishandled it. There are many other people who I met and who related some tidbits to me. I thank all of you.

It is my sincere hope that in this book I have provided some insight into not only the life of my father but also the lives of the many children of immigrant parents who lived in his time as well as the many men and women who fought in defense of this country. We owe all of you a debt of gratitude.

Charles J. Brucato, Jr.
Milford, Massachusetts
November 2, 2023

BIBLIOGRAPHY

Alexander, Colonel Joseph H., USMC (Ret), Closing In: Marines in the Seizure of Iwo Jima, p. 8

Arrest 18 In Milford Raids-12 Troopers, Local Police Take Action, All Men Plead Guilty, Milford Daily News, June 2, 1951

Atomic Bombings of Hiroshima and Nagasaki, Wikipedia 1945

Bartley, Whitman S., *Iwo Jima: Amphibious Epic,* Washington, D C: Historical Branch, G-3 Division Headquarters, U.S. Marine Corps, 1954

Baseball Brevities, Milford Daily News, April 9, 1932, p. 4

Baseball Brevities, Milford Daily News, April 11, 1932, p. 4

Baseball Brevities, Milford Daily News, May 11, 1932, p. 6

Baseball Brevities, Milford Daily News, May 12, 1932, p. 6

Baseball Brevities, Milford Daily News, June 19, 1932, p. 4

Baseball Brevities, Milford Daily News, September 7, 1932, p.4

Baseball Brevities, Milford Daily News, September 12, 1932, p.3

Baseball Brevities, Milford Daily News, June 29, 1933, p. 5

Belated Spirt Gives Milford 14-0 Victory, Milford Daily News November 7, 1932, p. 6

Bellantuonio Shuts Out Franklin as H. S. Romps 8-0, Milford Daily News, May 10, 1932, p. 6

Brewster, Art, *Purple Captain,* Worcester Telegram & Gazette (date and page unknown)

Broudy, Jake, *Sports Talk,* Worcester Telegram and Gazette, (date and page unknown)

Brucato, Charles J., Brucato, *Brucato Rates Stoico – Lumenti Best in School's History,* Milford Daily News, June 11, 1953, p. 13

Brucato, Charles, *My Greatest Sports Thrill* Milford Daily News, February 19, 1951, p. 6

Brucato Gets Bounced at Clinton-So Does Milford, Milford Daily News, May 27, 1950, p. 6

Brucato Homers as Milford Drubs Douglas Nine, 8-1. Milford Daily News, July 15, 1946, p. 4

Brucato Resigns as Soda Shoppe Manager; Hangs Up His Spikes, Milford Daily News, February 24, 1948, p. 6

Brucatto Stars as Junior Legion Team Beats Whitins 8-1, Milford Daily News, July 7, 1930, p. 4

Cahill, S.J., Rev. Raymond F. X. *The Quiet Crusader*, 1976, P. 24 (quoting Jack "Pookey" Brennan)

Capt. Charles Brucato Heads Attack with Two Doubles and A Triple, Milford Daily News, May 17, 1933

*Cenedella Case Tossed Into Lap of Mass. Supreme Ct, .*Milford Daily News, September 13, 1951, p. 1

Chambers, Colonel Justice Marion, *Third Battalion, Twenty-fifth Marines An Oral History*, p. 7.

Chapin, John C. USMCR, *The 4th Marine Division in World War II*, History and Museums Division, Washington, D.C. 1974 reprint of 1945 edition

Charlie Brucato Is Chosen Ball Captain, Milford Daily News, June 20, 1932, p. 4

Civil War Breaks Out in Korea, Milford Daily News, June 26, 1950, p. 1

Cock Fight in Milford Raided by State Police; 87 Arrested, Milford Daily News, p.1

Collier, Jim *Purple Pennings*, The Tomahawk, April 28, 1936, p. 8

Death for Two Atom Spies–Rosenberg and Wife to Die, Milford Daily News, April 5, 1951, p. 1

Decuers, Larry, The National WWII Museum, June 27, 2020

Diamond Dust, Worcester Telegram & Gazette, (date and page unknown)

Diamond Notes, Milford Daily News, July 13, 1931, p. 4

Dickie, John, *Cosa Nostra, A History of the Sicilian Mafia*, (Holden & Stoughton 2015)

Disastrous Innings Bring Defeat to Milford Legion Team 9-6, Milford Daily News, August 18, 1930, p. 4

Draper Men Retiring, Milford Daily News, March 1, 1951, p. 7

Early Move by Japan Not Expected, Milford Daily News, December 6, 1941, p. 1

Eastman, Deborah, Lamontagne, Anne, and Lovell, Marilyn, *Images of America Milford*, Arcadia Publishing, Charlestown, South Carolina, 2014, p.107

Fire Uncovers Still in Milford Barn, Milford Daily News, June 1, 1931, p. 1

5000 See Local Legion Team Win State Title, Milford Daily News, August 11, 1931, p. 1

Game Notes, Milford Daily News, October 1, 1951, p. 8

Gearan, John, *HC Feats Nothing Next to Real Game*, Worcester Telegram, May 19, 1985

Gridiron Gossip, Milford Daily News, November 2, 1931, p. 5

Gridiron Gossip, Milford Daily News, September 24, 1932, p.4

Gridiron Gossip, Milford Daily News, November 12, 1932, p. 5

Gridiron Gossip, Milford Daily News, November 28, 1932, p. 4

https://en.wikipedia.org/wiki/1955

Hamwey, Ken, *Milford's League of Nations*, Milford Daily News, October 16, 1999, p. 24

Hamwey, Ken, *Treadeau Beats Out Brucato*, Sports Extra Section, Milford Daily News, June, 29, 1988, p. 3

Hearder, Harry, *Italy, A Short History*, (Cambridge University Press 1990, 12th printing 2014)

https://godfather.fandom.com/wiki/Omerta

Hill, Arthur, *Marine Corp Gazette*, Nov. 1945, p.27

H.S. Grid Squad Has Taste of Scrimmage; Brucato Shows Well, Milford Daily News, September, 1930, p

Hoffman, Carl W., Saipan: The Beginning of the End, 1950

Hundreds Journey to Manchester to See Regional Game, Milford Daily News, August 16, 1930

Japan 'Hedges' in Reply to United States, Milford Daily News, December 5, 1941

Jones, Stanley, *Greater Milford Area Sports*, Souvenir Edition Milford Daily News, June 7, 1980,

Jones, Stanley, *Infighting Hurt Joe Before KO*, Milford Daily News, October 27, 1951, p. 1

Jones, Stanley, *Speaking of Sports*, Milford Daily News, September 27, 1951

Jones, Stanley, *Speaking of Sports*, Milford Daily News, October 11, 1951, p. 14

Jones, Stanley, *Speaking of Sports*, Milford Daily News, October 23, 1951, p. 4

Jones, Stanley, *Speaking of Sports*, Milford Daily News, April 1, 1952, p. 5

Jones, Stanley, *Speaking of Sports*, Milford Daily News April 4, 1952, p. 6

Jones, Stanley, *Speaking of Sports*, Milford Daily News May 2, 1952, p. 8

Junior Legion Squeezes Out Victory, 6-5, Milford Daily News, June 30, 1931

Junior Legion Puts Calcimine on Lowell, 14-0, Milford Daily News, July 25, 1931

Keahey, John, *Seeking Sicily*, (Thomas Dunne Press 2011)

Kenny Whiffs 19 As Milford High Wins, 8-0, Milford Daily News, June 15, 1932

Leatherneck Magazine, "War on Japan's Doorstep" Nov.,1964

Local Juniors Lose Wild Game to Websterites, Milford Daily News, July 13, 1931, p. 4

Local Juniors Squeeze Out Victory 3-2, Milford Daily News, July 31, 1930, p. 6

Local Jr. Leaguers Plaster Worcester, Milford Daily News, July 10, 1930, p. 6

Local Legionnaires Massacre Walpole's Legion Club 16-3, Milford Daily News, July 7, 1932. p. 5

McGinnis, Robert E. '34, 1933 Oak Lily and Ivy Yearbook, p. 57

Madigan, Tim *Their War Ended 70 Years Ago. Their Trauma Didn't*, Washington Post, Sept.11, 2015

Mendon Chief and Girl Murdered, Milford Daily News, January 11, 1950, p. 1

M.H.S. Squad Ends Its Season by Holding Big Walpole Eleven to Tie, Milford Daily News, November 28, 1930, p. 6

Milford Blows Up as Walpole Parades 13-0, Milford Daily News, May 11, 1931, p. 4

Milford Crushes Maynard 34-0 To Snap League Milford Daily News, October 16, 1950, p. 6

Milford Gridders Top Groton by 28-0 Score, Milford Daily News, October 26, 1931, p. 5

Milford High Beats Clinton High in 10th 4 to 3, Milford Daily News. May 28, 1931, p.6

Milford High Drops Opener to Clinton in Drizzle, 12-0, Milford Daily News, September 30, 1952, p. 8

Milford High Football Team Feted By Sons of Italy Lodge, Milford Daily News, January 30, 1953, p. 6

Milford High May Emerge from Darkness This Fall, Milford Daily News, September 7, 1950, p. 12

Milford High Squad Steadily Improves in Scrimmages, Milford Daily News, March 29, 1951, p. 14

Milford High Squad Tramples Walpole, 38-0, Milford Daily News, November 27, 1931, p. 7.

Milford High's Victory String Cut by Norwood, Milford Daily News, June 9, 1932, p. 5

Milford High Stars Preparing for Big Game with St. Mary's Eleven, Milford Daily News, November 16, 1950, p. 16

Milford High Wins Tourney Crown, Milford Daily News, June 17, 1948, p. 6

Milford Jogs Over Clinton for 20-0 Win, Milford Daily News, October 3, 1932, p.4

Milford Junior Leaguers Down Chicopee Falls Team 6-1, 8-2, Milford Daily News, July 28, 1930, p. 4

Milford Little League Managers Submit Player Rosters, Milford Daily News, May 13, 1952, p. 6

Milford Marine is Killed, Milford Daily News, October 2, 1950, p. 1

Milford Loses Game 16-2 But Wins Protest, Milford Daily News, August 3, 1932, p.4

Milford Soda Shoppe Whales Rockdale 7-0 in One-Sided Skirmish, Milford Daily News, August 8, 1947, p. 6

Milford Stops Stubborn Marlboro Defence (sic) 14-0, Milford Daily News, October 13, 1932, p. 4

Milford Underdogs Hold Marlboro to 0-0 Deadlock, Milford Daily News, October 9, 1950, p. 6

Milford Wins Eastern State Title, Defeats Concord 3-1, Milford Daily News, June 8, 1953, p. 7

Milford Wins Flag With 7-2 Victory Over Clinton, Milford Daily News, June 12, 1952, p. 7

Milford Wins in Last Inning Rally, 7-6, Milford Daily News, August 1, 1931, p.

Miss Oliva Graduates with Honors, Milford Daily News, May 19, 1951, p. 1

New Milford Board of Selectmen Face New Bumps on Rough Road of 1949, Milford Daily News, March 7, 1949, p. 1

24 Nabbed in Milford Raid, Milford Daily News, February 19, 1951, p. 1

Norwich, John Julius, *Sicily, an Island at the Crossroads of History,* (Random House New York 2015)

1941 Oak Lily and Ivy, Football Section

1942 Oak, Lily and Ivy, p. 72

1947 Oak Lily and Ivy, p. 72

1947 Oak Lily & Ivy, p. 79

1948 Oak Lily & Ivy, p. 78

1948 Oak Lily & Ivy, p. 71

1950 Oak Lily and Ivy, p. 71

1950 Oak Lily and Ivy, p. 80

1951 Oak Lily & Ivy, p. 70

Pal, Dr. Preet, Woman Junction, Aug.13, 2020

Parvez, Hanan, *PsychMechanics,* May18, 2021

Puleo, Stephen, The Boston Italians, (Beacon Press 2007)

1936 Purple Patcher

1938 Purple Patcher

Saints' Stock Rises for Big Saturday Game, Milford Daily News, May 26, 1931, p. 4

Salamone, Filippo. Sicilian Wisdom: Proverbs, Poems, and History in The Sicilian Language, Kindle Edition

Seeks to Put Lift in Milford High Line, Milford Daily News, October 26, 1940

Sharp Blocking Milford High Astonishes Marlboro 55-6, Milford Daily News, October 14, 1952, p. 9

Sooey Twirls Great Game as H.S. Wins 5-4, Milford Daily News. May 19, 1931, p. 4

St. Mary's Team Downs Milford High 8-1, to Capture Daily News Cup, Milford Daily News, June 8, 1931, p. 4

State Police Raid Card Game In Milford; Eight Arrested, Milford Daily News, August 7, 1951, p. 1

Stoico Named Most Valuable Player at Milford High Football Banquet,Milford Daily News, January 26, 1951, p. 8

Strip Cenedella of Powers, Milford Daily News, August 6, 1951, p. 1

Tosches, Nicholas J., *New Milford Board of Selectmen Face New Bumps on Rough Road of 1949,* Milford Daily News, March 7, 1949, p. 1

Tri-Championship Milford High Baseball Team Honored at Banquet, Milford Daily News, September 23, 1948, p. 6

Two Dice Raids in Milford 24 Are Arrested, Milford Daily News, September 2, 1950, p. 1

Two Federal Men and Milford Police Get 60-Gallon Haul, Milford Daily News, July 29, 1930, p. 1

Tyson, Carolyn A., A Chronology of the United States Marine Corps, 1935-1946 Vol II

U.S. Bomber Circles the World, Milford Daily News, March 2, 1949. P. 1

Ward Found Insane Avoids Murder Trial, Milford Daily News, August 2, 1950, p. 1

Webb, Jonice, *Childhood Emotional Neglect,* Psychology Today, Dec.4, 2021

West, Jack, *Purple Pennings,* The Tomahawk (Holy Cross newspaper), November 10, 1936, p. 4

World Mourns the Passing of Thomas Alva Edison, Milford Daily News, October 19, 1931, p. 1

ABOUT THE AUTHORS

CHARLES J. BRUCATO, JR., HAS BEEN A PRACTICING ATTORney in his hometown of Milford, Massachusetts, for the past forty-five years. He and his boyhood friend, Aldo B. Consigli, founded the law firm of Consigli and Brucato PC, where they practiced together during those years. In his career, he tried cases in both the Massachusetts courts and United States District Courts in both Massachusetts and the Southern District of New York. He has also argued appeals in the Massachusetts Appeals Court and in the United States Circuit Courts of both the First and Second Circuits.

He is a graduate of Deerfield Academy, has a BA from the University of Vermont and a JD from Boston College School of Law. He was admitted to the Massachusetts Bar in 1973 and the United States District Court Bar shortly thereafter. He served for many years on the board of directors of the Massachusetts Academy of Trial Attorneys and is a past president of the Milford Bar Association.

While in college, he was a pitcher on the varsity baseball team, a brother in the Kappa Sigma Fraternity, and a columnist in the weekly school newspaper. He also pitched in the Cape Cod Baseball League and the Boston Park League. He has coached both youth baseball and football and been a volunteer coach of the Milford High School baseball and football teams. He served as president of the Milford Legion Baseball Club for several years.

After graduating from college, he was commissioned as a second lieutenant in the United States Army in 1969, graduated from the Officer's Field Artillery School at Fort Sill, Oklahoma in 1973, and was a field artillery officer in the Middleboro Unit of the Massachusetts National Guard.

He is married to Angela (nee Parente), and they have two children, Charles J. Brucato III and Lisa M. Brucato Burns, and six grandchildren, Georgia, Grace, and Gemma Brucato, Dylan Burrell, and Madelyn and Ryan Burns. They live in Milford, summer at Cape Cod, and spend the winter months in St. Petersburg, Florida.

JOHN M. BRUCATO DEDICATED THIRTY-SIX YEARS OF HIS life to education. He began his career as a teacher-coach at Milford High School in 1978. He then served as dean of students, athletic director, and head football coach at Miami Country Day School in Miami, Florida, from 1982 to 1985. In 1986, he returned to Milford High School where he taught psychology and coached football, track and field, and cross country. In 1997, he became the head football and wrestling coach at Lawrence Academy in Groton, coaching two years in the Independent School league. Thereafter, he served as assistant principal and then principal of Milford High School for fifteen years. He finished his career as executive director of the Advanced Math and Science Academy (AMSA), one of the top charter schools in Massachusetts located in Marlboro, Massachusetts.

He is a graduate of Milford High School where he was an outstanding player on the varsity football, baseball, and wrestling teams. He is a graduate of Trinity College with a BS in psychology and earned his master's degree in educational leadership at Framingham State University in 2006.

During his tenure at Milford High School, he was actively involved with the Massachusetts Secondary School Administrators Association. He was on the board of directors of that association for several years

and served as president in 2007. He was also active in the Massachusetts Interscholastic Athletic Association, serving as chairman of its
state wrestling committee for three years and as its vice president in
2010. In 2007, he was named Massachusetts State Principal of the
Year and in 2013 he was given the Voice of Hope by Employment
Options in Marlboro for his advocacy in assisting individuals afflicted
with mental illness.

An avid writer, he authored, *Creating a Learning Environment: An Educational Leader's Guide to Managing School Culture* (2005) and co-authored
Questions and Answers about Block Scheduling: An Implementation Guide (1999).

He is married to Linda Carlson Brucato. They have three children,
Jonathan, Jacob, and Gianna, and one grandchild, Noah Brucato.

Made in the USA
Middletown, DE
09 September 2024

60575227R00189